OTAGO GERMAN STUDIES
Edited by E.W. Herd and August Obermayer
Vol. 2

Department of German, University of Otago,
Dunedin, New Zealand

A
GLOSSARY
OF
GERMAN
LITERARY
TERMS

Edited by
E.W. Herd
August Obermayer

Department of German
University of Otago
Dunedin
1983

©1983 by the Editors

ISSN   0111—3283
ISBN   0—9597650—0—X

Department of German
University of Otago
P.O. Box 56
Dunedin
New Zealand

Printed in New Zealand

FOREWORD

This Glossary is designed for use by undergraduate students as an initial source of information. It does not replace any of the existing excellent *Sachwörterbücher*. It is however unique in that it aims specifically to provide a ready and inexpensive source of reference for English-speaking students and for scholars of other disciplines with only a limited knowledge of German, who are confronted with technical terms from German literary scholarship.

The Glossary contains 1379 entries, and approximately 250 of these have been dealt with in the form of short explanatory essays, contributed by 62 scholars from New Zealand, Australia, England, Scotland, Wales, Canada and the United States. The authors of these contributions are indicated by their initials. Entries without initials are the responsibility of the editors.

In order to keep the size and the cost of the Glossary within bounds appropriate to undergraduate students, it has been necessary to make a selection of the most commonly encountered literary terms. Bearing in mind the needs of English-speaking students, we have excluded terms which are synonymous in German and English, and also literary terms of relevance only to non-German literatures; we have tried to concentrate on important or typical German literary terms, on terms which are used in different ways in English and German, e.g.: *Romantik, Fiktion, Literaturkritik, Vers* etc., and on certain terms of a technical nature, such as metrical terms, or terms derived from Greek and Latin, such as the names of the Muses, which are the same in German and in English, but are largely unknown to present-day students. Any selection is of course arbitrary and can be criticized for sins of omission and commission. Editors faced with the need to select can only adhere to certain guiding principles and use their discretion.

We have deemed it useful to students to give dates of birth and death of writers, where no other indication of the age in which they lived is given in the text. Dates given for literary works are the dates of first publication, whenever these can be ascertained.

The technical production of the Glossary has been entirely from the resources of the University of Otago. The Editors would however wish to record their gratitude for the indispensable financial support of the German Embassy in Wellington and the Goethe Institute, Wellington. Their thanks are also due to many individuals, especially to Fiona Kennedy for her work in compilation and checking, to Joyce Walker for typing the manuscript, to Lyn Knarston and Peter Scott of the Medical Illustrations Unit for type-setting and design, to J.T. Robertson of the University Printery and to A.W.G. van Egmond of the University Bindery.

E.W.H.
A.O.

INTRODUCTION

Bold capitals are used for German entries only. Wherever an appropriate English translation could be established it appears in brackets after the entry; e.g.: **PARODIE** (parody).

The = sign is used to denote synonyms; e.g. **STREAM OF CONSCIOUS-NESS** (stream of consciousness) = Bewußtseinsstrom means Stream of consciousness as used in German is exactly the same as its English equivalent but there is also a German synonym.

Italics are used only for titles and foreign words appearing in the explanatory text.

The sign → is used only in the sense 'refer to' and the appropriate reference appears in capitals immediately after the sign; e.g.: → LITERATURWISSEN-SCHAFT means look up the entry *Literaturwissenschaft*.

Abbreviations used are:

A.D.	after Christ
B.C.	before Christ
c.	circa
cf.	compare
e.g.	for example
ed.	edited
esp.	especially
et al.	et alii
etc.	et cetera
f. (ff.)	following
FRG	Federal Republic of Germany
GDR	German Democratic Republic
i.e.	that is
M.A.	Middle Ages
med.	mediaeval
MHG	Middle High German
N.B.	nota bene
N.T.	New Testament
O.E.	Oxford English Dictionary
OHG	Old High German
O.T.	Old Testament
U.S.A.	United States of America
vs.	versus
St.	Saint

ABENTEUER → AVENTIURE

ABGESANG

Concluding section of the tripartite *Minnesang–* or → MEISTERSANG-STROPHE. Two parts of equal length, and with the same rhyme scheme, called → STOLLEN, constitute the → AUFGESANG. The third part, usually differing in both length and rhyme scheme, is called the *Abgesang*. → SONETT.

ABHANDLUNG

1. Systematic and thorough discussion of a particular subject; treatise.
   → DISKURS, → ESSAY.

2. Archaic term for → AKT.

ABSOLUTE POESIE (absolute poetry)

Term signifying in its most general sense the ideal of an autonomous poetic creation which derives entirely from the artist's creative imagination activating the linguistic material without having recourse to any representation of empirical reality or values beyond the self-contained artistic ones. Thus such poetry is not concerned with describable subject-matter but with the manifestation of the creative act itself. It relies on the inherent powers of language controlled by artistic discipline. The traditional emphasis on feeling, emotion and sensual representation in poetry gives way to conscious operations and abstractions.

In a more specific sense *absolute Poesie* refers to Baudelaire's poetic theory and practice, prefigured by Poe (1809–1849), and to some extent to the French symbolists in general. For Baudelaire (1821–1867) "imagination disassembles [décompose] reality; according to laws originating from the depth of the soul it gathers the parts (thus arrived at) and makes a new world of these" [. . .] "the first principle of poetry is . . . the human aspiration towards superior beauty".

Benn is the foremost German representative of *absolute Poesie* in his defence of the absolute poem as "the poem without faith, the poem without hope, the poem addressed to nobody". (Benn, *Probleme der Lyrik,* 1951). The term has been seen as having relevance in the context of mannerism, and as being related to *l'art pour l'art, poésie pure,* and abstract and concrete poetry.

H.H.

7

ABVERS

Second half of the →LANGVERS. →ANVERS.

AD SPECTATORES

Theatrical device which originated in the comedies of Aristophanes (c. 445–385 B.C.) and Plautus (c.250–184 B.C.); a character makes a direct address to the audience, stepping out of his role briefly to do so. His remarks are inaudible to the rest of the characters, and may hint at or indicate future events in the play. This is also a frequent comic device.

ADVENTSLIEDER

Carols or hymns sung during Advent describing the joyful anticipation of Christ's birth, and preparing for its celebration.

ADVENTSPIEL = Christspiel

Religious drama which dates back to the 6th century; popular with amateur groups for performance during Advent. The plot is usually taken from the Bible and concerns events in connection with the birth of Christ. → GEISTLICHES DRAMA.

ÄSTHETIK (aesthetics)

Field of enquiry concerned with the philosophy of art, the nature of artistic experience, and the criteria of artistic judgement. Plato (427–347 B.C.) and Aristotle (384–322 B.C.) emphasized the mimetic function of art and in 1750 A.G. Baumgarten's *Aesthetica* initiated modern discussions about the nature of beauty and its objective or subjective grounds. Later contributors include Hegel, Schelling, Croce and Cassirer.

The decline of representational art since the late 19th century has led to misgivings about the adequacy of the mimetic theory and to an emphasis on art's symbolic and expressive functions. Adorno attempts a synthesis of such views when he argues: "Art does not convey knowledge about reality because it photographically or 'perspectively' represents reality, but because, on the basis of its autonomous nature, it expresses those things that are concealed by the empirical forms of knowledge".

The last thirty years have seen a proliferation of aesthetic theory. This includes developments in semiotics, a discipline which regards the art object as a variable sign mediating between sender and receiver; structuralists and post-structuralists, redefining both the internal structure of the art object and the sociology of art; and the *Rezeptionsästhetik* (→ REZEPTION) of Jauß and Iser, which "attempts to understand the changing intelligibility of works by identifying the codes and interpretive assumptions that give them meaning for different audiences at different periods".

ÄSTHETIZISMUS (aestheticism)

A point of view which insists on the primacy of aesthetic experience and rejects its subordination to moral, social, or political ends. Normally associated with 'high culture', elitist thinking, it is a rejection of the bourgeois world and a defence of the 'ivory tower' of art for art's sake. It aims to transform life itself into a work of art, hence its interest in the figure of the dandy, who seeks to cultivate the idea of beauty in his own person and to devote his life to the exploration and satisfaction of his passions. *Ästhetizismus* was promoted in England by Walter Pater in *Studies in the History of the Renaissance* (1873), which includes an essay on Winckelmann, perhaps the representative 18th century aesthete; and in *Marius the Epicurean* (1885) Pater explores its classical antecedents. *Ästhetizismus* became a marked feature of *fin de siècle* art and literature, as in the work of Oscar Wilde (1854–1900) and Aubrey Beardsley (1872–1898); and was linked with the notion of decadence (→ DEKADENZ-DICHTUNG) by a group of French poets who published the journal *Le Décadent* in 1886. *Ästhetizismus* is usually associated with German writers c.1890–1910 including Schnitzler, Rilke, George and his circle, and is central to the early works of Hofmannsthal such as *Der Tor und der Tod* (1900). In the 20th century its best known example is Thomas Mann's *Der Tod in Venedig* (1912), where the whole-hearted pursuit of artistic form, whether in literature or in life, is shown as leading to a fatal sense of dislocation in normal living.

K.F.

ÄUSSERER REIM → KETTENREIN

AGITPROPSTÜCK

Abbreviation of *Agitations— und Propagandastück*. Type of drama used as a vehicle for political propaganda practised in socialist countries by amateur groups.

AKROSTICHON (acrostic)

A poem or verse in which the initial letters of each line form a word or name (possibly that of the author or dedicatee) when read vertically. If they form a regular alphabetical sequence, this is termed an abecedarius.

AKT (act) = Aufzug

The major division of a drama. Although Greek plays were continuous, there were obvious pauses, marked by the appearance of a chorus. As Aristotle (384–322 B.C.) implied, the dramas fell generally into five sections. Horace

(65—8 B.C.) insisted on the importance of five acts, a division observable in the Latin tragedies of Seneca (4 B.C.—65 A.D.). This was accepted in the → RENAISSANCE, and followed by the French dramatists and also the Elizabethans. The five-act structure can be seen as corresponding to stages in the dramatic action: exposition, complication, climax, falling action and catastrophe (Freytag's 'pyramid' theory of dramatic construction). Such a structure, especially for tragedy, was observed until the late 19th century, when, following Ibsen, the fourth and fifth acts were combined. In the 20th century, with the breakdown of traditional forms, more examples of two and three act plays (tragedy and comedy) are found, alongside plays structured on scenic or episodic lines, without division into acts.

M.M.

AKTIVISMUS → EXPRESSIONISMUS

AKZENT (accent) = Betonung

The *Akzent* stresses the parts of words and sentences in an utterance. We differentiate between the *Akzent* of a syllable (*Silbenakzent*), a word (*Wortakzent*) and a sentence (*Satzakzent*). In each of these cases, the *Akzent* may be produced by the following elements: (i) intensity of stress (*Tonstärke*, also *expiratorischer Akzent, dynamischer Akzent, Druckakzent*); e.g. the word *Le-se-map-pe* has a strongly-stressed syllable *Le-* (*Starkton*), a weakly-stressed *-map-* (*Schwachton*) and two unstressed syllables *-se-, -pe,* (*Nebenton*); (ii) pitch (*Tonhöhe*, also *musikalischer Akzent, Tonakzent*), which is generally highest in the strongly-stressed and lowest in the unstressed syllable (this order may be reversed in questions); (iii) quantity (*Tonlänge*, also → QUANTITÄT, *quantitativer Akzent*) which is determined by acoustic duration, e.g. long in 'Mehl', medium in 'Metronom', short in 'Segel'. The *Versakzent* brings to the natural flow of language a rhythmic and metric formality by applying the elements described under (i) — (iii).

U.B.

AKZENTUIERENDE DICHTUNG (accentual verse)

Verse in which the intensity of stress determines the metrical pattern as opposed to → QUANTITIERENDE DICHTUNG. The German accent is determined by stress. → AKZENT.

ALEXANDRINER (alexandrine)

Verse form of French origin: iambic hexameter of twelve or thirteen syllables, with a fixed caesura which usually falls after the sixth syllable: xx́ xx́ xx́||xx́ xx́ xx́ (x).

ALLEGORESE

Interpretation of myths or religious texts with the assumption that in addition to their lexical, syntactical and contextual meaning they contain a secret or even divine message; e.g.: the interpretation of the love poetry of the *Song of Songs* as a religious text. → ALLEGORIE, → EXEGESE, → INTERPRE-TATION.

ALLEGORIE (allegory)

The usage of the Greek term *allegoria* (= 'speaking otherwise than one seems to speak', 'figurative language') evolves in such a way that it early assumes a number of meanings in literature and literary criticism, which are interconnected.

1. In → RHETORIK it has a place in the section on ornamentation, where, together with irony, emphasis, synecdoche and hyperbole, it is treated as a figure of speech within the unit of sentence length which encodes a general concept or subject in the form of an image or "other subject of aptly suggestive resemblance" (OED), whose meaning, in contrast to the → SYM-BOL, must be known to the interpreter if it is not to remain enigmatic. The notion of justice, for example, is allegorized in the image of a blindfolded woman with a sword in one hand and a pair of scales in the other; or love as the winged boy-god with bow and arrow. In the course of the history of literature a whole dictionary of such allegorical images has been accumulated and these reflect traditional and historical areas of aesthetic argumentation within a code which is learned in society. The → EMBLEM represents a special development of allegory.

2. From the unit of sentence length allegory expands to become the subject of full texts in which the individual image and the whole stand for specifically encoded themes which characterize aspects of the literary argumentation of given societies within the European tradition: famous examples are Horace's use of the allegory of a ship in a raging storm denoting the current situation of the state; rescue from shipwreck as portraying the end of a turbulent love affair; or more generally, Homer's *Odyssey* as the allegory of man's search for the meaning of life. The literature of traditionalistic periods such as the late Antiquity, the M.A., the Renaissance and the Baroque develops this use of allegory into highly cerebral systems, with special interest in parody and satire. Although Romantic literature largely prefers the symbol to allegory, Goethe uses it again in *Faust II* (1832).

3. By the 4th century B.C. a method of interpreting texts had been developed which imposed allegorical meaning on texts whose literal sense was no longer acceptable to or understood by society, as was the case with the Homeric epics, the O.T. and, in particular, the *Song of Solomon*. This biblical love poem was allegorized as Yahveh's dialogue with Israel or, later, as the

soul's with its saviour. In the 2nd century A.D. the method of locating four different meanings within the text was introduced: (a) the historical meaning – the non-allegorical, literal interpretation (e.g. Jerusalem as the city of the Jews); (b) the allegorical meaning – the christological and ecclesiological interpretation (Jerusalem as the Church of Christ); (c) the tropological meaning – the moral interpretation (Jerusalem as the individual soul addressed and exhorted by God); (d) the anagogical meaning – the eschatological interpretation (Jerusalem as the City of God or Paradise). This method has been firmly established since the time of St. Augustine (354–430). A closely related method is the typological or figural method which interprets Adam, Isaac, Jacob, Job and even Ulysses as prefigurations of Christ (→ PRÄFIGURATION). Both methods have had great influence on ' modern thinking on hermeneutics (→ HERMENEUTIK) as they present possibilities of applying past aesthetic argumentation to present situations.

W.V.

ALLITERATION (alliteration) = Anreim

Consonance of the initial sounds in stressed words or syllables. (*H*aus und *H*of, *M*ann und *M*aus).

A special form of alliteration is the *Stabreim* which is the oldest principle of Germanic rhyme: the initial sounds of stressed words or syllables within a → LANGVERS rhyme; any vowel may constitute a rhyme with another vowel but consonants must be the same;

e.g.: dat sih *u*rhettun *a*enon muotin
  *H*iltibrant enti *H*adubrant untar *h*eriun tuem (*Hildebrandslied*).
→ REIM.

ALMANACH (almanac)

Originally tables of the days of the year, with relevant astronomical data attached. Later, with the gradual inclusion of more entertaining and informative material, the almanac became a year-book of institutions, societies or firms; e.g.: → MUSENALMANACH, *Gothaischer Theater Almanach, Inselalmanach, Verlagsalmanach.* → KALENDER.

ALTDEUTSCHE STROPHE → MEISTERSANGSTROPHE

ALTERNIERENDE DICHTUNG

Poetry which consists of strictly alternating stressed and unstressed or long and short syllables. Only iambic or trochaic metres (which may disregard the accentuation of normal speech) are possible.

ALTPHILOLOGIE

The study of ancient languages and literatures. → NEUPHILOLOGIE, →PHILOLOGIE.

AMBIGUITÄT (ambiguity) → DOPPELSINN

AMBIVALENZ, AMBIVALENT

Both the noun and the adjective denote an ambiguity of meaning, not so much in a single word, although this is also possible, but rather in more complex literary units such as images or lines, paragraphs, chapters, or stanzas, or more commonly, entire works. The term was first used in psychology to designate contradictory experiences and feelings, e.g. a love-hate relationship; this simultaneous attraction toward and repulsion from an object, person, or action is, etymologically speaking, the original sense of the word (cf. Latin *ambivalens*). Occasionally, *Ambivalenz* is confused with, or employed as a synonym of, → AMBIGUITÄT, a term only recently adopted from English usage; indeed *Ambivalenz* and *ambivalent* are themselves rather new in German literary terminology. The brief chapter, *Ambivalenz*, of Benn's *Roman des Phänotyp* (1949) gives both an excellent example and a general definition of this whole concept, as well as ample illustrations.

R.G.

ANAGNORISIS (anagnorisis)

The tragic hero's discovery or recognition of crucial facts or circumstances of which he was previously ignorant. According to Aristotle (384–322 B.C.) (*Poetics*) anagnorisis, → HAMARTIA and → PERIPETIE constitute the three basic elements of the tragic plot.

ANAGRAMM (anagram)

The new word or sentence which results from a rearrangement of the letters in another word or sentence; e.g. Peilkarastres = Kaspar Stieler.

ANAKOLUTH (anacoluthon)

Inconsistency of syntax: the change to a new grammatical construction without completing the previous one; may be a grammatical error or a deliberate stylistic device;

e.g.: Sie schlägt, die Rüstung ihm vom Leibe reißend,
   Den Zahn schlägt sie in seine weiße Brust (Kleist, *Penthesilea*).

ANAKREONTIK (anacreonticism)

The term is derived from the name of a Greek lyrical poet, Anakreon (c.570–480 B.C.), and of a collection of sixty pseudo-anacreontic poems, the *Anacreontea*, published by Henricus Stephanus in 1554. The themes and diction of these poems exercised considerable influence in France, Italy and England; in Germany the anacreontic style became the predominant form of lyric expression towards the middle of the 18th century. Anacreontic poetry contrasted sharply with the sombre mood of the Baroque (→ BAROCK) in that it celebrated the pleasures of life, singing of wine and women, spring and dancing, love and friendship. Reference to the mythological figures of Bacchus, Amor and Venus occurred as frequently as the description of stylized pastoral landscapes. Following the model of the *Anacreontea* the poems were often, but not always, written in unrhymed verse; they also attempted to parallel the graceful imagery of the Greek odes. Friedrich von Hagedorn (1708–1754), Ludwig Gleim (1719–1803), Johann Peter Uz (1720–1796) and Johann Nikolaus Götz (1721–1781) are the best-known German representatives of Anacreonticism, but even Lessing wrote a collection of poems entitled *Lieder von einem anakreontischen Freunde*, and Goethe provided the crowning touch with his poem to Friederike, *Kleine Blumen, kleine Blätter* (1771).

H.W.N.

ANAKRUSIS (anacrusis) = Auftakt

Unstressed short syllables which precede the first stressed or long syllable of the verse line, thus resulting in trochaic or dactylic metres only.

ANALYTISCHES DRAMA

Drama in which the plot is not presented in chronological sequence, but begins at the point when events which took place before the drama started, have reached their climax. The reader/spectator becomes familiar with the earlier events as the play progresses; e.g.: Sophocles (497–406 B.C.) *Oedipus the King.* → VORGESCHICHTE.

ANAPÄST (anapaest)

Metrical foot of three syllables, the first two unstressed or short, and the third stressed or long. (xxx̃)

ANAPHER (anaphora)

Rhetorical and poetic device: the repetition of a word or phrase at the beginning of several consecutive phrases, sentences, or lines of verse;

    e.g.:   Wie flog, was rund der Mond beschien,
            Wie flog es in die Ferne!
            Wie flogen oben überhin
            Der Himmel und die Sterne! (Bürger, *Lenore*).
→ EPIPHER.

ANEKDOTE (anecdote)

1. A short narration of an event in a person's life or of a personal characteristic, often an item of gossip, with a single distinct point.

2. Brief narrative aiming at the characterization of an historical period, a personality or a social phenomenon by presenting a single, striking and interesting event. It is narrated with the utmost stylistic economy. Its attitude of strict objectivity helps to endow the individual case with general significance. Its sources are oral tradition, early historiography and, later, journalistic feature stories: its pointed ending and pungent wit makes it similar to the joke. In the German literary tradition, the *Anekdote* has been regarded as an important literary art form since the satires and pamphlets of Humanism. Many of the successful chap-books (→ VOLKSBUCH) of the 16th century are collections of *Anekdoten* (e.g. *Eulenspiegel*, 1515; *Die Schildbürger*, 1597). The master of the popular and didactic *Anekdote* of the Enlightenment, was J.P. Hebel (1760–1826); some of the subtly ambivalent stories of Kleist (1777–1811) have become a paradigm for the genre. The tightly knit *Anekdoten* in Bernhard's *Der Stimmenimitator* (1978) show the genre in a new function, giving examples of the absurdity of the modern world.

L.B.

ANFANGSREIM

Rhyming of the initial words of two or more lines of verse;

e.g.:   Krieg! ist das Losungswort.
Sieg! und so klingt es fort. (Goethe, *Faust II*).

ANGLIZISMUS (anglicism)

Literal translation of an English idiom into another language; e.g.: once more = *einmal mehr* instead of *noch einmal*.

ANLAUT

Initial sound of a syllable or word. → AUSLAUT.

ANMERKUNG

Annotation, short explanatory note or critical comment in a literary or critical work. → FUSSNOTE.

ANREIM → ALLITERATION

ANSPIELUNG

Veiled allusion or reference to someone or something the author assumes is familiar to the audience or reader.

ANTIHELD (anti-hero) → **HELD**

ANTIKE

The term *die Antike* has been in common use in scholarly language since the age of Gottsched (1700–1766), as a collective term for 'The Ancients', the world of classical Greek and Roman antiquity, with its literature, art and philosophy, the main source, along with Christianity, of European civilization. In Goethe's writings, we learn from the *Goethe-Wörterbuch*, among about 100 occurrences of *Antike* about a third denote the period. In the rest the word refers to some Greek or Roman work of art, as in the name of the famous Mannheim collection of casts, the *Antikensaal*. In modern literary and art criticism and history the meaning is usually 'The Ancients' as opposed to 'The Moderns', whose age has since the 1890s commonly been called collectively by the newly coined term *Die* →MODERNE (i.e. *Welt* or *Zeit*).

W.H.B.

ANTIQUA

Roman type as distinct from → FRAKTUR (Gothic type).

ANTIQUAR (second-hand bookseller)

ANTIQUARIAT (second-hand bookshop)

ANTISTROPHE (antistrophe) = Gegenstrophe → **STROPHE**

ANVERS

First half of the →LANGVERS. →ABVERS.

APHORISMUS (aphorism)

Term given to pithy statements expressing in a clever and original fashion the insight of an individual. Although often used loosely to refer to all sorts of sundry short works, the aphorism, when viewed as a literary genre, or sub-genre, displays certain formal characteristics. It is essentially a short form and as such demands succinctness of expression. The point of view it conveys is that of an individual — as compared to the distillated wisdom of collective experience characteristic of the proverb (→SPRICHWORT).

Choosing merely to state its message rather than develop a logical argument, the aphorism represents a gratuitous moment of spontaneous insight. In order to achieve the necessary balance of poetic form and intellectual content, the aphorism relies heavily on distinctive, original language and frequently makes use of figures of speech — as in the following example by Karl Kraus: "Einen Aphorismus zu schreiben, wenn man es kann, ist oft schwer. Viel leichter ist es, einen Aphorismus zu schreiben, wenn man es nicht kann."

G.B.

APOKOPE (apocope)

Omission of the final letter or syllable of a word.

APOLLINISCH (Apollinian) → DIONYSISCH

APOLOGETIK (apologetics)

Discipline developed for the defence of Christianity against non-Christian philosophies. → APOLOGIE.

APOLOGIE

Speech or treatise in defence of a person, institution, philosophy, religion or opinion.

APORIE (aporia)

Figure of speech in which the speaker expresses doubt as to the possibility of solving the problem before him.

APPARAT (apparatus) = kritischer Apparat

Annotations of a critical edition which may appear in the form of footnotes, as an appendix or even as a separate volume. The apparatus contains information and documentation about the manuscripts, printed versions and editions of the text, and additions and/or omissions and changes undertaken by the editor. → TEXTKRITIK.

ARBEITERDICHTUNG = Proletarierdichtung

Arbeiterdichtung connotes various eras, but refers principally to writing by left-wing authors of middle and working class origin in the period 1918–1933, who in 1928 formed the *B.P.R.S.* (*Bund proletarisch-revolutionärer Schriftsteller*) with the journal *Die Linkskurve*. However, this group rejected the term *Arbeiterdichtung* in order to distinguish themselves from the work of earlier non-revolutionary working class writers, which tended to "demonise machinery and imbue work with an almost religious aura" (Gallas, *Marxistische Literaturtheorie*, 1972). The latter, amongst them Max Barthel (1893–1975), Heinrich Lersch (1889–1936), Josef Winckler (1881–1966), in 1912 formed the *Bund der Werkleute auf Haus Nyland* and later became active supporters of Nazi ideology. Hence the *B.P.R.S.* felt the term 'proletarisch-revolutionäre Literatur'

17

better characterized the socialist commitment of their writing. Some *B.P.R.S.* members who later became well-known GDR authors are: Johannes R. Becher (1891–1958), Willi Bredel (1901–1964), Otto Gotsche (1904–), Hans Marchwitza (1890–1965), Ludwig Turek (1898–1975). Certain Western critics have used the term *Arbeiterdichtung* in reference to the so-called → BITTER-FELDER WEG in the GDR, but this is not consistent with GDR usage.

Arbeiterdichtung has also been used to connote writing by the West German *Gruppe 61* and its offshoot, the *Werkkreis Literatur der Arbeitswelt* e.g. Max von der Grün (1926–), Erika Runge (1939–), Günter Wallraff (1942–) et al. Gerlach (*Bitterfeld*, 1974) contrasts this writing, which portrays the individual as passive victim of technology in an alienated labour process, with works of the Bitterfeld movement showing men as masters of technology in a creative labour process.

B.E.

ARCHIV (archive)

Place in which historical records are kept. There are specialized archives such as the *Deutsche Literaturarchiv* in Marbach.

ARISTOTELISCHES DRAMA = kulinarisches Theater

Terms coined by Brecht (1898–1956) to describe dramatic forms he considered no longer relevant to the 'theatre of the scientific age': the traditional, carefully constructed and closed dramaturgy which derived from the precepts of Aristotle (384–322 B.C.) and his interpreters. His main objection to Aristotle was ideological: because of the social implications, he took issue with the latter's view of the purpose of tragedy as catharsis – i.e. the purification in the spectator of the emotions of fear and pity by the imitation of actions that evoke these emotions. The identification of spectator with actor, and of actor with character, was always opposed by Brecht, and from 1933 he systematically developed an anti-Aristotelian theory of the drama which was opposed to a naturalistic and empathy-based presentation of character. In place of the well-made play with its conservative conventions, Brecht developed a theory of the 'epic' (→ EPISCHES THEATER) and, subsequently, 'dialectical' drama. This anti-metaphysical, materialistic drama placed more emphasis on the spectators' critical attitude towards the events of a play, and showed the individual figures to be changeable, contradictory and inconsistent.

M.M.

ARLECCHINO (Harlequin) = Harlekin

Stock character from the → COMMEDIA DELL'ARTE. He is normally the hero's servant, and is constantly engaged in hilarious intrigues and schemes, thus attracting much of the laughter.

ARMENBIBEL (Biblia pauperum)

Med. edition of the Bible, in the form of a pictorial presentation of significant events in the life of Christ; aimed at the poor and illiterate. → BILDER-BIBEL.

ART NOUVEAU → JUGENDSTIL

ARTES LIBERALES, ARTESLITERATUR = Freie Künste, = Sieben freie Künste

After St. Augustine (354—430), it was generally accepted that the free and educated man must be able to master seven *artes* (disciplines). In about 600 this became an institutionalized concept of education, divided into the *Trivium*: grammar, rhetoric, and dialectics, and the *Quadrivium*: arithmetic, geometry (also comprising geography), astronomy, and music (also comprising physics).

ARTIKEL (article)

1. Prose composition in a newspaper, journal etc., usually non-fictional, dealing with a specific subject in an independent manner. = Aufsatz.

2. Word indicating the gender of a noun (definite or indefinite article).

ARTUSROMAN

Courtly epic (→ HÖFISCHE DICHTUNG) based on the Celtic tales about Arthur, a 6th century chieftain reputed to have led the Britons in the battles against the Anglo Saxons. Breton entertainers propagated the tales in France, where they were transformed and amalgamated into longer epics. The outstanding French poet, on whose work a number of MHG *Artusromane* are based is Chrétien de Troyes (born c. 1140—1150, died before 1191). The principal characters of the *Artusroman* are the knights of Arthur's court (Erec, Iwein, Parzival, Gawan, Lanzelot). The highest chivalric ideal is vested in 'King' Arthur, and it is his court which attracts the knight. It is from Arthur's court that the knight departs to prove himself in a series of *Aventiuren* (→ AVENTIURE) and to which he returns to add his renown to that of the illustrious company. Arthur's court is thus the chivalric point of reference against which the progress of the hero is measured. The highly popular *Artusroman* served as the framework for some of the most profound poetic statements on the human condition in knightly terms at the turn of the 12th century (Hartmann von Aue, *Erec, Iwein*; Wolfram von Eschenbach, *Parzival*). It was also used as a vehicle for the compilation of mere adventure stories (Heinrich von dem Türlin, *Der Aventiure Crône*).

P.Oe.

ASSONANZ (assonance) = Gleichklang

Repetition or similarity of vowel sounds in neighbouring stressed words or syllables;

e.g.: Noch spür ich ihren Atem auf den Wangen:
Wie kann das sein, daß diese nahen Tage
Fort sind, für immer fort, und ganz vergangen?
(Hofmannsthal, *Terzinen über Vergänglichkeit*).

ATEKTONISCH = offene Form → GESCHLOSSENE FORM

AUBADE → TAGELIED

AUFBAU

Organized structure of a work, the manner in which its elements are combined to form a coherent whole.

AUFFÜHRUNG (performance)

Presentation of a dramatic or musical work to an audience.

AUFGESANG

The opening section of the Minnesang— und →MEISTERSANGSTROPHE, consisting of two →STOLLEN. →ABGESANG. →SONETT.

AUFKLÄRUNG (Enlightenment)

In general any movement advocating a rational, unprejudiced, sceptical, scientific and reformatory approach to life. More specifically it is a European movement with its roots in the 16th century but dominant in the 18th century. Its philosophies go back to the English thinkers Bacon (1561—1626), Hobbes (1588—1679), Locke (1632—1704) and Hume (1711—1776) and the French philosophers Descartes (1596—1650), Bayle (1647—1706), Montesquieu (1689—1755), Diderot (1713—1784), with Rousseau (1712—1778) leading on to new ideas. They prepare the way for the French Revolution. In Germany the *Aufklärung* is usually dated from 1720—1785 (Goethe's classicism) but it continues as an undercurrent to the end of the Romantic period, the earliest of often concurrent but also successive trends, since → STURM UND DRANG builds on *Aufklärung* as → KLASSIK does on *Sturm und Drang* and → ROMANTIK on *Klassik*. It is introduced by Leibniz (1646—1716) with his rational theology of pre-established harmony but takes a more practical turn with the similarly optimistic philosophies of Thomasius (1655—1728) and Christian Wolff (1679—1754), supported by Mendelssohn (1729—1786), Lichtenberg (1742—1799) and Nicolai (1733—1811). It is tempered and expanded by pietist trends

(→ PIETISMUS) leading to a cult of sensibility and earlier baroque trends rationalized to Rococo (→ ANAKREONTIK). The literature of the *Aufklärung* is dominated by the theories of Boileau (1636–1711) and Gottsched (1700–1766), later modified by Bodmer (1698–1783) Breitinger (1701–1776) and Lessing (1729–1781). They demand well-defined genres, the dramatic unities, avoidance of the unreal, clarity and good taste, all aimed at teaching and delighting. Literature is to serve the purposes of *Aufklärung* i.e. virtue, pleasure and human brotherhood. It was carried by the emerging bourgeois classes and was hostile to the Church, authoritarian institutions and all sources of intolerance. Its doctrines are summed up in Lessing's *Nathan der Weise* (1779). Representative German writers are Gottsched (1700–1766), Haller (1708–1777), Gellert (1715–1769), Wieland (1733–1813) and Lessing.

S.H.

AUFLAGE (edition)

Total number of copies of a book etc. published at one time. N.B.: eine Auflage von 1,000 = a run of 1,000 copies.

AUFRISS

Concise and systematic description of a discipline.

AUFSATZ (essay, article) = Artikel

Short prose composition in a newspaper or magazine dealing with a particular topic. → ABHANDLUNG, → ESSAY.

AUFTAKT → ANAKRUSIS

AUFTRAGSDICHTUNG

Poetry which an author is commissioned to write.

AUFTRITT

1. Entrance: appearance of a character on stage.
2. Scene: division of an act. → AKT, → SZENE.

AUFZUG → AKT

AUKTORIALES ERZÄHLEN

Term which came into prominence with the appearance of Franz K. Stanzel's *Die typischen Erzählsituationen im Roman* (1955) and *Typische Formen des Romans* (1964), in which Stanzel proposes a typology of the novel based on three basic narrative situations (points of view): *auktoriale, Ich*– and *personale*

Erzählsituation. Authorial narrative is characterized, according to Stanzel, by the presence of an identifiable narrator who intervenes in and comments on the narrative. Although this authorial narrator may appear at first sight to be identical with the author, this is not the case. The narrator is as much a creation of the author as are the characters of the novel, and as much an integral part of the novel structure. As opposed to the *Ich—Erzähler*, the authorial narrator is usually not involved in the action of the narrative, but relates events from a distance. As opposed to the *personale Erzählsituation*, where the narrative voice is reduced to a minimum and attention is focussed primarily on the characters, the authorial narrator has a personality which is revealed in his style of presentation and his comments on the narrative. The authorial narrator may be named in the novel, like Serenus Zeitblom in Thomas Mann's *Doktor Faustus* (1947) or may be completely anonymous; he may claim complete or only limited knowledge of events and motives. → ERZÄHLER, → PERSPEKTIVE.

E.W.H.

AULABÜHNE

Stage for the performance of → SCHULDRAMA (→ JESUITENDICHTUNG) in the *aula* (assembly hall) of a school.

AUSDRUCK (expression)

Communication of the inner and emotional make-up of the speaker by the full employment of all linguistic means (vocabulary, syntax, rhythm, metre, figures of speech etc.)

AUSDRUCKSKUNST → EXPRESSIONISMUS

AUSDRUCKSWERT

The capacity of linguistic structures to communicate an emotional message, in addition to their lexical meaning.

AUSGABE (edition) = Edition

Form in which a work is published. The term is often used with qualifying additions:
Ausgabe letzter Hand (last edition during the author's lifetime)
autorisierte Ausgabe (authorized edition)
broschierte Ausgabe (soft-cover edition)
→ DIPLOMATISCHE AUSGABE
editio castigata, castrata, expurgata, kastrierte Ausgabe, purgierte Ausgabe (editions for a special purpose, e.g. their use in schools, bowdlerized edition)
Erstausgabe, editio princeps (first edition)
Gesamtausgabe (complete works)

kritische Ausgabe, historisch-kritische Ausgabe (critical edition)
Lederausgabe (leather-bound edition)
Leinenausgabe (hard-bound edition with linen cover)
Lizenzausgabe (edition printed under licence)
Originalausgabe (original edition)
Taschenausgabe (pocket edition)
Taschenbuchausgabe (paperback edition)
Volksausgabe (inexpensive edition)

AUSHÄNGEBOGEN

Advance sheets the printer sends to the publisher and/or author to indicate the progress and quality of the printing.

AUSLAUT

Last sound of a syllable or word. →ANLAUT.

AUSLEGUNG (exegesis)

Analytical interpretation of a text. → EXEGESE, → INTERPRETATION.

AUSSTATTUNG

Collective term for the décor, costumes and props of a play.

AUSSTATTUNGSSTÜCK (revue) = Verwandlungsstück

Play in which décor, costumes and props are of prime importance.

AUTOGRAPH = Dichterhandschrift

Text written in the author's own hand.

AUTORENEXEMPLARE

Copies (of his published work) which according to his contract, the author is entitled to receive free of charge.

AUTORKORREKTUR

An author's corrections or revision. →BÜRSTENABZUG, →FAHNENKOR-REKTUR, →HAUSKORREKTUR.

AUTORISIERTE AUSGABE (authorized edition) → AUSGABE

AVENTIURE = Abenteuer

A term used in MHG epic poetry to denote an 'adventure' or incident. The

Aventiure usually involves a test of the knight's prowess and skill and therefore serves as a means by which he may increase his renown.

The term is also used to denote a segment of an epic (chapter, canto), or an epic as a whole. →ARTUSROMAN.

P.Oe.

BADEZELLENBÜHNE = Terenzbühne

Stage form of the → SCHULDRAMA common in the 16th century. The upstage area behind the empty forestage was divided by curtains into cell-like cubicles. Each cubicle represented the interior of a house or room. As this type of stage was not suited to changes of scene, the actors moved from one cubicle to the next, to indicate a change of location. The incorrect term → TERENZ-BÜHNE arose because illustrations of this type of stage were common in early editions of the Roman writer Terence (c. 195–159 B.C.).

BÄNKELSANG = Moritat

The art of the *Bänkelsänger* or *Moritatensänger*, who from the beginning of the 17th to the mid-20th century performed songs based on popular melodies, *Bänkellieder* or *Moritaten*, at the fairground and market-place. *Bänkelsang* was characterized by its sensational subject-matter, describing murders, executions, robberies, violent love affairs, natural disasters and also political events, often coupled with a strong didactic or moralistic intention. The *Bänkelsänger* functioned both as an entertainer and, although his songs were not always directly topical, as a 'walking newspaper', his aim being to sell the text of the *Moritat* to the public. Indispensable properties of *Bänkelsang* were the *Bank*, the platform on which the singer performed; the *Schild*, the poster on which the action of the *Moritat* was depicted in single episodes; and musical accompaniment on the barrel-organ.

While the *Bänkelsänger* sang, indicating each episode on the *Schild* with a pointer, another member of the troupe would hawk copies of the text. Because of its potential mass audience, elements of *Bänkelsang* were fused with the literary ballad, notably by poets of the 1848 Revolution, who introduced parody and a sharper political content, then in the late 19th and early 20th century by Wedekind (1864–1918) and Holz (1863–1929), who adapted *Bänkelsang* to a cabaret context. Although traditional *Bänkelsang* has been superseded in popular culture by film and the recording industry, it has survived in part in the ballads of poets such as Brecht (*Die Moritat von Mackie Messer*, 1928), Kästner (1899–1974), Rühmkorf (1929–), Christa Reinig (1926–) and Biermann (1936–).

W.S.S.

BALLADE

Category of verse, which over the last 200 years has developed from an interweaving of literary and popular elements. According to Goethe (1749– 1832), the *Ballade* is characterized by its mixture of the three major genres, a definition by and large valid today. It is *lyrical* in its affinity to song, its use of the refrain; *dramatic* in its dialogue, tempo, concentrated scenes, turning-points; and *epic* in its narrative content and impersonal story-telling tone. Frequently, it revolves around some tragic historical, legendary or mythological incident. The literary *Ballade* or *Kunstballade*, of which the first example is said to be Bürger's *Lenore* (1774), evolved out of the 18th century interest in folk song. Goethe and Schiller (1759–1805) brought the *Ballade* to a high point in the late 18th century, transforming it from a simple depiction of mysterious natural phenomena (*Erlkönig, Der Fischer*) to a vehicle for moral instruction (*Der Gott und die Bajadere, Der Handschuh, Die Kraniche des Ibykus*). The Romantic era saw a revival of interest in the popular and musical qualities of the *Ballade*, poets such as Brentano (1778–1842) and Eichendorff (1788–1857) endowing it with the simplicity and lyricism of the → VOLKS-LIED (*Auf dem Rhein, Waldgespräch*). Although the *Ballade* was favoured by many 19th century poets e.g. Mörike (1804–1875), Storm (1817–1888), Keller (1819–1890), Meyer (1825–1898), it had lost much of its vitality by the beginning of the 20th century. But Heine (1797–1856), by injecting humour and satire into it, (*Jammertal, Lobgesang auf König Ludwig I*), antici-pated later writers such as Wedekind (1864–1918) (*Brigitte B.*), who also found inspiration for the literary *Ballade* in the popular → BÄNKELSANG and the French → CHANSON. This tradition was continued by Brecht (1898–1956), who firmly established the *Ballade* as an instrument of social and political protest (*Legende vom toten Soldaten, Die Ballade vom Wasserrad*) (→ POLITI-SCHE DICHTUNG). Brecht's influence is evident in contemporary practitioners of the *Ballade*, such as Biermann (1936–) (*Ballade auf den Dichter François Villon*) and Enzensberger (1929–) (*Mausoleum*). The term *Ballade* has widened in the 20th century to include almost any narrative poem; the alternative term *Erzählgedicht* has thus been proposed by Heinz Piontek (1925–) to supersede it. The typical *Ballade* stanza is that of the *Volkslied*, although numerous variations are to be found.

W.S.S.

BARDE (bard)

Med. Celtic court poet, whose function was to sing and compose songs celebrating heroic deeds, and relating historical events; usually to the accompani-ment of a harp.

BAROCK (Baroque)

The word 'baroque' is derived from the Portuguese *barocco* meaning an irregularly shaped pearl, and was first applied in the 17th century as a term of abuse to characterize forms of art and architecture that did not adhere to the regular classical models. Today the term describes one of the great European styles in architecture, the visual arts, music and literature, which flourished from the late 16th to the early 18th centuries. Its salient features are its dynamic character and intensity, its ornateness and rich expression, its preoccupation with the yearnings of man for a higher spiritual existence.

It was during the baroque period that German literature made rapid progress in many fields towards the high standards and achievements in other countries of Western Europe. This may be claimed of the courtly and religious poetry, for which Martin Opitz provided a book of prescribed rules and patterns in the classical tradition, his *Buch von der Deutschen Poeterey* (1624). The sonnet with Fleming (1609–1640), Gryphius (1616–1664), Hofmannswaldau (1617–1679) and the church hymn with Gerhardt (1607–1670), Spee (1591–1635) in particular experienced their first flowering in the history of German literature. The same holds true for the serious drama of the age, whose development culminated in the Latin plays of the Jesuits (→ JESUITENDICHTUNG) and the tragedies of Andreas Gryphius. Both genres demonstrated the vanity and frailty of worldly existence, both similarly propagated the Christian message of man's ultimate salvation. It is this dualism which not only formed the central idea of the baroque tragedy and martyr play, but also determined their structure, style and imagery, all of them rich in contrast. The novel is generally regarded as representing the finest achievement of 17th century German literature. This evaluation is certainly justified in the case of Christoph Grimmelshausen's *Simplicissimus* (1669), which depicts the life and changing fortunes of its title hero against the background of the chaotic times of the Thirty Years War. Adhering to the picaresque tradition (→ SCHELMENROMAN) in its outer form, the novel succeeds in presenting a profound and comprehensive picture of a world darkened by suffering and sorrow and of a protagonist, who, after withstanding successive personal calamities, comes to realize the futility of his worldly endeavours and decides to end his life as a God-fearing hermit.

Johann Gottfried Herder (1744–1803) has termed the baroque period in German literature an 'emblematic age' (→ EMBLEM). The phrase is suggestive of the abundance in all literary genres of pictorial and ornamental devices such as the metaphor (→ METAPHER) and simile (→ VERGLEICH), sign and symbol (→ SYMBOL), allegory (→ ALLEGORIE) and emblem. They were employed to heighten the effect of the literary work and to impress the style-conscious, learned reader or theatre-goer, for the conventional imagery of the time did not originate from personal experience, but was deeply rooted in the classical heritage.

H.W.N.

BAUERNDICHTUNG

Literature which depicts aspects of village life, although it is more often than not written by city dwellers. → DORFGESCHICHTE, → DORFROMAN, → HEIMATDICHTUNG.

BEARBEITUNG

Any change or revision of a work carried out by a person or persons other than the author. → FASSUNG.

BEDEUTUNG

Meaning of a word, sentence or work.

BEDEUTUNGSLEHRE → SEMANTIK

BEDEUTUNGSWANDEL (semantic change)

The complete or partial change of meaning undergone by a word over an extended period.

BEIORDNUNG → PARATAXE

BEISEITESPRECHEN (aside)

Theatrical device where a character on stage makes a remark which is only audible to the audience but not to the other characters.

BEKENNTNIS, BEKENNTNISDICHTUNG (confession) = Confessiones, = Selbstbekenntnis

Literature which concentrates on the inner development and psychological self-discovery of the first-person narrator.

BELEGEXEMPLAR

Copy of the text which the author or publisher is entitled to receive free of charge.

BELLETRISTIK (belles-lettres) = schöne Literatur

Term for imaginative literature, as distinct from non-fiction. → DICHTUNG, → LITERATUR.

BENEFIZ (benefit)

Performance of a play, concert, opera or ballet for the benefit of an actor, singer, dancer, author or a charity.

BERICHT

Concise and ordered report of facts or events, excluding all extraneous matter. → BOTENBERICHT.

BESCHREIBUNG (description, depiction)

Description of phenomena which makes full use of stylistic and rhetorical devices in order to communicate the author's impressions, and his emotional reaction to them.

BESPRECHUNG (review) → REZENSION

BESSERUNGSSTÜCK

Sub-genre of the → ZAUBERSTÜCK. The aim of the *Besserungsstück* is the correction of human failures or foibles. This is usually achieved with the help of supernatural powers. → VOLKSKOMÖDIE.

BESTIARIUM (bestiary)

Med. collection of natural histories of animals, which are woven into moralizing fictional narratives.

BETONUNG → AKZENT

BEWUSSTSEINSSTROM → STREAM OF CONSCIOUSNESS

BIBLIA PAUPERUM → ARMENBIBEL

BIBLIOGRAPHIE (bibliography)

1. List of books and articles consulted.
2. Description (author, title, publisher, date and place of publication, number of pages, size), collection or selection of books according to specific criteria; e.g.: bibliography of an author, a specific topic, or books printed in a country within a given period. = Bücherkunde.

BIBLISCHES DRAMA (biblical drama)

As distinct from → GEISTLICHES DRAMA any play which is based on material from the Bible, and is not written for the celebration of a religious event.

BIEDERMEIER

1. Term originally coined by Ludwig Eichrodt (1827–1892) and Adolf

Kußmaul (1822–1902) in the title of their collection of parodic lyric poetry, *Gedichte des schwäbischen Schullehrers Gottlieb Biedermaier und seines Freundes Horatius Treuherz* published in the Munich *Fliegende Blätter* between 1855 and 1857. In this context it referred to someone belonging to the lower middle class, limited, prosaic, provincial and conservative.

2. Term applied to style of interior decoration in post-Napoleonic Germany, and then to painting of the same period, particularly the work of painters emphasizing the small idyllic details of everyday life, such as Ludwig Richter (1803–1884), Moritz von Schwind (1804–1871) and Carl Spitzweg (1808–1885).

3. Term applied by extension to denote the cultural-historical epoch 1815–1848. → RESTAURATIONSZEIT, → VORMÄRZ.

4. Applied to the literature of the years 1815–1848, the term suggests a distinction between the writers of this period and earlier Romanticism on the one hand, and later Realism on the other hand. The difficulty is however that the writers of this period do not form a homogeneous group. *Biedermeier* suggests characteristics (idyllic, conservative, apolitical etc.) which are not applicable to the writers of the *Junge Deutschland* movement, and other writers of the time such as Stifter (1805–1868) and Mörike (1804–1875) cannot satisfactorily be included. As a literary term, *Biedermeier* has not gained universal acceptance and has not yet been satisfactorily defined.

E.W.H.

BILD → **SPRACHLICHES BILD**

BILDERBIBEL

Illustrated edition of the Bible, possibly with an incomplete text. → ARMENBIBEL.

BILDERLYRIK (carmina figurata) = Carmina figurata, = Figurengedichte.

Poetry in which the stanzas, (or the poem as a whole), are typographically arranged in the shape of some symbolic object which has some connection with the content or themes of the poem. This type of poetry was especially popular during the baroque period. → BAROCK.

BILDERSCHRIFT (pictographic writing)

Non-phonetic script which uses pictorial symbols to depict words or concepts; e.g.: hieroglyphics, Chinese characters. → LAUTSCHRIFT, → SILBENSCHRIFT.

BILDGEDICHT → GEMÄLDEGEDICHT

BILDNIS (image)

A *Bildnis*, perhaps better rendered in English by 'graven image' is in literary criticism a fixed opinion or stereotyped view of someone or some group of people. The image is derived from preconceptions about a character's social function (e.g. the doctor, the soldier, the business-man) which exclude awareness of individuality, or preconceptions about a group with a common characteristic (e.g. Jews, terrorists, students) which ignore the possibilities of individual variations and differences. Although the concept is not a new one (e.g. Shylock's rejection of the image of the Jew in *Merchant of Venice* III, i), the term *Bildnis* gained currency particularly in the work of Max Frisch (1911–). → MASKE, → ROLLENSPIEL.

E.W.H.

BILDUNG

The development of a person's intellectual and emotional attributes to their fullest potential. *Bildung* is much more than the acquisition of skills and knowledge; it includes the development of a keen sense of ethical values, dignity, tolerance, judgement and the ability to draw on the achievements of intellectual and artistic developments and incorporate them into a mode of life suitable to the individual concerned and acceptable to society as a whole. "Accordingly our language, appropriately enough, is wont to use the word *Bildung* both of a product of formation and of the process". (Goethe, *Zur Morphologie*, 1817).

A.O.

BILDUNGSROMAN

The name invented in 1870 by Dilthey for the exceptionally influential type of German novel he saw in Goethe's *Wilhelm Meisters Lehrjahre* (1795f.) one in which the centre of interest is to be found not so much in the adventures of the hero, himself a passive character, as in the effects which his experiences are seen to have in his growth to maturity and clarity of purpose, after perhaps fumbling beginnings. Such a novel is often a veiled autobiography of the author, full of general reflections on life in the tradition of German Classicism, with its aim of full self-development, inspired by the art and wisdom of the past and present. Literary historians see the *Bildungsroman* foreshadowed in Wieland's *Agathon* (1766), and even in Wolfram's *Parzival* (c.1210). Typical examples after Goethe are Novalis's *Heinrich von Ofterdingen* (1802) Eichendorff's *Ahnung und Gegenwart* (1815), Keller's *Der grüne Heinrich* (1854), Freytag's *Soll und Haben* (1855), Stifter's *Der Nachsommer* (1857), Raabe's *Der Hungerpastor* (1864) and Thomas Mann's *Der Zauberberg* (1924). Closely related and often overlapping types are the → ENTWICKLUNGSROMAN, in which the hero's life-story is associated with general features of his time, and the *Erziehungsroman*, which stresses the influence of educational institutions.

W.H.B.

BINNENERZÄHLUNG

In a → RAHMENERZÄHLUNG, the story or stories within the framework.

BINNENREIM (internal rhyme)

Rhyme within the verse line; e.g.: Mir ist bange, daß du lange vergangen bist. (Rilke, *Das jüngste Gericht*).

BÎSPEL (exemplum)

MHG literary form: short didactic story, which illustrates and describes a situation or condition and draws a moral lesson from it.

BITTERFELDER WEG

Bitterfelder Weg denotes a cultural policy current in the GDR from the late 1950s to the mid 1960s. In an avowed attempt to bridge the gulf between art and ordinary people, and emphasizing the social function and educative potential of art in this process, the S.E.D. (Socialist Unity Party) and the Writers' Union promoted a twofold policy: (i) to encourage professional writers to use easily understood language, to treat contemporary themes, to familiarize themselves with production processes and workers' living conditions by spending time in industry or on the land; (ii) to encourage workers to take up the pen ("Greif' zur Feder, Kumpel!"), forming writing circles at their workplace and becoming active participants in culture, not merely passive consumers. The policy was formulated at the first Bitterfeld Conference (24th April 1959), sponsored jointly by the Mitteldeutscher Verlag and a socialist work brigade at the Bitterfeld electrochemical factory where it was held. Literary works regarded as products of *Bitterfeld* are: Franz Fühmann's *Kabelkran und blauer Peter* (1961), Karl-Heinz Jakobs's *Beschreibung eines Sommers* (1961), Brigitte Reimann's *Ankunft im Alltag* (1961) whose title became synonymous with the thematic orientation of the *Bitterfelder Weg*, Erwin Strittmatter's *Ole Bienkopp* (1963), Erik Neutsch's *Spur der Steine* (1964). The *Bitterfelder Weg* reasserted the method of Socialist Realism (→ SOZIALISTISCHER REALISMUS) in the face of 'bourgeois decadent' literary influences (→ FORMALISMUS) feared in the post-XXth Soviet Party Congress 'thaw'. The second Bitterfeld Conference (24th April 1964) praised the achievements of this policy but paradoxically also signalled its end, and the *Bitterfelder Weg* has all but disappeared from the literary scene in the GDR today.

B.E.

BLANKVERS (blank verse)

Unrhymed decasyllabic line of poetry, usually iambic pentameter.

BLAUE BLUME (blue flower)

Term first used by Novalis in his novel *Heinrich von Ofterdingen* (1802). The *blue flower* became the symbol of all Romantic aspirations and feelings.

BLINDES MOTIV

Motif which occurs only once and is not followed up. →MOTIV.

BLUBO

Abbreviation of *Blut— und Bodendichtung:* collective term for a trivial form of → TENDENZDICHTUNG favoured by the Nazis; the idealizing of the peasant's closeness to the soil and his special blood ties to his kinship group were the principal features. →HEIMATDICHTUNG.

BLÜTENLESE (anthology)

Collection of texts selected according to certain criteria; e.g.: love poetry, women's literature etc.

BOGEN = Druckbogen

Unfolded sheet of paper which after printing is folded and cut to size.

BOTENBERICHT

Dramatic device of reporting by messenger actions and events, which for various reasons have not taken place on stage, and which may have a significant effect on the plot.

BOULEVARDKOMÖDIE

Unassuming, and frequently artistically mediocre comedy whose main aim is success at the box-office.

BRECHUNG

General term for any occasion where metrical and syntactical structures do not coincide. → ENJAMBEMENT, → REIMBRECHUNG.

BREITE → EPISCHE BREITE

BRETTL → KABARETT

BRIEFROMAN (epistolary novel)

Novel largely or totally composed of fictitious letters; e.g.: Goethe's *Die Leiden des jungen Werthers* (1774).

BRIGHELLA

Stock male character from the → COMMEDIA DELL'ARTE; a clever scheming servant who usually relied on → ARLECCHINO to carry out his plans.

BROSCHIERTE AUSGABE (soft cover edition) → AUSGABE

BROSCHÜRE (pamphlet, booklet)

Short publication, usually stapled together with a soft cover, treating a subject of contemporary interest.

BRUCHSTÜCK → FRAGMENT

BUCHGEMEINSCHAFT (book club) = Lesering

Association where members may buy books substantially reduced in price.

BUCHMALEREI (illumination) → MINIATUR

BUCHMESSE

Annual book fair where publishers exhibit their latest productions.

BÜCHERKUNDE → BIBLIOGRAPHIE

BÜHNE (stage)

Elevated platform on which dramatic performances take place; (fig.) theatre, drama, arena. → AULABÜHNE, → BADEZELLENBÜHNE, → DREH-BÜHNE, → GUCKKASTENBÜHNE, → SHAKESPEAREBÜHNE, → SIMUL-TANBÜHNE, → SUKZESSIVBÜHNE.

BÜHNENANWEISUNG (stage direction) = Szenenanweisung

Instruction in the text of a play which specifies the production requirements such as gestures, exits, entrances, sound effects, lighting etc.

BÜHNENAUSSPRACHE

Standardized pronunciation of High German, obligatory for all theatres.

BÜHNENBEARBEITUNG

The modification or adaptation of a dramatic work for a performance.

BÜHNENBILD (set)

Décor of a play, scenery.

BÜHNENMANUSKRIPT

Text prepared for the performance of a drama; may be the actual manuscript before it is printed or the adaptation of an already printed text.

BÜRGERLICHER REALISMUS → REALISMUS

BÜRGERLICHES TRAUERSPIEL (bourgeois tragedy)

Sometimes confused with → WEINERLICHES LUSTSPIEL, *Bürgerliches Drama* and → TRAGIKOMÖDIE. Sub-genre that arose in the middle of the 18th century with Lessing's *Miß Sara Sampson* (1755). Further outstanding examples are Lessing's *Emilia Galotti* (1772), Schiller's *Kabale und Liebe* (1784) and later Hebbel's *Maria Magdalena* (1844). Guthke counts 24 *Bürgerliche Trauerspiele* by 1800. Similar dramas in Britain and France, e.g. Lillo (1693–1739), Diderot (1713–1784), merely substantiated the German tradition, whereas the sentimental novels of Samuel Richardson (1689–1761) had some direct influence. Both contemporary theory, e.g.: Lessing (1729–1781), Nicolai (1733–1811), and recent scholarship refute the assumption that the notion of class was determining. A better criterion is the private, homely nature of the *Bürgerliche Trauerspiel*, facilitating empathy and compassion (*Mitleiden*) as against the cold admiration engendered by heroic drama and its public setting. Since the private (bourgeois) world of the family is shown to be the nucleus of sincere human relations, the bourgeois class indirectly projects itself as the most human, universal and perfect of classes. *Bürgerliches Trauerspiel* stands in a dramatic tradition questioning the exclusive right of the noble aristocrat to tragedy. Social criticism is outspoken in only a few examples, Schiller (1759–1805), Hebbel (1813–1863).

S.H.

BÜRSTENABZUG (brush-proofs, galley-proofs) → AUTORKORREKTUR, → FAHNENKORREKTUR, → HAUSKORREKTUR

BÜTTEN (handmade paper)

BUKOLIK → HIRTENDICHTUNG

BUNDESTHEATER

Austrian term referring specifically to the three theatres which are financed and administered by the federal government: *Volksoper, Staatsoper* and *Burgtheater*. Also known as → STAATSTHEATER.

BURLESKE (burlesque)

1. Exaggerated and incongruous imitation of a person or literary style, for

satiric and comic effect.

2. Short satirical comedy, which employs caricature and overstatement in order to ridicule the peculiarities of a person, or of a specific literary taste.

BUTZENSCHEIBENLYRIK

Pejorative term first used by Paul Heyse in a letter (7th April 1884) to Emanuel Geibel, to mock a trend of poetry fashionable in the late 19th century. This type of poetry imitated Scheffel's *Trompeter von Säckingen* (1854) and *Gaudeamus* (1868); it idealized the exploits of med. emperors, life in med. cities and castles, and romanticized the M.A. generally.

CAESUR → ZÄSUR

CANTO (canto) = Gesang
Subdivision of an epic poem. → EPOS.

CAPITANO
Stock character from the → COMMEDIA DELL'ARTE; the braggart soldier.

CAPRICCIO
A fancyful, light-hearted, sketchy piece of prose. Because of its vagueness the term is used very rarely.

CAPTATIO BENEVOLENTIAE (modesty topos)
Rhetorical figure in which the author seeks the goodwill of his audience; e.g.: "I conjure you all that have had the evil luck to read this ink-wasting toy of mine. . ." (Sidney: *An Apology for Poetry*). → DEVOTIONSFORMEL.

CARMEN (poem)
This term was originally used to designate any metrically structured formal utterance, such as a prayer, incantation, etc. However, it can now apply to an epic or didactic poem, or even to a drama but this usage is rare.

CARMINA FIGURATA → BILDERLYRIK

CASUS → KASUS

CHANSON (chanson)
In med. times, a sung poem or a poem with musical accompaniment, usually strophic, with a refrain, and of varying metrical forms. The chanson was often a lyric on the theme of love. The term is now taken to mean a witty, impudent and succinct song for the cabaret stage. → BALLADE, → CHANSON DE GESTE.

CHANSON DE GESTE (chanson de geste)
Med. French narrative poem which was sung or recited with musical

accompaniment; frequently treating historical or mythical figures and events. It was usually decasyllabic, strophic, divided into laisses, and assonanced, later rhymed. The oldest surviving example is *La Chanson de Roland*, written c. 1100.

CHAP-BOOK → **VOLKSBUCH**

CHARAKTERISIERUNG (characterization)

The presentation and description of characters in a text so that the reader/ spectator has an impression of their appearance and personality, and their thoughts, words and actions may be seen to be commensurate with the type of person they are portrayed as.

CHARAKTERKOMIK

The comic effect derived from flaws in the character (e.g. greed, pride, vanity etc.) rather than from the situation. → SITUATIONSKOMIK.

CHARGE

Supporting role, which although small, requires a vivid and strong portrayal by the actor; e.g.: the *Kapuziner* in Schiller's *Wallenstein*.

CHEFREDAKTEUR → **REDAKTEUR**

CHIASMUS (chiasmus)

Rhetorical figure: the juxtaposition of two phrases or clauses which are identical in syntax, but have an inversion in word order; e.g.: Die Kunst ist lang, und kurz ist unser Leben. (Goethe, *Faust I*).

CHIFFRE (coded message)

In post-Goethean poetry figure of speech which — unlike symbol, metaphor and comparison — no longer establishes an understandable link with a recognizable outside reality within a generally accepted system of values and traditions, but reflects, as a result of the breakdown of such a system, a reality which is uniquely that of the poet's own making. It first gains prominence, therefore, in the myth-creating poetry of Hölderlin (1770–1843), (e.g. *Strom* = pathway of the Greek gods, link between Germany and Greece, between Hölderlin's own time and the Greek past) and in the poetry of the German Romantics. Since its meaning depends not on convention but on the given context of the poem and of the work as a whole, the *Chiffre* establishes multiple cross-references, hence its ambiguity and wealth of associations, e.g. *blau* in the poetry of Benn (1886–1956) with its connotations of mediterranean, dionysian, preconscious and instinctual, and the *Vogel* chiffre in the poetry of Günter Eich

(1907–1972). This summarizing or 'network' effect is often lacking in those cases where the term is more loosely used to describe what T.S. Eliot (1888–1965) called *objective correlative*. →METAPHER, →SYMBOL, →VERGLEICH.

A.V.

CHOR (chorus)

The chorus is the origin and a basic element of ancient Greek tragedy. A group of people speaking with one voice and somehow related to the protagonists accompanied the action, taking part in, reflecting and interpreting it. Attempts to revive the ancient chorus were made in the 17th and 18th centuries in German tragedy (e.g. Gryphius calling it *Reyen* and Klopstock in his *Hermann* plays using ancient ode forms). The development culminates in Schiller's *Braut von Messina* (1803) and its preface *Über den Gebrauch des Chors in der Tragödie*. For Schiller the chorus is the crowning element of the idealistic tragedy, because "it transfers the commonplace actual world into the old poetical one". It is the *Indifferenzpunkt* "that which lies at the exact medium between the ideal and the sensible" (*Sinnlichen*) in that it is "in itself, not an individual but a general conception; yet it is represented by a palpable body which appeals to the senses with an imposing grandeur". Wilhelm von Humboldt sums up Schiller's ideas with ingenuity: "The chorus [. . .] is the final summit on which it is possible to remove tragedy from the sphere of reality and mundane life, and it perfects the pure symbolism of the work of art", (letter to Schiller, 22nd Oct. 1803). Although Schiller felt that the incorporation of the chorus into his tragedy had made him a "contemporary of Sophocles" (letter to Humboldt, 17th Feb. 1803), he soon had imitators who were quick to adopt this feature of classical tragedy. After the initial enthusiastic reception of *Die Braut von Messina*, however, which critics described as the climax of modern tragedy, interest in the chorus faded quickly. Realism in the 19th century had no use for such an unnatural element in theatre. Some 20th century playwrights have revived it mainly for parodic purposes (e.g. Brecht in *Die heilige Johanna der Schlachthöfe*, 1932 or Frisch in *Biedermann und die Brandstifter*, 1958).

C.G.

CHORAL (chorale)

1. Sacred song, hymn.

2. Plainsong, a simple melody sung or chanted in unison, with free speech rhythms rather than a strict metrical form.

CHOREOGRAPHIE (choreography)

Design or arrangement of dance, esp. ballet.

CHORLIED

Text intended for presentation by a chorus. →CHOR.

CHRISTSPIEL → ADVENTSPIEL

CHRONIK

Presentation of historical facts in chronological order.

CLAQUE (claque), **CLAQUEUR** (claqueur)

A claque is a group of people hired to initiate and sustain applause for a performing artist, a claqueur is a member of such a group.

CLIO → KLIO

CODEX (codex) = Kodex

Forerunner of the modern book; in Roman times wooden or ivory tables connected by hinges, rings or strips, in the M.A. replaced by parchment.

COLLAGE = Kollage

Literary technique which selects excerpts of texts from a variety of sources (sometimes including material in foreign languages) and collates and compiles them into a new work or part of a new work. Not to be confused with → MONTAGE.

COLOMBINA (Columbine) = Smeraldina

Stock character from the → COMMEDIA DELL'ARTE; a cheeky chambermaid, daughter or servant of → PANTALONE and lover of → ARLECCHINO.

COMEDIE LARMOYANTE → WEINERLICHES LUSTSPIEL

COMMEDIA DELL'ARTE

Form of Italian comedy which flourished in the 16th and 17th centuries. It was above all a popular entertainment, welcomed by both court nobles and villagers, all of whom were given the opportunity to watch performances by the various touring troupes of actors which sprang up after 1550. There is no fixed definition of the form or content of the comedies performed, because complete play texts were not used. However, they shared a number of features, which included improvisation, a great deal of physical action and slapstick comedy, the repeated appearance of well-known character types, and the use of masks.

Each performance was based on a plot outline; its central theme always seemed to involve young people in love, the jealousies and rivalries of old people, and the plots and intrigues of the servants, or *zanni*. The outlines were filled in with such elements as improvised clowning, bawdiness, slapstick, verbal and physical abuse and rapid action, all of which delighted the audiences. Improvisation was a highly specialized skill, and it was argued that actors who were capable of improvising were infinitely superior to actors who simply memorized and repeated a script. Although improvisation was an important element, it should be noted that the art was based on a series of conventions and set speeches, which were learned by heart, and used where appropriate. Comic effects were usually drawn from a stock of *lazzi* — tricks or comic turns — which would interrupt the action to provide clowning interludes, often equivalent to the familiar custard-pie routine. Actors specialized in particular character-types, and the familiarity which this gave them with their roles helped to build immense skills in improvisation, as well as developing a strong working rapport among the members of the company. Stock characters of the *commedia dell'arte* were drawn from Latin comedy, and included types such as the cunning slave, the braggart soldier, and the greedy or foolish old man. One of the best-known characters was → ARLECCHINO whose costume became the familiar suit of diamond-shaped multi-coloured patches. He was one of the principal *zanni*, and was responsible for keeping up the pace of the comedy, through acrobatic tricks, coarse jokes and cunning schemes. Other well-known *zanni* were *Pulcinella*, who often appeared with a huge hooked nose and a padded stomach, and acted out scenes of domestic tyranny with his wife. The figure of Mr Punch can be recognized in this character. → BRIGHELLA was another of the cunning servants, who played havoc with the business and love affairs of his master. The masters, usually old men, were *Pantalone*, the stereotyped foolish husband or father, who could be easily outwitted or degraded, and *Dottore*, a doctor or lawyer, the archetypal ridiculous scholar. The braggart soldier figure was presented by *Capitano*. The least interesting characters were the young lovers, whose presence was necessary for the plot. These and other characters were made recognizable in the first instance by the traditional masks and costumes which they wore (e.g., red and black for *Pantalone*, black for *Dottore*), and they always followed similar patterns of behaviour from one plot to the next.

Although *commedia dell'arte* began to die out in the 18th century, its powerful theatricality influenced many playwrights, including Molière (1622–1673), Goldoni (1707–1793) and even Shakespeare (1564–1616) all of whom drew on *commedia* characters. It also influenced the Viennese → VOLKSKOMÖDIE, pantomime (through the use of such figures as *Harlequin, Pierrot* and *Columbine*), and the work of modern playwrights such as Italy's Dario Fo. A 20th century equivalent of *commedia dell'arte* may well be a group like the Marx Brothers, who also played stock characters, working their way through familiar comic and slapstick routines.

L.W.

COMPUTERLYRIK (computer·poetry)

Lyric poetry produced by specially programmed computers.

CONCEITS → KONZETTI

CONFERENCE

Compering of a variety performance, cabaret or party by a *conférencier* (compère). →KABARETT.

CONFESSIONES →BEKENNTNIS

CONTRADICTIO IN ADJECTO

Figure of speech in which the quality present in an adjective is incongruous with the thing being described. e.g.: hölzernes Eisen. →OXYMORON.

COPYRIGHT →URHEBERRECHT

CORRIGENDA (corrigenda)

List of corrections of misprints appended to a text.

COUP DE THEATRE (coup de théâtre)

An unexpected and sudden development in a drama, which may radically change the outcome.

COUPLET

Witty song of frivolous or topical content; its several stanzas are all sung to the same tune and usually finish with the same refrain; used in comic opera and →VOLKSKOMÖDIE. →POSSE.

DA CAPO

Request made by an audience, after sustained applause, for the repetition of a performance or an item.

DADAISMUS (Dadaism)

From its first programmes for the *Cabaret Voltaire* in Zurich in 1916, the international avant-garde movement of Dadaism, productive until around 1922 in Germany, Paris and New York, furthered modernist art in direct contact with the public and created new forms such as sound poems by Hugo Ball (1886–1927), ready-mades by Duchamp (1887–1968) and early compositions in paper, fabric and wood by Hans Arp (1887–1966). Dadaist theory, based mainly on ideas of Ball and Walter Serner (1889–+?) stressed freedom, spontaneity and openness to radical change. Influenced by anarchism and mysticism, the Dadaists mocked traditional European institutions, beliefs and art forms as mere conventions, no longer creative and discredited by their association with the World War. The Dadaists worked with basic modes of expression in sounds (the name *Dada* derives from children's language), with basic shapes and odd conjunctions of everyday objects. Francis Picabia (1879–1953) and Man Ray (1890–1976) established Dada in New York, and from 1919 Dadaism found effective publicists in Berlin e.g. Huelsenbeck (1892–1974) and Paris e.g. Tzara (1896–1963) and was joined by major artists such as Max Ernst (1891–1976) and Schwitters (1887–1948). In Berlin, the left-wing, anti-war thrust of Dadaism was expressed most strongly in the satirical art of Grosz (1893–1959), Hausmann (1886–1971), Wieland Herzfelde (1896–) and Helmut Herzfelde (1891–1968) who published under the pseudonym of John Heartfield.

M.A.

DAKTYLUS (dactyl)

Metrical foot of three syllables, the first stressed or long and the two following unstressed or short. ($\acute{x}$xx). →METRIK.

DAMNATUR

Formula which means 'must not be printed'; negative verdict given by an official censor of the Roman Catholic Church. →IMPRIMATUR.

DARSTELLER

An actor or singer in pursuit of his profession; e.g. der Darsteller des Faust =

the actor playing the part of Faust.

DARSTELLUNG

Literary presentation of real or fictitious events, persons or experiences.

DATIERUNG

The dating of a text, edition etc.

DEBÜT (début)

The first public appearance of a performing artist.

DECADENCE → DEKADENZDICHTUNG

DECKNAME

Fictitious name of an author or of a literary character. → PSEUDONYM.

DECKUNGSAUFLAGE

Number of copies required to be sold in order to recover the production costs of an edition; including the author's honorarium but excluding the cost of advertising.

DEKADENZDICHTUNG

This term which has a more strongly negative connotation in German than in either French or English, denotes a widespread movement in European literature towards the end of the 19th century. *Dekadenzdichtung* is characterized by its awareness of being part of an oversophisticated culture thought to have reached its peak and to be heading towards its decay. Rejecting conventional values, it seeks beauty for its own sake and emphasizes a continuous striving for more intense sensations of every kind. It embraces resignation and pessimism and has a taste for themes of a morbid, exclusive and dreamlike nature. (→ ÄSTHETIZISMUS).

As a literary phenomenon, *Dekadenzdichtung* has its roots in the 19th century, where it is represented in the works of Byron (1788–1824), Baudelaire (1821–1867) and Heine (1797–1856). It finds its most distinct expression in France in the 1880s as a reaction against the Naturalist movement. Its ideals are best exemplified by Des Esseintes, the hero of J.-K. Huysmans's novel *A Rebours* (1884).

In German thinking, the idea of decadence is used by Nietzsche (1844–1900) to describe the cultural situation of his time as one of exhaustion and decay. He sees in Richard Wagner the exemplary decadent (*Der Fall Wagner*, 1888). In German literature the term *Dekadenzdichtung* can only be used with difficulty since it overlaps with the concept of Impressionism (→ IMPRESSIONISMUS).

For this reason it is only used for individual authors or works. A great contribution to this literature comes from Austria in the writings of Altenberg (1859—1919), Schnitzler (1862—1931), Beer-Hofmann (1866—1945) and in the early works of Hofmannsthal (1874—1929) and Rilke (1875—1926), all of which are however also described by the term Impressionism. Thomas Mann's *Buddenbrooks* (1901) and *Tod in Venedig* (1913) are seen as part of German *Dekadenzdichtung* as well as Heinrich Mann's *Im Schlaraffenland* (1900) and Friedrich Huch's *Peter Michel* (1901). After the turn of the century *Dekadenzdichtung* is challenged on the European level by Futurism (→ FUTURISMUS), and in Germany by *Heimatkunst* (→ HEIMATDICHTUNG) and Expressionism (→ EXPRESSIONISMUS).

E.K.

DEKOR, DEKORATION (décor, stage set) → **PROSPEKT**, → **SOFFITTE**, → **VERSETZSTÜCKE**

DELEATUR

Proof-reader's instruction to remove a letter, word or passage. The sign used to indicate this is the Greek delta (δ).

DEMUTSFORMEL → **DEVOTIONSFORMEL**

DENKSCHRIFT (memorandum)

Report to authorities on an important event of public concern.

DENKSPRUCH → **DEVISE**

DENKVERS (mnemonic verse) = Eselsbrücke, = Gedächtnisvers, = Merkvers

Rhymed lines of no literary value which help to remember rules and facts; e.g.: the battle of Issos, 333 B.C.: Drei, drei, drei
Bei Issos Keilerei.

DENKWÜRDIGKEITEN → **MEMOIREN**

DETEKTIVROMAN

One of the two basic types of the → KRIMINALROMAN. In contrast to the *Thriller* where the hunt for a criminal is told in a chronological sequence of dramatic episodes which are geared towards the future — the capture and conviction of the criminal — the *Detektivroman* is analytical in nature. Its action is oriented towards the past. The important event, always a crime and usually a murder, takes place at the beginning or has already taken place when the action of the novel starts. The tension, which is typical of the novel, results from the enigma the crime presents, and the efforts of a detective to solve it. The narrator's perspective is usually that of the detective, and his knowledge, as well as that of the reader, is limited accordingly. As a consequence the reader shares the intellectual efforts of the detective and — at the discretion of the author — explores numerous blind alleys together with him before they both experience the satisfaction of solving the case. Since the *Detektivroman* is best enjoyed if the reader competes with the detective, using his own imagination and sagacity, it is intellectually much more stimulating and rewarding than the *Thriller*, although according to circulation figures, the latter is much more popular.

H.W.

DEUS EX MACHINA (deus ex machina)

Theatrical device: the introduction of a highly unexpected and contrived element in order to effect a resolution of the plot; e.g.: a message or messages from the king or ruler (parodied in Brecht's *Dreigroschenoper*, 1928).

DEUTSCHE BIBLIOTHEK

National library of the FRG, which produces the *Deutsche Bibliographie* (German Bibliography); founded in Frankfurt a.M. in 1946. The East German equivalent is the → DEUTSCHE BÜCHEREI.

DEUTSCHE BÜCHEREI

Founded in 1912 in Leipzig to serve as a National Library, and now situated in the GDR, produces the *Deutsche Nationalbibliographie* (German National Bibliography). The West German equivalent is the → DEUTSCHE BIBLIOTHEK.

DEUTSCHES HOCHSTIFT → FREIES DEUTSCHES HOCHSTIFT

DEUTSCHKUNDE

Concept of German as a teaching subject which extends beyond the traditional notion of teaching German language and literature, embracing such areas as German history, geography, music, philosophy etc.

DEUTSCHORDENSDICHTUNG

The literature of the Order of the Teutonic Knights which flourished from 1300—1400 and had its centre in Marienburg in Prussia. The fusion of religious and knightly concerns is reflected in the favoured themes: either treatments of religious figures from the O.T., such as Esther, Ruth, Daniel and Job; or heroic tales like the Revolt of the Maccabees. Some works were written in Latin, but most were composed in East Middle High German, the official language of the order. The battle of Tannenberg in 1410 signalled the end of the order and its literature.

DEUTUNG

Explanation of the meaning of a literary text. → INTERPRETATION.

DEVISE (motto) = Denkspruch, = Wahlspruch

Phrase or maxim adopted by a person, family or institution as their rule of conduct; frequently inscribed on a coat of arms; e.g.: 'honni soit qui mal y pense' or 'Ich dien'.

DEVOTIONSFORMEL (modesty topos)

Phrase expressing the author's genuine or affected modesty. → CAPTATIO BENEVOLENTIAE.

DIÄRESE (diaeresis)

1. Separate pronunciation of two vowels which could be pronounced as a dipthong; this pronunciation may be indicated by the diaeresis above the second vowel. e.g.: *Aïda.*

2. Pause in a metrical line formed by the coincidence of the end of a word with the end of a metrical foot. → ZÄSUR.

DIALEKTDICHTUNG = Mundartdichtung

Literature in a local or regional variety of a language, a medium of *regional* identification, distinct from *national standard* varieties — FRG, GDR, Austrian, Swiss Standard German. Before the standardization of German, there was only dialect literature. *Dialektdichtung* is more significant in German than in English literature. Dialect is used in concrete poetry e.g. Achleitner (1930–), Artmann (1921–), Jandl (1925–)– Austrian; Eggimann (1936–), Marti (1921–)– Swiss; in film and drama: e.g.: Fassbinder (1946–1982), Qualtinger (1928–), Sperr (1944–), Turrini (1944–). Since the 1970s, as part of a regional resurgence, dialect literature has become a vehicle for social criticism and agitation. Earlier dialect writers include Hebel (1760–1826)– Alemannic; Reuter (1810–1874)– Low German; Nestroy (1801–1862), Raimund (1790–1836)–Viennese. Many have come to create their own orthography for what is usually a spoken code.
M.C.

DIALOG (dialogue)

Speech between two or more persons; the written conversation in a literary work.

DIARIUM → TAGEBUCH

DIASTOLE

Lengthening of a vowel which is naturally short for purposes of versification. → SYSTOLE.

DICHTER (poet)

Person who creates → DICHTUNG. Loosely: author, writer, poet.

DICHTERAKADEMIE

Union of writers whose aim is to advance and encourage literature; with membership by election.

DICHTERHANDSCHRIFT → AUTOGRAPH

DICHTERISCHE FREIHEIT (poetic licence)

A writer's freedom to deviate from conventional rules, facts, etc., where he considers it justified, for the creation of a particular artistic effect.

DICHTERKRÖNUNG

Creation of a poet laureate (*gekrönter Dichter*).

DICHTUNG

1. In the widest sense of the term *Dichtung* is synonymous with → LITERA-TUR esp. when it appears in compounds such as → GESELLSCHAFTS-DICHTUNG or → HIRTENDICHTUNG.

2. In a more specific sense *Dichtung* refers to those achievements of language which are aesthetically and artistically most satisfying. The term therefore implies a value judgement and is used synonymously with *Sprachkunstwerk* and *Poesie*.

A.O.

DICHTUNGSGATTUNGEN → GATTUNGEN

DICHTUNGSLEHRE → POETIK

DICHTUNGSWISSENSCHAFT

That part of → LITERATURWISSENSCHAFT which deals with → DICH-TUNG.

DICTUM → DIKTUM

DIDAKTIK → LEHRDICHTUNG

DIKTION

1. Manner of presentation of ideas and arguments.
2. Delivery, diction.

DIKTUM (dictum, saying) = Dictum

DINGGEDICHT

This term is usually applied to a relatively small number of German poems from the 19th and 20th centuries and is used to distinguish them from poetry that presents itself as the record of an intense personal experience (*Erlebnislyrik*). In the *Dinggedicht* the self of the poem (*das lyrische Ich*) remains in the background and the reader's attention is focussed on a visual reality (*Ding*) whose essence the poem seeks to capture. The term was coined to denote poems by Mörike (*Auf eine Lampe*, 1846), Meyer (*Der römische Brunnen*, 1891) and numerous of Rilke's *Neue Gedichte* (1907f). Its usefulness in wider applications has been severely diminished since German critics have employed it to foster the myth of *objective* poetry. The poetic vision in *Dinggedichte* is no less personal than in *Erlebnislyrik*; the difference lies in the way in which the poem presents itself to the reader, emotions being implicit rather than explicit. While *Dinggedichte* do not usually philosophize or moralize, they do suggest symbolic or metaphysical meanings in the visual realities they evoke. They are rarely content with detached description but are often highly mannered *interpretations* of visual experience. The best *Dinggedichte* present a counterpoint of stasis and movement: inanimate objects are brought to life as the *eye* of the poem travels over them, or else living and hence transient things are endowed by the poem with the permanence of a sculpture or painting.

A.S.

DINGSYMBOL

An object of symbolic meaning, the presence of which signals the occurrence of important events in a text.

DIONYSIEN (Dionysia)

Celebrations in honour of the god Dionysus held in the larger Greek cities lasting for six days, four of which were usually reserved for the performance of new dramatic works.

DIONYSISCH (Dionysian)

The antithesis between *dionysisch* and *apollinisch* developed during the Romantic period gained momentum with the appearance of Nietzsche's *Die Geburt der Tragödie* (1872).

Dionysisch refers to the vitalistic, ecstatic and irrational mode of experiencing the world. This mode of experience is reflected by equally explosive and ecstatic language. *Apollinisch*, in contrast, refers to a more rational, harmonious and ordered mode of experiencing the world and its expression.

A.O.

DIPLOMATISCHE AUSGABE (diplomatic edition)

Reproduction of a text, incorporating all errors and peculiarities as they appear in the original manuscript. →AUSGABE.

DIREKTE REDE (direct speech)

A speaker's original utterance, normally enclosed by quotation marks. →ERLEBTE REDE, →INDIREKTE REDE.

DISEUR, DISEUSE (diseur, diseuse)

Presenter of texts and songs on the cabaret stage. →KABARETT.

DISKURS (discourse, discussion, conversation)

May also refer to a treatise. →ABHANDLUNG.

DISPOSITION

Layout and organization of a speech, an essay or a literary text.

DISSERTATION

Thesis submitted by a university student for a doctoral degree. N.B. the German word *Dissertation* refers to doctoral theses only.

DISSONANZ

Discordance, harshness of language, which may be unintentional, or a deliberate stylistic device.

DISTANZ = Erzählerdistanz

The detachment of the author or narrator from the emotions and experiences expressed. →PERSPEKTIVE, →UNMITTELBARKEIT.

DISTICHON

Dactylic rhyming couplet, made up of one → HEXAMETER and one → PENTAMETER. In Greek and Roman poetry, the verse and metre of the elegy. →ELEGIE.

DITHYRAMBUS (dithyramb)

Choral song chanted by a mass chorus during the → DIONYSIEN. Now refers to a mode of literary expression which uses expressive and vitalistic language.

DIVA (diva)

Famous singer or actress.

DIVERTISSEMENT (divertissement)

Brief interlude of ballet performed in the course of an operatic or dramatic production.

DOKUMENTARTHEATER (documentary theatre)

A form of political theatre in vogue during the 1960s. As in film and television documentaries, the primary function of documentary theatre is the factual and often verbatim presentation of specific events, and its effect is achieved through the edition of the historical source material. Hence the plays are usually based on documents — most commonly the transcripts of trials e.g. Heinar Kipphardt, *In der Sache J. Robert Oppenheimer* (1964), Peter Weiss, *Die Ermittlung* (1964/65) and Hans Magnus Enzensberger, *Das Verhör in Habana* (1970). The term is sometimes (misleadingly) applied to all drama based on historical events during the National Socialist period e.g. Rolf Hochhuth, *Der Stellvertreter* (1963). →POLITISCHE DICHTUNG.

M.H.

DOPPELSINN (double meaning, ambiguity) = Ambiguität,= Mehrdeutigkeit

Occurs when a statement conveys more than one meaning, and is thus subject to multiple interpretations.

DOPPELTE EBENE

Literary device, especially frequent in lyric poetry. A second level of presentation is introduced, with the aim of avoiding uniformity, e.g. reality and myth, human and supernatural. → EBENE.

DORFGESCHICHTE

The most frequent form of → BAUERNDICHTUNG: a relatively short narrative, more often than not written by a city-dweller, which seeks to give a general picture of village life, by describing the customs, activities and problems of villagers, who show close affinities to nature and the soil and are usually unsophisticated. →HEIMATDICHTUNG.

DORFROMAN

Form of → BAUERNDICHTUNG. The narration is of greater length than the → DORFGESCHICHTE. → HEIMATDICHTUNG.

DOTTORE

Stock character from the → COMMEDIA DELL'ARTE; the archetypal ridiculous scholar.

DRAMA (drama)

The origins of the word (from the Greek, meaning 'action' or 'thing done') are reflected in Bentley's description of the basic theatrical situation as " 'A' impersonates 'B' while 'C' looks on." Inherent in drama is the notion of the performed event, the fact that, like an orchestral score, a play is realized through performance. In its broadest sense, drama is simply 'play' and can refer to any kind of performance from a production of *Faust* or *Macbeth* through the clowning of music-hall comedians to pantomime or ritualistic dance. Central to the theory of the drama remain such concepts as plot, structure, character and action. Classical writers compared the plot of a drama to the tying and untying of a knot, and the principle of dramatic conflict is implicit in this image. Aristotle (384–322 B.C.) placed greatest emphasis on the structuring of the incidents, insisting that drama is an imitation not of character but of action and life. Since his time, the critical debate over the respective importance of character and plot has continued unabated, while playwrights have experimented with the discarding of both.

M.M.

DRAMATIK

Collective term to encompass all dramatic literature; one of the literary genres. → GATTUNGEN.

DRAMATISCH

Emil Staiger's definition of 'dramatic' (*Grundbegriffe der Poetik*, 1946) reverses the familiar view of its derivation: instead of locating the origins of the term in the drama itself, he suggests rather that the stage is a creation of the spirit of dramatic poetry. Basing his argument upon an *idea* of the dramatic, rather than on specific works, he erects a metaphysical construct embracing, on the one hand, notions of suspense and tension, conflict and opposition, and, on the other, two styles – 'the pathetic' (rhetorical) and 'the problematic'. Both styles are end-oriented and appropriate to the dramatic writer's concerns, which are less with the objects and incidents themselves, than with the perspective from which he views these and the order he assigns to them. To describe the connections between the lyric, epic and dramatic modes, Staiger uses the analogy of the syllable, word and sentence, in which each stage represents a progression from the one before. Moreover, dramatic is not synonymous with 'theatrical': a work may lack those qualities we label dramatic and yet prove to be effective in its use of stage conventions. → EPISCH, → LYRISCH, → PATHOS, → PROBLEM.

M.M.

DRAMATISIERUNG (dramatization)

Creation of a stage version usually of a prose text.

DRAMATIS PERSONAE (dramatis personae)

1. The characters in a play; usually listed at the beginning of the text.

2. The list of characters at the beginning of a text or in a theatre programme. = Personenverzeichnis.

DRAMATURG

Resident artistic adviser of the theatre management, who is frequently a dramatist in his own right; he reads the manuscripts submitted to the theatre, adapts plays for performance if necessary and is often responsible for programme notes. The office of *Dramaturg* does not exist as a rule in English-speaking theatre.

DRAMATURGIE (dramaturgy)

1. The combined efforts of the → DRAMATURG and the producer; the skills and knowledge necessary for the staging of a play.

2. Theory of drama and theatre; e.g.: Lessing's *Hamburgische Dramaturgie* (1767—69).

DRAMOLETT

Very short piece for stage performance.

DREHBUCH (film script)

DREHBÜHNE (revolving stage)

A turntable attachment to a stage, which when rotated facilitates rapid changes of scenery.

DREIFELDERBÜHNE → SHAKESPEAREBÜHNE

DREIKÖNIGSSPIEL

Dramatization of the story of the Three Wise Men (Magi). This form of religious drama dates back to the 11th century in Germany, and was performed on the 6th January, the day of the Epiphany, a feast-day which celebrates the manifestation of Christ to the Magi. The *Dreikönigsspiel* later became fused with the → WEIHNACHTSSPIEL, because of the overlap in subject-matter. →GEISTLICHES DRAMA.

DREIREIM

Rhyming of three consecutive verse lines: a a a. →REIM.

DRUCK (print, printing)

DRUCKBOGEN →BOGEN

DRUCKERLAUBNIS →IMPRIMATUR

DRUCKERMARKE →DRUCKERZEICHEN

DRUCKERSPRACHE

The standardized version of German which was effected by the printing houses in the 16th century. →KANZLEISPRACHE.

DRUCKERZEICHEN (colophon) = Druckermarke, = Signet, = Verlagssignet, = Verlegerzeichen

Printer's mark: a sign or trademark identifying the printing office, and later the publisher, which originally appeared at the end of a text, and later on the title page.

DRUCKFEHLER (misprint, printing or typing error)

DRUCKJAHR (year of printing)

DRUCKORT (place of printing)

DRUCKPRIVILEGIEN

Privileges granted to printers and publishers as a form of protection against the unauthorized reprinting of their publications by other printers and publishers. These were applicable before copyright was introduced. → URHEBER-RECHT.

DRUCKSCHRIFT (publication, printed work)

DRUCKVORLAGE

The version of a text considered to be ready for printing (in printed or manuscript form with all necessary corrections) from which the type-setter works.

DUBLETTE (duplicate)

Second copy of a book, periodical etc; e.g. in a library.

EBENE

Level of presentation; e.g.: the level of reality, the level of dream or the level of the supernatural. → DOPPELTE EBENE.

EDITIO CASTIGATA (bowdlerized edition) → AUSGABE

EDITIO PRINCEPS (first edition) = Erstausgabe → AUSGABE

EDITION → AUSGABE

EDITIONSTECHNIK → TEXTKRITIK

EINAKTER (one act play)

EINBAND

Cover or binding of a publication.

EINBILDUNGSKRAFT (imagination)

The human capacity to form mental images, through which alone, according to Kant, (*Kritik der Urteilskraft*, 1790), we are able to synthesize our otherwise chaotic sense impressions into mental pictures of separate external objects. Kant calls imagination "a creative capacity which enables us to construct in our minds a second natural world out of the materials which the first provides." Goethe (1749–1832) celebrates this supreme human gift, which he calls *Phantasie*, in *Meine Göttin*, much as Keats (1795–1821) does in his *Fancy*. Several of the German Romantics speak of 'produktive Einbildungskraft' as the source of all poetry and philosophy. For modern German aesthetic theory, after the impact of Realism, Dilthey's *Die Einbildungskraft des Dichters* (1887) was a powerful plea for a return to the older conception of poetry as "an instrument for the understanding of the world worthy to rank beside *Wissenschaft* (i.e. science and scholarship) and religion."

W.H.B.

EINDRUCKSKUNST → IMPRESSIONISMUS

EINFACHE FORMEN ('primary forms')

Term coined by André Jolles in a book of this title published in 1929, in which he classifies and describes the original and basic forms of popular narrative literature. Jolles distinguishes nine different forms: → KASUS, → LEGENDE, → MÄRCHEN, → MEMORABILE, *Mythe*, → RÄTSEL, → SAGE, *Spruch* and → WITZ. These primary forms are viewed by scholars as originating in pre-literate culture and therefore as being part of the oral tradition in literature. The forms themselves are considered to be the expression in language of certain universal and enduring attitudes which humans adopt in their response to the world. As a consequence of this view, more recent research has extended the scope of the term *einfache Formen* beyond narrative literature to include also the various basic forms of lyric poetry.

M.S.

EINFÜHLUNG (empathy)

The emotional response to a work of art as distinct from an intellectual understanding of it.

EINHEITEN (three unities)

Aristotle (384–322 B.C.) first proposed unity of action in the drama (i.e. no material extraneous to the central plot). French and Italian dramatists extended this concept, adding unity of place and time: the play was to be restricted to one location, and the time scheme was to approximate as closely as possible to the actual duration of the performance, or at most span a single day.

EINHEITLICHKEIT

Uniformity and appropriateness of style throughout a work.

EINLEITUNG

1. Introduction, foreword, preface; the preliminary section of a literary work or discourse which prepares or explains what follows. = Geleitwort.

2. Exordium: the initial part of a classical drama, which introduces the characters and reveals the subject of the play.

EINSILBIGER REIM → MÄNNLICHER REIM

EKLEKTIZISMUS (eclecticism)

Mode of creation which does not develop its own technique and philosophy but selects elements from existing ones.

EKLOGE (eclogue)

Type of pastoral poem, frequently written in the form of a dialogue between rural characters such as shepherds and shepherdesses. → HIRTENDICHTUNG, → IDYLLE.

ELABORAT

Piece of writing in which the author's efforts and exertions are clearly apparent, so much so that it frequently appears laboured and stolid.

ELEGIE

In Greek and Roman literature, a poem written in elegiac distichs (→ DISTICHON).

In modern German literature, however, it is the mood of melancholy, reflection, longing and sadness which characterizes the *Elegie*, rather than the metre. → JEREMIADE, → KLAGELIED.

ELLIPSE (ellipsis)

Stylistic device: omission of word(s) in a sentence resulting in an incomplete syntactical construction.

ELOGE (eulogy, panegyric)

Speech in praise of a person.

EMBLEM (emblem) = Sinnbild

The emblem originated from the study of Egyptian hieroglyphics by the Italian humanists (→ HUMANISMUS) whose aim was to create the modern equivalent of the ancient signs. Andrea Alciati published the first emblem-book, *Emblematicum libellus* (Augsburg, 1531), which not only went through more than 150 editions itself but also had a large following in all the major European countries. In its classic form the emblem consists of three parts: the *inscriptio* or motto, the *pictura*, and the *subscriptio* or epigram, which functions as a commentary on both picture and motto. Although the *pictura* is of prime importance in the tripartite structure of the emblem, it is only through the *inscriptio* and *subscriptio* that a deeper, hidden meaning of the picture is revealed and that often a moral maxim or a universal truth is established. The synthesis of pictorial and literary presentation was reflected in the terminology of the emblematists themselves, when they defined emblems as *Picta Poesis* or *Gemälpoesy*. This new art form gained particular importance in the 16th and 17th centuries, profoundly influencing European literature in all its branches. In Germany emblematic references and imagery were frequently used in the poetry and drama of the Baroque. → BAROCK.

H.W.N.

EMENDATION (emendation)

Correction and revision of a faulty and/or fragmentary text, in accordance with the principles of → TEXTKRITIK.

EMIGRANTENLITERATUR → EXILLITERATUR

EMPFINDSAMES LUSTSPIEL → WEINERLICHES LUSTSPIEL

EMPFINDSAMKEIT = Sentimentalismus

Term applied to a literary and social development c. 1740–1780 concerned with intensive cultivation of sentiment, sensibility and introspection. Sources include self-scrutiny practised in pietist circles (→ PIETISMUS), the epistolary novels of Samuel Richardson (*Pamela*, 1740; *Clarissa Harlowe*, 1749), the works of Laurence Sterne (1713–1768), and Rousseau's *La nouvelle Héloïse* (1761). Associated with enthusiasm for nature, fascination with death, especially in Edward Young's *Night Thoughts* (1742/3) and Macpherson's *Ossian* (1765), and close identification of love and friendship. The ability to feel intensely and to weep readily is often taken as a sign of a character's moral worth. Its excesses were later attacked in England by Jane Austen's *Sense and Sensibility* (1811) where the latter indicates "an overrefined and excessive susceptibility".

In Germany *Empfindsamkeit* was associated with Klopstock's *Messias* (1748) and lyric poetry, the poets of the *Göttinger Hain*, and Gellert's *Leben der schwedischen Gräfin von G.* (1747/8). In Goethe's *Die Leiden des jungen Werthers* (1774) Lotte looks out at a landscape as a storm passes over and breathes the word "Klopstock!" The following lines typify the diction of *Empfindsamkeit*: "Ich erinnerte mich sogleich der herrlichen Ode, die ihr in Gedanken lag, und versank in dem Strome von Empfindungen, den sie in dieser Losung über mich ausgoß. Ich ertrug's nicht, neigte mich auf ihre Hand und küßte sie unter den wonnevollsten Tränen". *Empfindsamkeit* appears in → COMEDIE LARMOYANTE and in Lessing's *Miß Sara Sampson* (1755) but was later attacked by him for its *Schwärmerei* and parodied by Goethe in *Der Triumph der Empfindsamkeit* (1777), which ridicules *die Empfindsamen* in the Darmstadt circle also described in *Dichtung und Wahrheit* (1811 ff.)

K.F.

EMPHASE (emphasis)

Phonetic device: the increase of stress or the raising of the voice in order to accentuate a word or a phrase; indicated in printing by italics, spacing, underlining etc.

ENDREIM

The rhyming of sounds from the last stressed syllable onwards as opposed to

Stabreim (→ALLITERATION); e.g.: Herzen/Schmerzen. →REIM.

ENDSILBENREIM

The rhyming of the last unstressed or short syllables of two or more lines; e.g.: Herzlein/Zweiglein. →REIM.

ENGAGEMENT

1. An author's strong personal commitment to moral, political, or religious beliefs which is reflected in his work. → ENGAGIERTE LITERATUR.

2. Engagement; employment of a performing artist.

ENGAGIERTE LITERATUR = Littérature engagée (committed literature)

German form of the French term *littérature engagée*, coined by Jean-Paul Sartre in 1945 and discussed most fully in his essay *Qu'est-ce que la littérature?* (1947). The usual English term is 'committed literature', denoting literature which is committed to an idea or cause, and more especially to a political or social movement. It is to be distinguished from → TENDENZLITERATUR, since its practitioners insist on the primacy of literature over propaganda. Sartre maintains that *engagierte Literatur* is always in the service of socialist democratic revolution against established authority, appealing to the idea of liberty. "En un mot, la littérature est, par essence, la subjectivité d'une société en révolution permanente." Literature is activity: "Parler c'est agir . . . L'écrivain engagé sait que la parole est action". This activity however results from the free choice of the writer, and it is therefore not correct to suggest that the literature of the socialist states in which writers have to conform to guide-lines established by the ruling political party is *engagierte Literatur*. Although Sartre insisted that only works in prose could be properly called *engagierte Literatur*, the term can be equally well applied to the political ballad or chanson. → POLITISCHE DICHTUNG.

E.W.H.

ENGLISCHE KOMÖDIANTEN

Professional travelling theatre groups which came from England to the Continent. Their presence in Germany can first be documented in 1586 in Dresden. There is evidence that after 1592 some of these groups remained in Germany, and by filling their vacancies with German actors gradually became German groups. Initially, their performances were in English. This necessitated a very naturalistic and sometimes exaggerated acting style, which they retained when they became German groups.

A troupe consisted of ten to fifteen actors and about seven musicians. They presented (sometimes crude) adaptations of plays by Shakespeare (1564—1616), Marlowe (1564—1593), Kyd (1558—1594) etc. but introduced into each play the role of clown which was usually played by the director of the group (→ PICKELHERING). This clown figure acted as a guide and commentator for the audience and sometimes assumed the function of the Greek chorus. Travelling theatre groups in Germany flourished until the end of the 18th century but declined due to the establishment of theatre buildings which had their own ensembles in residence.

A.O.

ENIGMA → RÄTSEL

ENJAMBEMENT (enjambement) = Hakenstil, = Versbrechung, = Zeilensprung

The overflow of the syntactical structure into the next metrical line; the end of a verse line and the end of the sentence do not coincide;

e.g.: Wer, wenn ich schriee, hörte mich denn aus der Engel
Ordnungen? und gesetzt selbst, es nähme
einer mich plötzlich ans Herz. . . (Rilke, *Duineser Elegien*)

ENTSTEHUNGSGESCHICHTE

History of the origin and development of a (literary) work, tracing influences, sources, different versions etc.

ENTSTEHUNGSZEIT

The time span from the first conception of a work to its final version.

ENTWICKLUNGSROMAN

Type of novel prevalent in the 18th and 19th centuries, which characterizes the development of the German rather than the European novel. Although the term is loosely used of 20th century novels such as Thomas Mann's *Zauberberg* (1924) or Hesse's *Glasperlenspiel* (1943), the *Entwicklungsroman* rests upon presuppositions which are no longer valid. The development of the main character, usually a sensitive and exceptional individual, is traced from initial doubt, confusion or ignorance to a maturity which reflects the ideal of the author and, to some extent, of his age. Concentration on the growth of the individual frequently indicates the presence of autobiographical elements. The first presupposition essential to the *Entwicklungsroman* is that behind all the changes, errors and set-backs in the progress of the individual towards harmonious development there is a fundamental continuum of personality, which is finally revealed in its essential purity; the second is that this development can be traced adequately in conformity with universally valid psychological laws; and the third is that the milieu in which the individual lives can be adequately described in static terms. Whatever other 'modern' elements the *Entwicklungsroman* may contain, these presuppositions distinguish it clearly from the novel of the 20th century. The earliest *Entwicklungsroman* is Wieland's

Agathon (first version 1766, second 1773, third 1794); the prime example of the genre is Goethe's *Wilhelm Meisters Lehrjahre* (1795–96); and the latest examples are Keller's *Der grüne Heinrich* (first version 1854, second 1879–80) and Stifter's *Der Nachsommer* (1857). Novels in other European literatures, such as *David Copperfield* (1849), may have certain affinities with the *Entwicklungsroman*, but usually tend to place more emphasis on actual social conditions. Related terms are → BILDUNGSROMAN, which stresses the classical ideal of → BILDUNG, and *Erziehungsroman*, which suggests a more strictly pedagogical approach to the development of the individual.

E.W.H.

EPIGONENDICHTUNG (literature written by epigones)

The literary work of those who come after great creative writers, and who cannot free themselves from the influences of the preceding periods and authors, and imitate previous literature in an unimaginative and unconvincing fashion.

EPIGRAMM (epigram)

1. Inscription on monument, building, tomb etc. = Inschrift.

2. Very brief and succinct poem, usually consisting of a couplet which utilizes satire, irony and wit to make a specific point. = Sinngedicht;
    e.g.:   Wie willst du weiße Lilien zu roten Rosen machen?
              Küß eine weiße Galathee, sie wird errötend lachen.
    (Friedrich v. Logau)
    Latin epigrams frequently use → DISTICHON.

EPIK (narrative literature, epic poetry)

1. General term which encompasses all forms of narrative literature (*erzählende Dichtung, Erzählkunst*). The basic attitude in *Epik* is one of observing the action from a distance (→ EPISCH). The narrator, however, can make his presence felt to a greater or lesser extent. Its basic forms are narrative and report. The focus is on action rather than characters and it may be placed either in a realistic landscape or in a world of fantasy. (e.g. Goethe's and Schiller's exchange of ideas on a definition of epic and dramatic forms of art). Primary forms (→ EINFACHE FORMEN) like legend, myth and folk-tale can be regarded as basic or early forms of *Epik*. The main short forms of narrative are anecdote (→ ANEKDOTE) and novella (→ NOVELLE). Further short forms are fable and idyll, 'large' forms the novel, saga and the epic poem. → PROSA.

2. Sometimes *Epik* is held to be synonymous with heroic poetry (*Epos*). The epic poem is a long narrative incorporating myth, legend, folk-tale and history and it is frequently of national significance (→ NATIONALEPOS). There are two main strands: (a) the primary epic, which belongs to the oral

tradition and is composed orally and recited; only much later is it occasion-ally written down; (b) the secondary epic, which is conceived in written form. To the former belong: *Gilgamesh* (19th–18th centuries B.C.), *Odyssey* (c.800 B.C.), *Beowulf* (c.8th century), the *Elder Edda* (c.800–1200). In the latter group fall: Virgil's *Aeneid* (c.29 B.C.), which later served as the chief model for Milton's literary epic *Paradise Lost* (1667), furthermore the anonymous *Chanson de Roland* (c.1100), the *Nibelungen-lied* (c.1200), Tasso's *Gerusalemme Liberata* (1581). The epic was ranked by Aristotle as second only to tragedy, and by Renaissance critics as the highest genre of all. →GATTUNGEN.

V.K.

EPILOG (epilogue)

1. Short speech given by a principal character to the audience at the end of a play.

2. Conclusion added to a novel, or long poem.

EPIPHER (epiphora)

Rhetorical and poetic device: the repetition of a word or phrase at the end of consecutive lines of verse or phrases; e.g.: Nacht ist es: nun reden lauter alle springenden Brunnen. Und auch meine Seele ist ein springender Brunnen. . . (Nietzsche, *Nachtlied*). →ANAPHER.

EPISCH

1. In its most general sense *episch* means 'narrative'; *epische Dichtung* generally speaking means 'prose'. →PROSA.

2. *Episch* may be used more specifically as the adjective of *Epos*; when used thus *epische Dichtung* means 'epic poetry'. →EPIK.

3. For Emil Staiger (*Grundbegriffe der Poetik*, 1946) *episch* denotes one of the three qualities (→ DRAMATISCH, → LYRISCH) which according to their distribution in a given text constitute its relationship to a genre (→EPIK, →DRAMATIK, →LYRIK).

    Episch in this sense is a mode of presentation. It is the presentation of a situation, an event or a landscape from a certain perspective, which is always detached from and outside what is presented. This presentation is characterized by the objectivity and composure of the presenter (narrator) who aims at relating things with equanimity. →ERZÄHLER.

A.O.

EPISCHE BREITE

The characteristic mode of epic narration which features frequent deviations from the main theme, the inclusion of anecdotes and episodes, the use of detailed description, flashbacks etc.

EPISCHE WIEDERHOLUNG

Repetition of certain words or phrases throughout a text, which occurs frequently in epic narration. → EPITHETON, → LEITMOTIV.

EPISCHES PRÄTERITUM

The use of the imperfect tense as a narrative tense, where the imperfect form does not indicate a temporal relationship.

EPISCHES THEATER (epic theatre) = nichtaristotelisches Theater

Term coined by Brecht (1898—1956) to designate a kind of drama and style of production which he created and developed. *Episches Theater*, in direct contrast to the theatre of illusion or aristotelian theatre, as Brecht called it, uses every device at its disposal to destroy any illusion of reality and to prevent the audience from identifying with the figures and situations in front of them. (→ VERFREMDUNGSEFFEKT). Brecht requires the audience to be critically detached, to relax and to reflect on the lessons to be learnt from the events presented on stage. The audience is expected to leave the theatre instructed and improved, therefore it must be kept alienated from the action on stage. There is still pleasure to be derived from this type of theatre, i.e. the pleasure and exhilaration of discovery, of a new insight, and there is also room for emotions, such as 'love of justice, the urge to freedom or justified anger'. These emotions should be evoked by a performance and the 'critical attitude' which should result from any encounter with epic theatre can, according to Brecht, never be passionate enough. → ARISTOTELISCHES DRAMA.

A.O.

EPISTEL (epistle)

1. Letter.

2. Letter written by an apostle in the N.T.

EPITAPH (epitaph)

1. Funeral speech.

2. Inscription on a tombstone, memorial plaque, etc. = Grabschrift.

3. Memorial stone or plaque.

EPITHETON (epithet)

Adjective or adjectival phrase which defines a particular quality. Recurring epithets are frequent in epic narration. → EPISCHE WIEDERHOLUNG.

64

EPODE (epode) →STROPHE

EPOPÖE →EPOS

EPOS (epic poetry) = Epopöe

The word is of Greek origin and means a long verse narrative. Distinguishing features are great length, regular metre and the presentation of the deeds of gods and heroes. The Western tradition begins with Homer (c.800 B.C.), continues with Virgil's *Aeneid* (c.29 B.C.). Med. examples are: the *Nibelungenlied* (c.1200), *La Chanson de Roland* (c.1100) and the earlier Icelandic sagas. Since the → RENAISSANCE, epic poetry has been replaced by prose, particularly the novel, as the main mode of extended narration. →EPIK.

ERATO (Erato)

Muse of love poetry. →MUSEN.

ERBAUUNGSLITERATUR (devotional literature)

Refers to the vast and manifold traditions of religious and devotional literature written — in prose and verse — with the specific intention of awakening and stimulating pious emotions and contemplation. Devotional literature is usually intended to be read at home individually or in an intimate circle of friends or family. The streams of Mysticism (→ MYSTIK) of the 14th and 15th centuries and the Pietism (→ PIETISMUS) of the 17th and 18th centuries in particular produced a rich and valuable devotional literature usually aimed at and read by theologians and an elite of educated and literate laymen. Although devotional literature does not exclude any particular genre, it developed a number of characteristic forms of its own, e.g.: tracts (→ TRAKTAT), consolations (*Trostbüchlein*), collections of sermons (*Predigten*) and prayers for the year (→ POSTILLEN), autobiographical confessions. With the change and the dramatic increase in the reading public and the general secularization of literature during the 18th and 19th centuries devotional literature lost much of its importance and reputation. Now written predominantly for the common reader it has become often trivial, sentimental and politically reactionary.

F.V.

ER-FORM (third person narration)

ERFÜHLUNG

The emotional perception of phenomena: a concept which is of great importance in Romanticism and Impressionism.

ERINNERUNGEN →MEMOIREN

ERLEBNIS

In literary criticism this term refers to any significant experience of the writer which is transformed into an artistic form. This aesthetic process may result in a considerable discrepancy between the original experience and its artistic manifestation. Hence, there have developed two important modes of literary criticism which seek to interpret the author's work by means of uncovering these key experiences. The one finds this information by means of biographical detective work, and the other, the psychoanalytical school, probes the poet's unconscious for these experiences by analysing recurring motifs and images.

ERLEBTE REDE (style indirecte libre) = Style indirecte libre

In prose works a specific technique for rendering the mostly unuttered thoughts of a person. Compare the following examples, one for direct speech (→ DIREKTE REDE) and one for reported speech (→ INDIREKTE REDE): Sie sagte: "*Muß ich* das wirklich tun? ": Sie fragte sich, ob sie das wirklich tun müsse. In *erlebte Rede* this becomes: *Mußte sie* das wirklich tun? As can be seen from the examples, *erlebte Rede* formally combines particular elements of direct speech and reported speech, offering the author the advantages of both: it employs, on the one hand, the immediate, direct perspective of the person who utters his or her thoughts directly without having to put them into direct speech (which is rather clumsy because thoughts, in real life, are not normally uttered verbally) and, on the other hand, it retains the objective, detached perspective of the writer who does not have to interrupt his flow of words through the awkward grammatical constructions required by reported speech. Thus, *erlebte Rede* enables the author to incorporate a character's innermost thoughts and feelings into his own discourse in a very subtle and highly sophisticated way. It follows that *erlebte Rede* is esp. used in works with a psychological approach. When applied consistently within the narrative it is called the → STREAM OF CONSCIOUSNESS technique.

U.B.

ERREGENDES MOMENT

The first definite hint of the impending conflict in a drama; the point at which the plot changes from the exposition to the climax.

ERSCHEINEN

The release of a publication to the book trade.

ERSCHEINUNGSJAHR (year of publication)

ERSCHEINUNGSORT (place of publication)

ERSTAUFFÜHRUNG (première) = Première

The first performance of a dramatic or musical work in any given country, or of a new translation or adaptation etc. →URAUFFÜHRUNG.

ERSTAUSGABE (first edition) →AUSGABE

ERSTDRUCK

1. Preliminary printing of a work, prior to official publication.
2. The first publication of a work in a journal, magazine etc. before it appears in book form.

ERSTLING, ERSTLINGSWERK

The first published or unpublished work of an author.

ERWEITERTER REIM →REICHER REIM

ERZÄHLENDE DICHTUNG →EPIK

ERZÄHLER (narrator) = Narrator

In general usage *Erzähler* denotes anyone who recounts a story, and is therefore used as a term for any writer of narrative prose (as in the title of Hugo von Hofmannsthal's anthology, *Deutsche Erzähler*, 1912). In literary criticism, however, the term is synonymous with the English *narrator* or *narrative voice*, and refers to a fictional figure in a narrative, not to be identified with the author, who tells the story from a particular point of view (→ PERSPEKTIVE). This narrator figure can be a fully-drawn character participating in the action of the narrative, speaking in the first-person singular (*Ich-Roman*) as in Thomas Mann's *Bekenntnisse des Hochstaplers Felix Krull* (1954) or through the medium of his letters, as in Goethe's *Die Leiden des jungen Werthers* (1774). In the third-person novel (*Er-Roman*) the narrator can be at any point on a scale between a fully-developed figure, as Serenus Zeitblom in Thomas Mann's *Doktor Faustus* (1947) to complete anonymity, as in Goethe's *Die Wahlverwandtschaften* (1809). Even where, as in the *nouveau roman*, the attempt is made to eliminate the narrator altogether, we still have to presume the presence of a narrative voice. Many modern novelists have experimented with a multiplicity of narrative voices, as for instance William Faulkner in *The Sound and the Fury* (1929) or Gerd Gaiser in *Schlußball* (1958). The narrator-figure can be used to control the point of view; he can claim, implicitly or explicitly, omniscience, or can admit the limitations of his knowledge, as in Siegfried Lenz's *Stadtgespräch* (1963); he can address the reader directly (the 'dear reader' technique, used for instance — for comic effect — by Wilhelm

Raabe, 1831–1910); he can comment on the action and can introduce material extraneous to the narrative, as in *Huguenau oder die Sachlichkeit*, the third volume of Hermann Broch's trilogy *Die Schlafwandler* (1931/32) (→ AUKTO-RIALES ERZÄHLEN). The narrator can also be to varying degrees conscious of his own function as narrator, and aware of his own abilities or weaknesses, as in Christa Wolf's *Nachdenken über Christa T.* (1968). The varied and sophisticated use of the narrator or narrative voice as an essential element of the novel is one of the major developments of the novel form in the 20th century.

E.W.H.

ERZÄHLERDISTANZ → DISTANZ

ERZÄHLHALTUNG → PERSPEKTIVE

ERZÄHLKUNST (fictional art) → EPIK

ERZÄHLPERSPEKTIVE → PERSPEKTIVE

ERZÄHLSITUATION (point of view) → AUKTORIALES ERZÄHLEN, → PER-SPEKTIVE

ERZÄHLUNG

This is the most neutral and general of the group of terms (including → NO-VELLE, → KURZGESCHICHTE, → ANEKDOTE, etc.) which refer to short or medium length fiction. Its generality is shown by the related words → ERZÄH-LER, 'narrator' or 'storyteller', *erzählen*, 'to narrate' or 'to tell a story', and → ERZÄHLKUNST, 'fictional art', all of which may be applied to fiction of any kind or length. It is not properly used for fiction of novel length, a → RO-MAN in German; nor for a story employing subject-matter which is fantastic or supernatural, e.g.: → MÄRCHEN. But it is used freely over the rest of the spectrum of fictional works, when not displaced by one of the more restricted terms such as → NOVELLE, although here too there is considerable overlap and variability of usage. For example, Kleist (1777–1811) called his collected short fiction *Erzählungen*, though they are commonly referred to as *Novellen*. Some scholars have taken the view that an *Erzählung* differs from a *Novelle* by being less carefully and artistically composed; but though this view has some currency, the more common view is that *Erzählung* is simply a looser, more inclusive and general term.

J.M.E.

ERZÄHLZEIT, ERZÄHLTE ZEIT

Erzählzeit is the time taken to read a narrative (or to tell a story), as opposed to *erzählte Zeit* — narrated time, the time-span covered by the narrative.

An investigation of the relationship between *Erzählzeit* and *erzählte Zeit* can illuminate aspects of structure and of narrative techniques. The 19th century novel, covering a whole lifetime in a number of pages requiring say 10 hours to read, will clearly use a technique of selection and will have a structure marked by peaks of development. Some modern novels e.g.: Broch's *Der Tod des Vergil* (1945) deal with an *erzählte Zeit* much more approximate to the *Erzählzeit* and show therefore differences in structure and technique.

E.W.H.

ESELSBRÜCKE → DENKVERS

ESSAY

The term, derived from Montaigne (*Essais*, 1580) and Bacon (*Essays*, 1597 ff.), was first used by a German author, instead of the previously preferred *Versuch*, in the title of Hans Grimm's *Essays* (1859). *Essay* means the same in German as in English, but in neither language has it been satisfactorily defined. It is a short prose form, dealing with any subject-matter of general concern, but without trying to present a single strand of logical argument or to reach a firm conclusion. Unlike the scientific treatise, the essay has a value which is not diminished by later advances in the subject. The style of the essay is at least as important as the content, and is often marked by careful elegance and deliberate subjectivity. The point of view is tolerant and sceptical (Montaigne), serene and wise (Bacon). In German *Essay* should be distinguished from → ABHANDLUNG = scientific treatise, → TRAKTAT = polemical writing, and → FEUILLETON, which deals with more ephemeral matters and pays less importance to elegance of style. The term → AUFSATZ approximates more closely to *Essay*, but shares with → ABHANDLUNG the primacy of content over form and style. Recent scholarship has used the term *Essay* and in particular its derivatives → ESSAYISMUS and *essayistisch* to denote those elements in a novel which are not strictly narrative. The use of the term *essayistisch* in novel critisism has become very lax, and is sometimes used (incorrectly) to characterize a particular type of novel (such as Uwe Johnson's *Das dritte Buch über Achim*, 1961).

E.W.H.

ESSAYISMUS

Term used in novel criticism to denote those elements of the novel which are not strictly narrative and display characteristics of the → ESSAY, (i.e. careful elegance, deliberate subjectivity etc.). Robert Musil (1880–1942) used the term in his novel *Der Mann ohne Eigenschaften* in a quite specific way:

> There was something in Ulrich's nature that worked in a haphazard, paralysing, disarming manner against logical systematisation, against the one-track will, against the definitely directed urges of ambition; and

it was also connected with his chosen expression, 'Essayism', even although this something in him contained precisely those elements that he had, in the course of time and with unconscious care, eliminated from that concept. The translation of the word 'essay' as 'attempt', which is the generally accepted one, only approximately gives the most important allusion to the literary model. For an essay is not the provisional or incidental expression of a conviction that might on a more favourable occasion be elevated to the status of truth or that might just as easily be recognised as error (of that kind are only the articles and treatises, referred to as 'chips from their workshop', with which learned persons favour us); an essay is the unique and unalterable form that a man's inner life assumes in a decisive thought. Nothing is more alien to it than that irresponsibility and semi-finishedness of mental images known as subjectivity; but neither are 'true' and 'false', 'wise' and 'unwise', terms that can be applied to such thoughts, which are nevertheless subject to laws that are no less strict than they appear to be delicate and ineffable. There have been quite a number of such essayists and masters of the floating life within, but there would be no point in naming them.

Musil thus does not use the term essay as a generic term but rather as a psychological category and consequently *Essayismus* as a term to denote a certain perception of life, practised by 'the masters of the floating life', possibilitarians who think "how everything could 'just as easily' be and [. . .] attach no more importance to what is than to what is not".

A.O.

EUROPAMÜDE

Form of pessimism developed by the poets of the *Junge Deutschland*, esp. Heine (1797–1856) and Willkomm (1810–1886), who were obsessed with the notion that Europe was a dying continent, and consequently idealized life in the New World (America).

EUTERPE

Muse of song. →MUSEN.

EXEGESE

The interpretation of texts, esp. the Bible, according to established principles. → ALLEGORESE, → HERMENEUTIK, → INTERPRETATION.

EXEMPEL (example) = Paradigma

Paradigm of positive or negative aspects inserted into a speech or text in order to illustrate a certain viewpoint.

EXEMPLAR

Copy of a printed publication or manuscript.

EXILLITERATUR = Emigrantenliteratur

In spite of its seemingly broader scope the term refers to the German-speaking writers who were swept out of their homelands — Germany, Austria, Czechoslovakia, etc. — by the Fascist wave of the 1930's and 1940's. Certainly there have been emigrations before (and since), but the mass exodus of artists, philosophers, journalists, poets and novelists from the area of the so-called *Großdeutsches Reich* is unique. Renowned men and women — whose names will have to stand here for countless others — such as Brecht (1898–1956) and Wolfskehl (1869–1948), Feuchtwanger (1884–1958) and Döblin (1878–1957), Anna Seghers (1900–) and Nelly Sachs (1891–1970), Heinrich Mann (1871–1950) and Thomas Mann (1875–1955) had to flee from country to country in search of shelter. No wonder that many ended in despair and suicide, Benjamin for example at the Spanish border, Toller (1893–1939) in the city jungle of Manhattan, Hasenclever (1890–1940) in a French internment camp, Tucholsky (1890–1935) in nearby Sweden and Stefan Zweig (1881–1942) in faraway Brazil. Others formed small communities, in Sanary-sur-mer, New York, Santiago de Chile, Los Angeles, Mexico etc., to carry on the business of German literature, founding journals, writing plays, poems and novels, denouncing the barbarities of the epoch. Loners like Zuckmayer (1896–1982), who became a farmer in Vermont, struck out on their own.

Of course the works thus produced vary greatly according to the individuality of their authors, the philosophical traditions in which they were embedded, the subjects with which they dealt and the genres into which they were cast. But somehow they all bear the marks of the extraordinary circumstances under which they were conceived. Understanding German literature in this century is impossible without studying the rich body of letters created by the German exiles and the historical events underlying them.

E.S.

EXKURS (excursus)

Detailed and often lengthy discussion of a point raised in a text, esp. a scholarly work; may appear as a footnote or appendix.

EXPIRATORISCHER AKZENT → AKZENT

EXPRESSIONISMUS (expressionism) = Ausdruckskunst

A European phenomenon encompassing most art forms; predominant in German literature c. 1910–1925. Expressionism was partly a reaction against → NATURALISMUS and → IMPRESSIONISMUS and partly the aesthetic manifestation of the peculiarly explosive atmosphere which resulted in the eruption of World War I.

Prominent themes such as the search for a new concept of humanity ('der neue Mensch'), the battle between the generations, esp. between father and son and the conflict between the sexes leading to a more open and explicit portrayal of sexual relationships, are presented in equally revolutionary language. Daring neologisms, the breaking up of conventional grammatical and metrical structures, the elimination of articles and prepositions, the use of hyperbole and ellipsis and the ecstatic cry ('der ekstatische Schrei') characterize the style of expressionist literature. Some expressionist writers developed a distinct political commitment which is referred to as *Aktivismus*.

German expressionist writers produced prose, drama and lyric poetry but their lasting achievement is thought to be their lyric poetry. Expressionism in German literature is represented by Stadler (1883–1914), J.R. Becher (1891– 1958), Stramm (1874–1915), Lasker-Schüler (1869–1945), Sternheim (1878– 1942), Benn (1886–1956), Hasenclever (1890–1940), Wedekind (1864–1918) et al. →MODERNE.

A.O.

EXTEMPORE →STEGREIF

FABEL

1. **Fable.** Short didactic narrative in which animals assume human customs, behaviour and speech for the purpose of exemplifying a moral thesis or illustrating a truth. Aesop (c.550 B.C.) is said to have introduced this genre to European literature by collecting such texts, mainly from India. The genre has been used ever since; in the 20th century predominantly for political satire. The relationship between animal and human qualities has been stereotyped (e.g. the fox is cunning, the snake is false, the lion majestic etc.) so that little characterization is necessary.

   In German the term *Fabel* is usually restricted to the meaning 'beast fable' (*Tierfabel*).

2. The basic story-line or plot-structure of a narrative or a play, combining the subject-matter (→ STOFF, *Vorwurf*) and the central motif (→MOTIV).

   A.O.

FACHBUCH (textbook)

Book containing the description of a discipline or craft by an authority on the subject. →SACHBUCH.

FACHLITERATUR

The available textbooks on a discipline or craft written by authorities on the subject. →FACHBUCH.

FÄLSCHUNGEN (literary forgeries) = literarische Fälschungen

Works which have been concocted with the intention of hoodwinking the public as to their true origin or authorship; or works which have been written in fraudulent imitation of another author's style.

FAHNENKORREKTUR (galley proofs)

Preliminary proofs which have not yet been arranged in pages, and on which corrections are made. →AUTORKORREKTUR, →BÜRSTENABZUG, →HAUS-KORREKTUR.

FAHRENDE →SPIELLEUTE

FALKENTHEORIE

Part of the theory of the → NOVELLE as Paul Heyse expounded it in the introduction to his collection of *Novellen* (*Deutscher Novellenschatz*, 1871). Each *Novelle* should have a definite individual character or profile, "a strongly marked silhouette whose outlines, expressed in a few words, would make a characteristic impression, in the manner in which the contents of that story of the Falcon in Boccaccio's *Decamerone* (1349–1353), narrated in five lines, impress themselves profoundly on the memory". The Falcon is "the specific thing which distinguishes this story from thousands of others". All 100 tales of the *Decamerone* are preceded by brief summaries. Heyse's desideratum is a reference to that of the 9th story of the 5th day, which runs as follows:

> Federigo degli Alberti loves and is not loved in return, and spending all in courteous fashion he impoverishes himself until he possesses only a falcon which, having nothing else, he gives to eat to his lady who has come to his house; she, knowing this, changes her mind, takes him as her husband and makes him rich.

While it is true that *Novellen* normally deal with some striking, distinctive subject, not every *Novelle* necessarily contains a central, concrete symbol, or → DINGSYMBOL, by which it is remembered.

P.M.

FALLENDE HANDLUNG (falling action)

The part of a dramatic plot in which the hero's fortunes decline; the part from the turning-point (→ WENDEPUNKT) to the end of a tragedy. → STEIGENDE HANDLUNG.

FALLHÖHE

The extent of a tragic hero's fall from glory to misery; concept developed as a justification for the theory that only people of high rank and noble birth make fitting tragic heroes (→ STÄNDEKLAUSEL). The more elevated the stature of the tragic hero, the greater and more tragic his fall, and the greater the emotional response of the audience. → KATHARSIS.

FASSUNG

Version of a text: sometimes an author may publish or write several different versions of the same text. → BEARBEITUNG.

FASTNACHTSPIEL

Type of non-religious play connected with carnival celebrations (before Lent) in the 15th and 16th centuries, produced esp. in Nuremberg by groups of young men, mostly artisans. The players were not professionals, and although in carnival costume like the audience, did not aim at any theatrical performance in the modern sense. There was no stage and no props; in the course of carnival entertainments a space would be cleared for a series of solo comedy acts, the whole performance being introduced and concluded by a praecursor or speaker (who might also be the author), and seldom totalling more than 300 lines, sometimes less than 100. At first the acts were independent entities, delivered by a series of performers appearing as carnival fools or anonymously, but in some *Fastnachtspiele* there is a tendency to relate the individual pieces more or less closely to one another, and in later examples the development of a plot and dialogue. In content, too, there is a development from the original carnival aim of coarse or obscene entertainment (esp. at the expense of the peasantry) to one of social criticism or moral didacticism. In both these developments the name of Hans Sachs (1494–1576) is significant.

R.F.

FERNSEHSPIEL (television play)

Drama esp. written for the medium of television which, like the film, can make use of the close-up but, unlike film, does not achieve the effect of the wide screen. *Fernsehspiele* are therefore usually of a more intimate nature and normally employ only a small number of actors.

FESTSCHRIFT

Special publication of a collection of essays in honour of a respected scholar, contributed by his friends, colleagues and students, on an important occasion such as his birthday or retirement.

FESTSPIEL

1. Festival; e.g.: *Salzburger Festspiele*.
2. Play written for a festive occasion or in commemoration of a person or an event.

FEUILLETON

1. Section of a newspaper devoted to the arts, science and leisure activities (excluding sports).
2. Term applied by extension to light literature dealing with topics of general interest in a subjective and entertaining manner, concentrating on apparently trivial points and occurrences. The best examples of the *Feuilleton* approach the form of the →ESSAY.

FEUILLETONISMUS

The presentational mode of the →FEUILLETON.

The term is often used in a derogatory way signifying forced witticism, fashionable name-dropping and superficial argument.

FIBEL

1. First reader at primary school level.
2. Standard textbook of a discipline or craft.

FIGUR

1. Any person featuring in a creative text.
2. → RHETORISCHE FIGUR (figure of speech).

FIGURENGEDICHTE → BILDERLYRIK

FIKTION

Term derived from the Latin *fictio*, meaning something made. In general usage it frequently denotes the opposite of a factual account, and can be used derogatively to imply falsification.

In literary criticism the German term refers to the imaginative presentation of events which do not necessarily have any correlative in the external world. Consequently *Fiktion* is an essential element of most literary works as opposed to factual and historical accounts. (→ LITERATUR, → REPORTAGE).

The distinction in usage is clear in the adjectives derived from *Fiktion*: *fiktiv* refers to the meaning in general use, and is equivalent to the primary meaning of English *fictitious; fiktional* refers to the meaning in literary criticism, which is expressed in English by (a work) *of fiction*, or by the adjective *fictional*. The German term is not synonymous with English *fiction*, which may be used to refer to prose narratives (e.g. Walter Scott is one of the great writers of English fiction): *Fiktion* may not be used in this sense. → WIRKLICHKEIT.

E.W.H.

FLICKWORT → FÜLLWORT (expletive word)

FLIEGENDE BLÄTTER

1. Loose pages in a book.
2. → FLUGBLATT (leaflet, broadsheet).

FLORIERTER STIL → GEBLÜMTER STIL

FLOSKEL

Set or empty phrase, a platitude, an embellishment of speech.

FLUGBLATT (handbill, leaflet, broadsheet)

A single sheet of paper, with printed text and possibly illustrations, used for the rapid dissemination of sensational news, or the propagation of certain opinions on political or religious topics, or matters of literary taste.

FLUGSCHRIFT (pamphlet)

Cheaply produced, and often anonymous publication of limited length, used for the same purpose as a → FLUGBLATT.

FORM (form)

Contrary to what applies to some other, seemingly identical and yet — however slightly — divergent concepts, the modern German usage of *Form* does not differ from that in contemporary Anglo-American literary criticism. On the one hand, this term is employed as liberally as its English counterpart, and is considered to be interchangeable with style (→ STIL), expression (→ AUSDRUCK), etc., the result being a conceptual arbitrariness which borders more often than not on sheer 'chaos' (J.T. Shipley, *Dictionary of World Literature*, 1964). On the other hand, the Aristotelian as well as Hegelian interplay or dialectic, both of form and content and of form and meaning, is cherished, and *Form* conceived of as the adequate, indeed necessary expression of → INHALT and → BEDEUTUNG not only in an aesthetic, but also in a philosophical sense. The word stems from the Latin *forma*; it was introduced during the 13th century to replace MHG *bilde* or *gestalt*. The latter term however was revived by early 20th century critics who, drawing on Goethe, on Shaftesbury's 'inward form', and ultimately on Plotinus, also favoured the dual notion of an 'intrinsic form' (*innere Form*) as opposed to one that is merely 'extrinsic' (*äußerlich*, frequently used in a derogatory sense); in fact, they even ventured to proclaim a specific *deutsche Form* (Oscar Walzel, *Gehalt und Gestalt im Kunstwerk des Dichters*, 1929). While such nationalism has now been abandoned, the duality of 'closed' vs. 'open' form, advocated by the art historian Heinrich Wölfflin, and applied by the same critics to entire epochs such as the → RENAISSANCE and the → BAROCK, can still be encountered, although its popularity has greatly diminished. This dualistic view persists nowadays only in a variation, used mainly in dramaturgical terminology, where it serves to differentiate between the two basic types of plays: 'classical' drama following the rules, which is defined as tightly knit, or 'closed', and 'epic' drama in the vein of Brecht (1898–1956) — though long preceding and far transcending him — which is described as loosely structured, or 'open' (Volker Klotz, *Geschlossene und offene Form im Drama*, 1960). → GESCHLOSSENE FORM.

R.G.

FORMALISMUS (formalism)

Refers to the method of literary criticism developed by the Formal School in Soviet Russia c.1915–1930. This school originated in revolt against sociological, psychological, and ideological Russian literary criticism, as well as against Symbolism, and saw itself as revolutionary, along with the Futurists and Constructivists of the early post-revolutionary years. Initially, Formalism rejected both literary history and the social role of literature in its emphasis on the work of art as artefact, with integrity and coherence, and on poetic (as opposed to practical) language as the primary literary fact. However, Formalism later redefined literary history as the evolution of genres, with 'low' forms (such as the detective story) often rejuvenating literature, and saw literature's social function as being "to make us see things, not to know them" (Shklovsky). Formalism's concept of form, which subsumed content and other raw 'materials' in the total work of art, influenced the Czech and Polish 'structuralist' schools of the 1930s, and can be seen as the precursor of current French structuralism. It has also had far-reaching reverberations for Marxist aesthetic theory. In the debates in the Soviet Union in the 1930s and the GDR in the 1950s, the extent to which Formalism deliberately aimed to overcome the form/content dichotomy was misinterpreted. Hence in these and other socialist countries Formalism has become a sweeping and pejorative term encompassing all formal experimentation (in contrast to the more content-orientated → SOZIALISTISCHER REALISMUS) and anything suspected of being a 'late bourgeois decadent' art form.

B.E.

FORMAT (size, format)

Term referring to the size of a book or sheet of paper; e.g.: folio, quarto, A4 etc.

FORMEL (formula)

A set form of words, a phrase; e.g.: greetings, wishes, openings and endings of letters etc.

FORMENLEHRE → MORPHOLOGIE

FORTSETZUNGSROMAN

Novel printed in instalments in magazines, etc. → ILLUSTRIERTENROMAN, → ZEITUNGSROMAN.

FRAGMENT (fragment) = Bruchstück

The surviving portions of an unfinished text.

FRAKTUR

Gothic type as distinct from → ANTIQUA (Roman type).

FRAUENDIENST

In the M.A., the chivalric service which knights gave to noble married women. →MINNE.

FRAUENLITERATUR

The traditional concept of *Frauenliteratur* is that of literature written by women, usually about women and intended primarily for women readers, defined according to society's definition of 'typical' or 'natural' feminine attributes. Thus it was assumed that women writers would depict home and family, exhibit more emotionality, a greater affinity for nature, less originality or aptitude for form or innovation and a tendency towards triviality. Women writers were supposed to be particularly suited to some literary genres, e.g. emotional lyric poetry and unsuited to others, e.g.: drama. Most influential works of literary history have, in the past, examined *Frauenliteratur* only superficially and according to such criteria, without regard for the historical, literary or social context. Since the mid-1960s with the new orientation of → LITERATURWISSENSCHAFT towards the social conditions and political aspects of literature, and more specifically as a result of the impetus of the women's movement, critics, and especially feminist critics, have begun to re-examine *Frauenliteratur*, looking at the works of women writers in the context of male-orientated literature in a patriarchal society, the conditions of literary production specific to women writers, and the question of the possibility of specifically 'female aesthetics'.

P.R.

FRAUENZEITSCHRIFTEN

18th century magazines written for the entertainment and education of women. Later they took up the fight for women's rights. Now they generally tend to be illustrated magazines with articles on topics such as cookery, the upbringing of children, and the house and garden. There are, however, several strongly political ones which write exclusively about feminist causes and ideas.

FREIE BÜHNE

Society formed 5th April 1889 in Berlin by Maximilian Harden, Theodor Wolff, Paul Schlenther, Heinrich and Julius Hart, Samuel Fischer, Otto Brahm, et al. with the goal of performing the dramas of the Naturalist writers for members only. This measure was in order to eliminate the censor, who disapproved of the public performance of these dramas.

FREIE KÜNSTE →ARTES LIBERALES

FREIE RHYTHMEN

Unrhymed lines of any length, which lack metre but instead use the natural rhythms of language. (→ RHYTHMUS).

Freie Rhythmen can be distinguished from prose by the fact that all the lines are similarly structured and sometimes grouped together into stanzas of various lengths. → FREIE VERSE.

FREIE VERSE

1. Rhymed verse lines of varying length and number of feet, which have the same metrical foot throughout, usually iambic or trochaic.

2. Rhymed verse which lacks metre and often features irregularity of line length. → FREIE RHYTHMEN.

FREIER SCHRIFTSTELLER (free-lance writer)

FREIES DEUTSCHES HOCHSTIFT

Organisation established in Frankfurt a.M. on the centenary of Schiller's birthday, 10th Nov. 1859, with the general objective of promoting and fostering scholarship, the arts, and education. Since 1863 it has been housed in the *Goethehaus* in Frankfurt a.M. and now its primary concern is the cultivation of the heritage of the German Classical period.

FREIHEITSDICHTUNG

Term given to the body of patriotic and political poetry written in support of the uprising against Napoleon between 1813 and 1815. Principal exponents are Schénkendorf, Arndt and Theodor Körner.

FREILICHTTHEATER (open-air theatre) = Naturtheater

FRONLEICHNAMSSPIEL (Corpus Christi play) = Prozessionsspiel

Loosely structured religious play depicting the various stations in the passion of Christ. → GEISTLICHES DRAMA.

FRONTISPIZ (frontispiece)

1. Illustration (formerly a copperplate) facing the title page.

2. Illustrated title page of a book.

FRÜHDRUCKE → INKUNABELN

FRÜHROMANTIK

Term commonly used in German literary history to denote the works and literary theories between 1795 and 1802 of Friedrich Schlegel, August Wilhelm

Schlegel, Friedrich von Hardenberg (Novalis), Tieck and Wackenroder, occasionally also those of Jean Paul, Hölderlin and Bonaventura (pseudonym of August Klingemann). The term *Frühromantik* lacks precision. Close co-operation existed between Friedrich Schlegel and Novalis who, inspired by the philosophy of Fichte (*Wissenschaftslehre*, 1794), developed a philosophical concept of '*romantische Poesie*'. *Poesie* — the term has a much wider range of meaning than the English 'poetry' — was destined "not merely to reunite the separate genres"of literature and to "link *Poesie* to philosophy and rhetoric. It would and should also mingle and fuse *Poesie* and prose [i.e. creative literature and critical writing], artistic *Poesie* and natural *Poesie*", but also make *Poesie* "lively and sociable, and life and society poetic." This concept of *Universalpoesie* was supplemented by the concept of → IRONIE according to which every artistic effort was to be seen as 'both playful and serious', as 'the freest of all licences, for through it one rises above one's own self' (Friedrich Schlegel, 1798). Consciousness of the growing alienation between man and society as well as nature gave rise to this theory which is directed towards human self-realization in accordance with the responsibilities of the individual as part of society.

While Friedrich Schlegel was mainly concerned with aesthetic concepts, Novalis added scientific, political and religious perspectives (*Die Christenheit oder Europa*, 1799). Friedrich and August Wilhelm Schlegel edited the journal *Athenaeum* (1798–1800) which contained some of the most important programmatic statements and also literary representations of this theory (Friedrich Schlegel, *Fragmente*, Novalis, *Blüthenstaub*, both 1798, *Hymnen an die Nacht*, 1800). During this time August Wilhelm Schlegel's house in Jena became a centre of discussion (*Jenaer Romantik*).

Tieck and Wackenroder in Berlin contributed largely to the rediscovery of med. and Renaissance art (*Herzensergießungen eines kunstliebenden Klosterbruders*, 1797), especially that of Albrecht Dürer. After Wackenroder's death Tieck became closely associated with Friedrich Schlegel and Novalis. At the same time Hölderlin, Hegel and Schelling together conceived *Das älteste Systemprogramm des deutschen Idealismus* (c.1795–96) proclaiming a 'new religion' which through an 'aesthetic art' would establish the 'allgemeine Freiheit und Gleichheit der Geister'. Thus the intellectual and artistic efforts generally subsumed under the term *Frühromantik* can be seen as a direct response to the historical situation in Germany after the French Revolution and during the subsequent *Koalitionskriege*.

G.S.

FÜLLE DES AUSDRUCKS

Richness of expression as manifest in the use of synonyms in → HENDIADYOIN, → PLEONASMUS etc.

FÜLLMOTIV (makeweight motif)

Self-contained subordinate motif which has no direct connection with the central motif and might easily be replaced by another. →MOTIV.

FÜLLUNG = Versfüllung

Number of unstressed or short syllables between the stressed or long ones in a metrical foot or line; may be strictly regulated as in classical metres, or free. →ALLITERATION.

FÜLLWORT (expletive word) = Flickwort

FÜNFAKTER (drama in five acts) →AKT

FÜRSTENSPIEGEL

Novel which addresses itself to a monarch or prince and provides advice about modes of government and behaviour; e.g.: Machiavelli, *Il Principe* (1532). →SPIEGEL.

FUNKTIONALISMUS

Concept of literature which views a work as an organic unity, each individual element of which fulfils certain functions which become apparent after a close examination of the whole structure. →LEITMOTIV, →SCHLÜSSELWÖRTER.

FURCHT UND MITLEID (pity and fear) →KATHARSIS

FUSS (Foot) = Versfuß

Metrical unit comprising a number of syllables, with at least one stressed or long syllable. The type of foot (feet) used determines the metre of a poem. →METRUM.

FUSSNOTE (footnote)

Short explanatory note or critical comment in a literary work which appears at the bottom of the page. →ANMERKUNG.

FUTURISMUS (Futurism)

An artistic movement founded in Italy in 1909 by Marinetti. It radically opposed everything traditional and developed a cult of the modern, for which the term *Modernalotria* was invented. By that the Futurists understood general glorification of modern life in all its manifestations, but their enthusiasm was esp. for modern technology and above all for fast,modern modes of transport — cars and planes —, since speed was believed to express the essence of all that was modern. The manifesto of the Futurists claims that: ". . . a screaming car

which seems to run on shrapnel is more beautiful than the *Nike of Samothrace*".
Art should be aggressive. War, "the only hygienic thing in the world", was
exalted along with militarism and patriotism. "The destructive acts of anarchists"
and "the despising of women" were both lauded. The language of literature was
to be radically revised, so that adjectives, adverbs and conjunctions would be
viewed as superfluous and emotional, likewise punctuation. The vehicles of
poetic declaration were to be nouns and infinitive forms of the verb. In German
literature, the poetry of August Stramm (1874—1915) is based on this principle.
In the *Technical Manifesto of Futuristic Literature*, published in 1912, Marinetti
formulates the programme as: "Destruction of Syntax. Unfettered fantasy.
Liberated words". An appropriate example of futuristic poetry is:

man — torpedo-boat
woman — harbour
crowd — breakers.

L.Z.W.

GALANTE DICHTUNG

French and Italian literary form fashionable in the late Baroque and Rococo periods, c.1700, which sought to entertain court circles by means of witty and elegant poems and songs depicting the frivolous side of aristocratic life. The most important sub-genres included poetical letters, odes, sonnets and epigrams. The *galante Roman* is the German manifestation of this; however, due to the different social conditions in Germany, it was no more than an empty literary convention intent on imitating the elegant French and Italian models, dalliance being the predominant theme.

GALANTER ROMAN → GALANTE DICHTUNG

GASSENHAUER

Pejorative term for an extremely popular song or tune, of little artistic merit.

GASTSPIEL (guest performance)

Performance given by a visiting actor, singer, dancer or troupe in another theatre by invitation.

GATTUNGEN (genres) = Dichtungsgattungen

1. The principal literary species which are constituted by basic modes of presentation and which have been recognized since ancient times although not restricted to the presently dominant tripartite scheme. This has been developed since Goethe referred to the three *Naturformen* → EPIK, → LYRIK, and → DRAMATIK and subsequent German literary scholarship has accepted this triad. There have been occasional attempts to establish a fourth *Gattung* (e.g. *Didaktik*) or even to disestablish them all (Benedetto Croce) but generally speaking the three *Gattungen* seem to be firmly established. A *Gattung* is characterized by the presence of a quality which is more fundamental than mere formal characteristics. Emil Staiger (*Grundbegriffe der Poetik*, 1946) proposed the predominance of one of the qualities of → EPISCH, → LYRISCH or → DRAMATISCH as designating criterion for the *Gattung*. Although this has been challenged, no really satisfactory criteria for the definition of a *Gattung* have been developed. The discussion

is still continuing. →POETIK.

2. *Gattung* can also refer to a group of texts which share the same formal characteristics (e.g. → SONETT) or the manner in which they treat their subject-matter (e.g. → ROMAN, → NOVELLE). It is, however, preferable to use the term *Arten* for these divisions and to reserve the term *Gattung* for the principal genres narrative, lyric, dramatic.

A.O.

GEBÄRDE (gesture)

Spontaneous reaction or movement of the body which is characteristic of a particular individual and may therefore reveal his true feelings and thoughts far more reliably than words. A *Gebärde* may be accompanied by words and thus highlight, underline, or even contradict the spoken word. →GESTE.

GEBLÜMTER STIL = florierter Stil

Style characterized by extremely florid and figurative language, which often appears pompous and artificial.

GEBRAUCHSLYRIK

Poetry written with a specific purpose in mind; e.g.: for the glorification of a monarch.

GEBROCHENER REIM

Extreme form of → ENJAMBEMENT; a syllable within a word is used as a rhyming syllable. →REIM;

    e.g.:   Hans Sachs war ein Schuh—
            macher und Poet dazu.

GEBUNDENE REDE

Language which has a definite metrical rhythm: verse as opposed to prose.

GEDÄCHTNISVERS →DENKVERS

GEDANKENFIGUR →RHETORISCHE FIGUR

GEDANKENLYRIK

Lyrical poetry which portrays mainly intellectual experiences; e.g.: Schiller: *Der Spaziergang.* →LYRIK.

GEDICHT

Term applied to any single literary composition written in verse, whether it be in the lyrical (e.g. Rilke, *Herbsttag*, 1902), the epic (*Das Nibelungenlied*, c.1200) or the dramatic mode (Schiller, *Wallenstein*, 1799). It should not be confused with → DICHTUNG or → LYRIK, although it necessarily belongs to the first category and frequently to the second. A *Gedicht* may be distinguished by its 'ordered' nature, both in its visual and its auditory aspect, its appearance on the printed page and its strongly rhythmical quality; but the range of variation is great. It may, for instance, be arranged in strophes of equal length within a strict metrical and rhyme scheme (Hofmannsthal, *Terzine über Vergänglichkeit*, 1894); or it may assume a looser, irregular structure such as that found in → FREIE RHYTHMEN (Goethe, *Prometheus*, 1774). In its usual, lyrical mode the *Gedicht* may be characterized as an emotional, intellectual and linguistic complex, which arises from the impulse to articulate an inner state or feeling and which employs language in its most musical, concentrated and self-conscious form. In the epic and dramatic modes the *Gedicht* conforms to the essential features of the respective genres, commonly utilizing rhyming couplets in the former (Wolfram von Eschenbach, *Parzival*, c.1210) and blank verse in the latter (Kleist, *Prinz Friedrich von Homburg*, 1821).

W.S.S.

GEFLÜGELTE WORTE

Well-known and sometimes hackneyed quotations or maxims.

GEGENSPIELER (antagonist)

In a drama or narrative the hero's principal opponent(s).

GEGENSTOLLEN → STOLLEN

GEGENSTROPHE (antistrophe) = Antistrophe → STROPHE

GEGENWARTSDICHTUNG (contemporary literature) → DICHTUNG, → LITERATUR

GEHALT → GESTALT

Within a theory of literature as aesthetic argumentation, *Gehalt* (content, but not to be confused with → INHALT, see below) comprises the *What*, whereas *Gestalt* (form) comprises the *How* of literary argumentation.

It is commonly assumed that both are dialectically linked together and that any separation of them is detrimental to the understanding of the meaning of a text. Nevertheless, for the purposes of a methodical procedure in literary criticism, it is helpful to differentiate between the analytic and synthetic aspects or levels in the structure of a work. The aspect of content includes, where appropriate, story, plot and motivation. The aspect of story (*Inhalt*) of a work refers to the sequence of events in order of time and place which exists in its own right and has its own tradition; as its source it has the material ($\rightarrow$ STOFF) which can range from myths to newspaper reports and which lies outside the specific work in which it is used; the plot (action) which refers to the sequence of events in their causal connection, and motive or motives, i.e. the causal agents, are the means by which the author turns the material into the individual work. The story can be regarded as presenting the theme of the work, whereas plot and motivation present the author's idea, his response to the questions inherent in the story. This latter aspect of the literary work forms the proper subject of the history of ideas.

Form, on the other hand, refers to the way in which the content is presented, for example as tragedy, novel or sonnet within the genres ($\rightarrow$ GATTUNGEN) of narrative, drama and the lyric. Furthermore, form encompasses the literary modes of irony, satire, parody and the grotesque. The relationship between content and form is the central subject of literary poetics and much debate has focussed on the question as to whether it is imposed by the author or is already inherent, as for example in the question as to whether a story, plot or motive is intrinsically either dramatic, epic or lyrical. The history of poetics shows many changes in the understanding of this relationship. The linguistic presentation cannot be separated from the consideration of the relationship between form and content; its specific method of study is the subject of stylistics.

Gehalt and *Gestalt* are united in the essential symbolic character of the work. Only in this dialectical unity does the work present a statement within the aesthetic argumentation of literature. On the symbolic level the critical potential of the notion of *Gestalt* is fully realized; the *Gehalt* of a work, however, is not finite but open to continuous expansion through interpretation which oscillates between the indefinite horizons of authorial intention and reader reception.

W.V.

GEISTESGESCHICHTE (history of ideas) = Ideengeschichte

The philosophical type of history of literature and art which marked the reaction in Germany, from the decade before the First World War to the end of the Second, against the $\rightarrow$ POSITIVISMUS of the later 19th century. What was meant by Positivism was its vigorous pursuit of well-founded facts as the essence of scholarship, e.g. in the work in Germanistics of the Scherer School. These scholars laid the factual foundations of their branch of learning in critical editions, biographies and bibliographies of the leading authors, and comparative literary studies of great scope, rivalling the natural sciences in their exact scholarship. As the German universities slowly re-established themselves after the war, leading scholars in the arts faculties turned back to Dilthey's conception of the *Geisteswissenschaften*, the Arts subjects. To understand an age, on this view, scholars must seek out and compare with each other the manifestations of its essential *spirit* (*Geist*) in its religion, philosophy, literature, art, scholarship and social institutions, or as many of these aspects as possible. Some leading exponents of this kind of approach were Unger, Walzel, Gundolf, Korff, Strich and Rehm.

W.H.B.

GEISTLICHE DICHTUNG

Literature which is based on the dogmatic and historical tradition of a particular faith, and is not necessarily written by the clergy.

GEISTLICHES DRAMA

As distinct from → BIBLISCHES DRAMA, a religious play which is written for the purpose of commemorating and celebrating particular events in the ecclesiastical year, and which is performed at the appropriate dates. → ADVENT-SPIEL, → DREIKÖNIGSSPIEL, → FRONLEICHNAMSSPIEL, → OSTERSPIEL, → PASSIONSSPIEL, → WEIHNACHTSSPIEL.

GEKREUZTER REIM → KREUZREIM

GEKRÖNTER DICHTER (poet laureate) → DICHTERKRÖNUNG

GELEGENHEITSGEDICHT (occasional poem) = Huldigungsgedicht

Poem composed to mark a specific occasion, such as a marriage, birthday, etc. or an important social or historical event.

GELEHRTENDICHTUNG

Literature which results from an extensive amount of research by a highly educated author, not necessarily a scholar.

GELEITWORT (preface, foreword) → EINLEITUNG

GEMÄLDEGEDICHT = Bildgedicht

Poem which has a painting or sculpture as its subject. → EMBLEM.

GEMEINFREIE WERKE

Literary works for which the copyright has expired.

GEMEINPLATZ → LOCUS COMMUNIS

GEMEINSPRACHE

The sum of those elements of a language (vocabulary, syntax, grammatical structure etc.) which are used and accepted by all competent speakers, and are not peculiar to a regional dialect or professional jargon.

GENERALPROBE (dress rehearsal)

Final rehearsal of a play before public performance.

GENIE → GENIEZEIT

GENIEZEIT = Genieperiode

Label commonly used as a synonym for → STURM AND DRANG, but while the latter term enjoys some general application in denoting any period or phase of youthful turbulence, *Geniezeit* refers specifically to the decade between 1770 and 1780 and the personal and literary values of a small group of writers, foremost among them being Goethe (1749–1832) and Herder (1744–1803). *Genie* is a broader term than the English *genius*. It does not primarily assert outstanding excellence, but implies creative originality (*Kraftgenie, Original-genie*) as distinct from the pursuit of established patterns. These writers exaggerated a trend, partly inspired by Rousseau (1712–1778), emphasizing in their lives and work the spontaneous expression of individual, fervid, even violent emotional states and rejecting the canons of 'Good Taste' set up earlier in the century. They valued the vital coherence of the living, breathing organism rather than the perfection of clockwork mechanism admired by their fathers. They placed primitive nature above sophisticated culture, and preferred the confessional lyric and the conflict of drama to more discursive epic forms of literature. One decade hardly deserves to be called an 'age', but as an explosion of genuine native genius, it echoed down the years.

J.S.

GENOS, –US → STILARTEN

GENREBILD (genre picture)

Short, vivid and realistic portrayal of everyday life situations.

GERMANISMUS

Literal translation of a German idiom into another language.

GERMANISTIK

Collective term to denote all scholarly pursuits of the history and culture of the Germanic peoples. This includes → LITERATURWISSENSCHAFT and → SPRACHWISSENSCHAFT, but also mythology, folklore, archaeology and jurisprudence.

Germanistik as an academic discipline was established by the brothers

Grimm and by Lachmann early in the 19th century. Because of the volume of the material a division into *ältere Germanistik* (up to and including MHG) and *neuere Germanistik* (from the beginning of New High German) was introduced later.

Nowadays the term *Germanistik* is often used synonymously with *Deutsche Sprach— und Literaturwissenschaft.* →PHILOLOGIE.

A.O.

GESAMMELTE WERKE (selected works)

Edition of a selection of works by an author. → AUSGABE.

GESAMTAUSGABE (complete works) → AUSGABE

GESAMTKUNSTWERK

Term coined by Richard Wagner (1813–1883) to designate his concept of musical drama, and by extension applied to any art work in which several art-forms are employed simultaneously.

GESANG → CANTO

GESANGBUCH (hymn-book)

Collection of religious songs used in liturgical services.

GESCHICHTSDICHTUNG

Literature in which historical events and personalities form the subject-matter; and which views history as a significant force.

Sometimes used as a vehicle for political propaganda, esp. to avoid censorship. e.g.: Stefan Heym, *Der König David Bericht* (1972).

GESCHICHTSKLITTERUNG

Inaccurate and possibly biased compilation of history.

GESCHLOSSENE FORM (closed form) = Tektonik

Geschlossene Form (closed form) and *offene Form* (open form) are 20th century critical terms evolved by the art historian Heinrich Wölfflin or his school. They proceeded from the difference in styles established by Wölfflin, between the Renaissance and Baroque: stasis (closed) as against movement (open), harmony as against unruliness, balance and equipoise as against asymmetry and exaggeration. Wölfflin's separation of styles has in its turn affinities with the Schlegel brothers' (August Wilhelm Schlegel 1767–1845 and Friedrich Schlegel 1772–1829) notions of the 'Classical' and the 'Romantic'. Applied to literature, the Wölfflinian terminology has less obvious usefulness as an historical description; rather it came to describe 'constants' which could be seen in the development of European and, more especially, German drama. It is no coincidence that the first attempt to apply 'open' and 'closed' to drama came during the Expressionist era in Germany, also a time of rediscovery of the German neo-Shakespearean tradition as exemplified by Lenz (1751–1792) and Büchner (1813–1837). One particularly influential extension since then has been the study by Volker Klotz (*Offene und geschlossene Form im Drama*, 1960), which has seen the closed e.g. Racine (1639–1699), Goethe (1749–1832), later Schiller (1759–1805) in terms of condensed form, humanistic or religious subject-matter, unified plot and logical exposition, with the open e.g. Lenz, Grabbe (1801–1836), Büchner, Wedekind (1864–1918), Brecht (1898–1956) exemplified by more diffuse structure, greater individual importance of scenes, less restriction on time and space, and an underlying atmosphere of scepticism or doubt. Significantly, neither Klotz nor any other exponent of this theory has been able adequately to apply it to the dramatist who most defies rigid formal classification: Shakespeare.

R.C.P.

GESELLSCHAFTSDICHTUNG

Literature written by members of the upper classes for the upper classes esp. during the 16th and 17th centuries. → GALANTE DICHTUNG, → HIRTENDICHTUNG.

GESPALTENER REIM

Rhyme which combines two or more short words into one rhyming unit; e.g.: hat es / mattes. → REIM.

GESTALT → GEHALT

GESTE (gesture)

1. A conventional stereotyped movement of the body which is widely understood and accepted as a substitute for words; e.g.: the repeated crooking of the forefinger meaning 'come here'.

2. Set gesture studied by actors and public speakers for the purpose of communicating certain emotions; e.g.: horror: opening the eyes and mouth wide. → GEBÄRDE.

GHASEL (ghazel)

Verse form of Arabian origin, in which after an initial rhyming couplet, the even lines of the poem echo this rhyme, and the odd lines are unrhymed. aa ba ca da. . .xa.

GLEICHKLANG → ASSONANZ

GLEICHLAUF → PARALLELISMUS

GLEICHNIS

The *Gleichnis* is an extended form of the → VERGLEICH. Like the → PARABEL it is a narrative which draws a sustained analogy between the material in the story and the lesson it is attempting to impart but unlike the *Parabel* it uses a direct comparison (so. . . .wie).

The distinction between *Parabel* and *Gleichnis* is not always made; e.g.: The parables of the N.T. in particular, are often referred to as *Gleichnisse*.

A.O.

GLOSSE (gloss)

Explanatory note or definition of a rare or difficult word in a literary work, which may appear as a footnote (→ FUSSNOTE), in the margin (→ MARGINALIEN, *Randglosse*) or between the lines (*Interlinearglosse*).

GOETHEZEIT

The cultural period from 1770–1830 in Germany which separates the 18th century characterized by the Enlightenment from the more scientifically oriented realistic 19th century. It is seen as the climax of German culture because of its achievements in music (e.g. Haydn, Mozart, Beethoven, Schubert, v. Weber), philosophy (Kant, Fichte, Hegel, Schelling, Schopenhauer), literature (Goethe, Schiller, Hölderlin, Kleist, Tieck, Eichendorff) and philology (Jacob and Wilhelm Grimm, Wilhelm v. Humboldt), and it is a period which saw the emergence of a strong education-minded middle class producing large numbers of intellectuals, a process of secularization and the development of a sense of national identity and pride. The flourishing of culture however, as so often in German history, coincides with a period of national disaster and humiliation: from 1789 to 1815 most German territories were involved in the struggle against revolutionary France, then, defeated by Napoleonic forces, they endured periods of occupation by French and Russian armies. The *Goethezeit* encompasses three literary movements and two generations which Korff called *humanistisch* and *romantisch*: some of the young → STURM UND DRANG writers of the 1770s developed into the *Klassiker* of the 1790s and acquired their basic intellectual outlook ˙*before* the French Revolution. The *Romantiker* emerged c.1800 and represented the *post*-revolutionary generation.

The period derives its name from the greatest literary figure of the time, Johann Wolfgang von Goethe (1749–1832), who established his fame in the early 1770s with his play *Götz von Berlichingen* (1773) and his novel *Die Leiden des jungen Werthers* (1774) and whose last work *Faust II* was published posthumously in 1832. In the intervening sixty years he promoted or participated in every major literary development, continually excelled in every genre and contributed to several areas of scientific research. Heinrich Heine in *Die romantische Schule* (1833) was the first to call this period "die Goethesche Kunstperiode".

The term only came into general use in the 1920s after Korff had published the first volume of his *Geist der Goethezeit* (4 vols. 1923–53). According to Korff the three basic elements shaping intellectual life in the *Goethezeit* were "the educated middle-class's dream of humanity", "the transformation of naive Christian religion into a philosophy of life" and "the necessity of art for humanity". While there is general agreement that → KLASSIK and → ROMANTIK are part of this period, scholars differ in their assessment of the irreconcilability of the world views of these two major movements. The current trend is to stress their common views rather than their disparities. Moreover, there have always been reservations about the term *Goethezeit*, because, in its claim that one person is its dominating figure it excludes too many aspects of the period.

C.G.

GONGORISMUS → SCHWULST

GOTHIC NOVEL → SCHAUERROMAN

GRABREDE (funeral oration)

Speech delivered at a funeral service.

GRABSCHRIFT → EPITAPH

GRÄZISMUS (Graecism, Hellenism)

Literal translation of a Greek idiom into another language.

GRAMMATISCHER REIM

The rhyming of words with the same roots, and sometimes their inflexions. This occurs frequently in → MEISTERSANG, and → MINNENSANG; e.g.: bekleiden / kleidet / kleit / leiden / leidet. → REIM.

GROBIANISMUS (grobianism)

A 16th century attempt to expose, and to curb the crudities and improprieties of the period, using a mode of presentation in which the format and style of the med. rules of etiquette were imitated, and boorishness, crudity and indecency were satirically presented as ideal modes of behaviour.

GROSCHENHEFT (penny dreadful)

Cheaply printed, sensational novel of no literary merit. → TRIVIALLITE-

GROSSSTADTDICHTUNG

Literature about life in large cities, which explores the soulless and soul-destroying nature of the modern metropolis, and the individual's struggle to maintain his identity and humanity within it.

GROTESKE (grotesque)

A narrative technique, style or perspective which focusses the attention of the reader on incompatible opposites, usually involving conflicting cultural values. In content this could consist of horror in humour, humour in horror; the demonic in the sublime, the sublime in the demonic; serious cultural values in an absurd context, absurd cultural values in a serious context. In function this could consist of photographic reality in an absurd situation; meticulous attention to trivial detail in an emotionally overpowering situation; strict logical sequence in an insane chaotic situation.

Groteske is frequently used in literary criticism to denote 'unpleasant' or associated negative concepts and is then defined in terms of the response of the reader, which raises problems of both subjectivity and reliability. In more recent critical literature these negative connotations have decreased to some extent. The major problem in defining the term lies in the inconsistency of its usage.

A.C.

GRÜNDERZEIT

The years following the Franco-Prussian war (1870/71), a period of frenzied financial speculation, nationalism and capitalism.

GRUNDRISS (outline)

Systematic presentation which covers the essential points of something without going into detail.

GSTANZL → SCHNADAHÜPFL

GUCKKASTENBÜHNE (proscenium stage)

Stage situated at one end of the auditorium separated from the audience by a curtain and making use of changeable wings and backdrops.

HAKENSTIL → ENJAMBEMENT

HALBZEILE → KURZVERS

HAMARTIA (hamartia)

According to the *Poetics* of Aristotle (384–322 B.C.), hamartia was the hero's 'tragic flaw' (a weakness of character) or error of judgement, which leads him to commit a mistaken act, which directly causes his downfall. Together with → ANAGNORISIS and → PERIPETIE, hamartia constitutes the tragic plot. → HYBRIS.

HANDLUNG (action, plot) = Vorgang

The framework of actions and events upon which epic narrative and drama are constructed. Aristotle's formula for dramatic structure in his *Poetics* — presentation, development, complication, crisis and resolution of the action — can be applied to most literary works from Greek tragedy to the western and the detective story. This basic narrative scheme with its organic pattern of beginning, middle and end is capable of indefinite variation. At one pole in the drama is the ideal of the closed action, represented in the 16th and 17th centuries by the neoclassical doctrine of the three unities (time, place, action) (→ EINHEITEN). At the other pole is the open structure of Shakespearean and Jacobean drama with multiple plots. The organic 'fiction' of a completed action is questioned or negated in much modern literature. In the modern novel plot in the traditional sense tends to dissolve into subtle analyses of social and psychological causalities underlying action. → NEBENHANDLUNG.

D.R.

HANDPUPPENSPIEL → PUPPENSPIEL

HANS-SACHS-BÜHNE = Meistersingerbühne

Type of podium stage named after the leading dramatist of the *Meistersinger*, which evolved in the mid 16th century. It consisted of a neutral forestage with a rear stage behind it, which was curtained off on four sides, and contained a trapdoor. It closely resembles the Shakespearean stage, in that it is a → SUKZESSIVBÜHNE, a progression beyond the multiple fixed acting areas of the med. → SIMULTANBÜHNE. → BÜHNE.

HANSWURST, HANSWURSTSPIEL = Harlekinade

Stock comic character: the naive and clumsy, yet shrewd peasant. In 1710 Joseph Anton Stranitzky revived the figure, and, giving it an identifiable costume, made it into a distinct comic type. *Hanswurst* became the central character of a number of comedies known as *Hanswurstspiele.* → VOLKSKO-MÖDIE.

HARLEKIN (Harlequin) → ARLECCHINO

HARLEKINADE → HANSWURSTSPIEL

HAUFENREIM → REIMHÄUFUNG

HÄUFUNG → WORTHÄUFUNG

HAUPT– UND STAATSAKTION

Pejorative term used by Gottsched (1700–1766) for the stock plays of the German travelling theatres (*Wanderbühne*) c.1700. *Hauptaktion* refers to the main play, while *Staatsaktion* refers to its historical and political content. The plays treated grand historical and political figures in a melodramatic fashion.

HAUPTFIGUR → HELD

HAUPTMOTIV → MOTIV

HAUPTROLLE (leading role) → ROLLE

HAUSKORREKTUR

The first corrections made in the printing office before proofs are sent to the author. → AUTORKORREKTUR, → BÜRSTENABZUG, → FAHNENKOR-REKTUR.

HAUSPOSTILLE → POSTILLE

HEBUNG (arsis)

The stressed or long syllable of a metrical foot.

HEIDELBERGER ROMANTIK

Term commonly used to denote the work of a group of writers around Clemens Brentano and Achim von Arnim between 1805 and 1808, when Brentano lived mainly in Heidelberg, where Arnim joined him in 1805–06 and

1808. Both were associated there with Joseph Görres and Friedrich Creuzer, professors at Heidelberg University. Main publications: Arnim/Brentano, *Des Knaben Wunderhorn* (1806–1808); Görres, *Die teutschen Volksbücher* (1807); Arnim (ed.), *Zeitung für Einsiedler* (1808), with contributions by Arnim, Brentano, Bettina Brentano, Görres, Wilhelm Grimm, Kerner, Uhland et al. Arnim, Brentano and Görres shared interests in the tradition of romantic literature, i.e. European literature since the M.A. (→ ROMANTIK), with special though not exclusive emphasis on German literature. While Görres's study of old German chap-books (→ VOLKSBUCH) represented historical research, Arnim and Brentano adapted or rewrote their source material, grafting on to it modern thought and psychology in order to demonstrate a timeless union between art and humanity in contrast to the inhumanity of any social and political reality. *Volk* (Arnim, *Von Volksliedern*, 1806), as the true source of poetry, was identified with the common people, but at the same time the word also adopted the meaning of 'nation', i.e. a political unity above all existing social and political divisions. The works of Görres, Arnim and Brentano thus invoked the spirit of a German national tradition at a time when large parts of Germany were occupied by the French.

Des Knaben Wunderhorn considerably influenced German poetry, e.g. Eichendorff (1788–1857), Uhland (1787–1862), Wilhelm Müller (1794–1827), Heine (1797–1856), Mörike (1804–1875) and stimulated German composers, e.g. Beethoven, Brahms, Strauss, Mahler. It also inspired further research in German popular literature (Jakob and Wilhelm Grimm, *Kinder– und Hausmärchen*, 1812 ff.; *Deutsche Sagen*, 1816 ff.).

G.S.

HEILIGENLEBEN, HEILIGENVITA

Popular med. version of a saint's biography, usually fictional rather than strictly factual. →LEGENDE.

HEIMATDICHTUNG

Developed at the turn of the century as a reaction against Naturalism, with its insistence on the factual and sordid details of existence in newly industrialized cities. The catch-phrase of *Heimatdichtung* was 'Los von Berlin!' It viewed *Heimat* as the unspoiled rural village environment, with traditional social structures, where the individual could recover from the malaise and fatigue of decadent urban life. The movement away from Berlin, a process of literary decentralization, saw the proliferation of regional literatures. This had the positive effect of educating new social classes as readers. Unfortunately, *Heimatdichtung* also incorporated the less savoury element of German thought which had developed during the 19th century: excessive Germanic consciousness with its associated doctrines of racial purity and anti-semitism. Thus *Heimatdichtung* was quickly seized upon by Nazi propagandists and consequently the term was discredited. (→ BLUBO). Since the Second World War, however, some critics have tried to rehabilitate it by arguing that any literature which draws its inspiration from a rural environment is *Heimatdichtung*.

C.B.

HEIMKEHRERROMAN

Type of fiction featuring servicemen returning from war, and exploring the problems of their readjustment to civilian life.

HELD

Historically not merely the central character of a drama or epic poem (e.g. *Heldenepos, Heldendichtung*), but one who is also endowed with exceptional qualities of moral courage and an almost superhuman strength deriving from his being favoured by the gods. The Romantic hero defied both gods and men in a search for the ultimate truth. The heroine, with some exceptions in classical drama, was a secondary, passive figure whose role was defined in relation to the hero. In current usage, the hero/heroine (or anti-hero) is no longer distinguished by particular virtues. He/she is simply the central character in a literary work, sometimes also called the protagonist. In German literature, this evolution of the term was exacerbated by the co-option of heroic terminology in Nazi ideology and rhetoric. This brought the term into disrepute, so that it has been replaced in current literary scholarship by the term *Hauptfigur*. An exception to this trend was the use, in the GDR during the 1950s and early 1960s, of the term → POSITIVER HELD in the context of the theory of Socialist Realism. → SOZIALISTISCHER REALISMUS.

B.E.

HELDENDICHTUNG (heroic epic poetry) → HELD

HELIKON (Helicon)

Beoetian mountain, which the ancient Greeks believed to be the seat of the Muses, and therefore sacred. → HIPPOKRENE, → MUSEN.

HELLENISMUS

Hellenistic period in Greece, which began with the exploits of Alexander the Great (356–323 B.C.) and continued until the beginning of the Roman Empire (30 B.C.).

HENDIADYOIN (hendiadys)

Figure of speech;

1. The co-ordination of two synonymous nouns; e.g.: mit Gaben und Geschenken.

2. The co-ordination of two words, one of which is dependent on the other; e.g.: 'Wir schlugen sie mit Schwert und Stahl' — when the literal meaning is 'mit Schwertern aus Stahl'.

HERAUSGEBER (editor)

Person responsible for preparing or revising the work of others for publication.

HERMENEUTIK, HERMENEUTISCHER ZIRKEL

Just as *hermeneutics* in English, the German term signifies the art and the practice of textual interpretation, as well as their methods and methodology; it is, therefore, largely synonymous with → INTERPRETATION and → DEUTUNG, → EXEGESE and → AUSLEGUNG. The latter pair of concepts, referring to biblical exegesis in particular, and thus to what used to be called *hermeneutica sacra* as opposed to *hermeneutica profana*, points to an issue which has been debated ever since Friedrich Schleiermacher (1768–1834) founded the modern science of hermeneutics, and Wilhelm Dilthey (1833–1911) applied Schleiermacher's insights to literary criticism: namely, whether or not there are, or ought to be, different kinds of interpretation corresponding to different kinds of texts. Schleiermacher and his disciples flatly reject such a distinction, as does Hans-Georg Gadamer in his influential study, *Wahrheit und Methode. Grundzüge einer philosophischen Hermeneutik* (1960), whereas others, e.g. the contemporary Italian theorist, Emilio Betti, have tried not only to maintain it, but to expand it even further. Regardless of this disagreement, however, every hermeneutic process consists of two steps, the first being the understanding (*Verstehen*) of the meaning (→ BEDEUTUNG) of a given text, the second its interpretation or exegesis proper, i.e. the explanation and elucidation of the meaning. Yet any interpretative approach is in turn caught, from the very beginning, in the so-called 'hermeneutic circle' (*hermeneutischer Zirkel*) which can be defined as the insoluble interdependence of part and whole; for, paradoxically, "the whole can be understood only through its parts, but the parts can be understood only through the whole" (E.D. Hirsch, *Validity in Interpretation*, 1967). While the circularity of hermeneutics may be untenable from a strictly logical point of view, it nevertheless must be accepted as indispensable for all textual understanding, and might indeed be extended to include the historicity of the critic himself (Joseph Strelka, *Methodologie der Literaturwissenschaft*, 1978). Hermeneutics as a modern science has not gone unchallenged though, either in Germany or in the English-speaking community. For instance Susan Sontag's massive attack on it (*Against Interpretation and Other Essays*, 1964, where she pleads for an 'erotics' of art and literature instead) has been echoed by at least some representatives of German criticism. There are scholars who hold that meaning in a literary text is not preordained, but rather generated by the activity of the reader (Wolfgang Iser, *Die Appellstruktur der Texte*, 1970), as there are poets who decree that reading — and consequently, interpretation or hermeneutics — amounts to nothing less than a totally arbitrary 'anarchic act' (Hans Magnus Enzensberger, *Bescheidener Vorschlag zum Schutze der Jugend vor den Erzeugnissen der Poesie*, 1976).

R.G.

HERMETISCHE LITERATUR (hermetic literature)

1. Body of religious, philosophical and occult writings from Egypt attributed to Hermes Trismegistos (the god of wisdom) dated approx. 3rd century A.D.

2. Product of a modern literary trend, which is highly esoteric, using private symbols and metaphors, and attempting to be as cryptic as possible.

HEXAMETER (hexameter)

Metrical line consisting of six dactyls (→ DAKTYLUS) or five dactyls and a trochee (→ TROCHÄUS) or a spondee (→ SPONDEUS).

HINTERTREPPENROMAN

Cheap sensational novel of sex and adventure. → TRIVALLITERATUR.

HIPPOKRENE (Hippocrene)

Spring on Mount Helicon (→ HELIKON), which → PEGASUS is said to have created by a stroke of his hoof; and according to Hesiod (c.7th century B.C.) was a source of poetic inspiration. → MUSEN.

HIRTENDICHTUNG (bucolic or pastoral poetry) = Bukolik, = Schäferdichtung

Literary genre originated by Theocritus (c.310–250 B.C.), which gives an idealized presentation of pastoral living. The life of shepherds and shepherdesses is portrayed in a highly sentimental fashion, as the poet looks nostalgically at their closeness to nature, and the blissful tranquillity and simplicity of their existence.

Hirtendichtung first appeared in German literature in the 17th century, initially in the form of translations from Romance languages and later in its own right as creative literature. Lyric poetry (→ EKLOGE, → IDYLLE), drama (*Schäferspiel*) and the novel (*Schäferroman*) were the principal modes of expression.

A.O.

HISTORISCH-KRITISCHE AUSGABE (critical edition) → AUSGABE

HISTORISCHE ERZÄHLUNG, NOVELLE, –R ROMAN, –S DRAMA, –S LIED

Forms of → GESCHICHTSDICHTUNG.

HOCHLITERATUR

Literature of acknowledged aesthetic merit, as opposed to → TRIVIAL-LITERATUR, and which is written by an identifiable author, as opposed to → VOLKSDICHTUNG.

HOCHSPRACHE

Language which in its spoken and written form adheres to set standards (as opposed to → UMGANGSSPRACHE). → BÜHNENAUSSPRACHE, → SCHRIFT-SPRACHE.

HOCHSTIFT → FREIES DEUTSCHES HOCHSTIFT

HÖFISCHE DICHTUNG (courtly literature) = Ritterdichtung

Vernacular literature produced largely by courtiers for the secular or ecclesiastical court. In the med. period (major literary production in MHG from c.1150 to 1250) the sung lyric and the recited verse epic are the two major forms. The lyric concentrates in particular on courtly love (→ MINNE, → MINNESANG), but there is also a vigorous tradition of political comment, above all in the work of the major lyric poet Walther von der Vogelweide (c. 1170–1230). The courtly epic takes its material from Classical sources (*Aeneid*, the Trojan wars, Alexander), from Celtic sources (→ ARTUSROMAN), from ancient Germanic sources (*Nibelungenlied*), from Christian legends and the Bible. The three major epic poets, all of whom wrote between c.1180 and 1225, are Hartmann von Aue, Gottfried von Straßburg and Wolfram von Eschenbach. French literature is the great intermediary for both the lyric and the epic tradition, and in both traditions the ideal courtly knight is the focus of the poetic statement. The effort to attain courtly excellence and renown, the apparently impossible task of affirming worldly chivalric ideals as well as fulfilling God's demand to renounce the world, is the underlying theme of courtly literature in the med. period. Its purpose is therefore not only to entertain, but also to educate and improve the courtly audience by confronting the social reality of the knight with an ethical and moral ideal and example.

The courtly literature of the Baroque era (17th century) again presents, by means of the lyric, the epic, and now also the drama, a courtly ideal for the benefit of the courtly audience.

P.Oe.

HÖRSPIEL (radio play)

Dramatic genre which originated in 1923 with the advent of radio. Because the *Hörspiel* has to forgo all visual impact and rely on the spoken word and acoustic effects alone it is not bound by the restrictions of the stage and can thus use time and space with much greater freedom than a stage play. As it requires greater concentration from its listeners however, the *Hörspiel* has to be shorter and usually does not last more than an hour. This in turn usually involves the discarding of a division into acts and scenes. Since the *Hörspiel* relies only on voices and sound effects, its requirements differ from those of the stage play, particularly in techniques of introducing and identifying characters.

A.O.

HOFTHEATER (court theatre)

Originally a prince's private theatre, later opened to the paying public, but subsidized and controlled by the ruling prince.

HOREN

1. Canonical hours; prayers appointed to be said at certain times of the day.

2. Goddesses of the seasons.

HOSENROLLE

Male role played by an actress.

HULDIGUNGSGEDICHT → GELEGENHEITSGEDICHT

HUMANISMUS (humanism)

1. The system of the literary and philosophical studies and writing of the scholars of the European Renaissance, which flourished in Germany in the 14th to 16th centuries. It was inspired by the literature and art of ancient Rome, and later still more by those of ancient Greece. The learned still thought in Latin, wrote in it and used it for teaching and discussion, so that a scholar soon felt himself at home in any university and national differences were minimal.

2. *Neuhumanismus*, the renewed concentration on Greek and Latin studies in Göttingen and other German universities in the second half of the 18th century, which had a marked influence on leading writers from Wieland onwards, and as a result of Wilhelm von Humboldt's reforms the similar concentration on classical studies, to the detriment of the natural sciences, in the curriculum of the Prussian grammar-schools (*Gymnasien*) for much of the 19th century.

W.H.B.

HUMANISTENDRAMA → SCHULDRAMA

HUMOR (humour)

This word has been acquiring meanings since antiquity and has not yet discarded any. However, it should be clear from the context if one of the older meanings such as body fluid, disposition, aberration in temperament, mood, whim, quirk or obsession is intended. Since the 18th century the word has been applied to two main areas: to describe a particular attitude of mind in a person and to characterize objective qualities in literary technique. It is generally agreed that a person who combines tolerance, cheerfulness and detachment with a contemplative turn of mind has *Humor*. German *Humor* tends to be less jolly, and more reflective than its English counterpart. An important constituent of *Humor* is the ability to take the long view of a situation, which considers present adversities and incongruities from the standpoint of infinity, and smiles both at the contrast thus obtained, and at the realization that the contrast will eventually be resolved. This ability to see human events in a much larger context is central to literary *Humor*. Here *Humor* denotes the clear-sighted but sympathetic portrayal of human idiosyncrasies. *Schwarzer Humor* and *Galgenhumor* are equivalent to the English black humour and gallows humour. The former jokes with the macabre, the latter displays cheerfulness in the face of imminent death. → KOMIK.

F.G.S.

HYBRIS (hubris)

The excessive pride or arrogance of a tragic hero which leads him to disobey the gods or violate a moral law, and consequently causes his downfall. → HAMARTIA.

HYMNE (hymn)

In ancient Greece, a song in praise of a god or hero. Later, the med. *Hymne* had a strictly religious function as a song in praise of God. The English term *hymn* still retains this meaning. In German, however, the term now denotes a poem in praise of a god, person, idea or country (*Nationalhymne*). There are no specific formal requirements, but an elevated and solemn style is the most important feature, the tone being more lofty than that of the → ODE with which it is often confused.

HYPERBEL (hyperbole)

Figure of speech: blatant overstatement or exaggeration, which is not intended to be interpreted literally.

HYPOTAXE (hypotaxis) = Satzgefüge, = Schachtelung

The subordination of clauses as distinct from → PARATAXE.

IAMBUS → JAMBUS

ICH-FORM (first-person narrative)

Narrative in which a character who himself plays a part in a story relates it in a quasi-autobiographical manner. → AUKTORIALES ERZÄHLEN.

IDEALISMUS

German literature of the → GOETHEZEIT can only be understood in the general context of contemporary idealistic thinking which is characterized by the basic contention that spiritual forces shape, govern and pervade the world and, in the final analysis, guarantee its meaning and cohesion; and that accordingly the act of perception can be seen as a process by which the human mind imposes its structures on reality (Kant) or even creates it (Fichte). "Life in Germany as it was then and as it is so vividly reflected in our literature was centred on an endeavour to grasp an all-embracing and divine sense of this world and from this there grew the desire to raise the level of man's existence, his individual dignity and the social orders. Total dedication to the great concepts generated by the human mind became for this age the existential justification for all moral values, ideals and standards. The metaphysical expression of this tendency was the interpretation of the universe in terms of itself — the ideal that the infinite was contained in the finite, of an ideal relationship perceived in a link joining all finite matter, a link fixed by time, space and causality, the oneness of God and the world." (Dilthey, *Die deutsche Philosophie in der Epoche Hegels*, publ. 1925).

Within this framework there are two mainstreams of idealism which have been characterized as the 'Idealism of Freedom' (*Idealismus der Freiheit*) and the 'Objective Idealism' (*objektiver Idealismus*) (Dilthey, *Die Typen der Weltanschauung und ihre Ausbildung in den metaphysischen Systemen*, 1911) or as the 'Idealism of Reason' (*Vernunftidealismus*) and the 'Idealism of Nature' (*Naturidealismus*) (Korff, *Geist der Goethezeit II*, 1930). The former emphasizes the dichotomy of mind and matter, soul and body, freedom and subjection, reason and instinct, subject and object, form and life, eternity and transience, immortality and mortality. Man is part of both worlds; his double nature compels him to endure the tensions between them. His greatest challenge is therefore to achieve existential harmony: a human Utopia. Schiller (1759–1805) is the most prominent *literary* representative of this mode of thinking. According to him, the manifestation and prefiguration of human harmony is art. The latter interprets what are seen as antagonistic forces by the Idealism of Freedom as polarities which are reconcilable (Herder) or reconciled in God (Schelling). Reality is a vast realm of increasingly more complex structures, the organizing principles of which are the same for all creation, both the most primitive inanimate thing and the most sophisticated living creature. Nature is thus a realm of analogies and evolutions. Goethe (1749–1832) is the greatest *literary* protagonist of Objective Idealism. – Both varieties of idealism share the ideal of humanity characterizing the *Goethezeit* as a whole: the belief in man as the centre of the world and his potential to develop further and gain a state of perfect human dignity and peace resembling on a higher level the all-embracing harmony of the early world.

C.G.

IDEENGESCHICHTE → GEISTESGESCHICHTE

IDENTISCHER REIM

The rhyming of identical words; e.g.: Herz/Herz. → REIM.

IDYLLE (idyll)

Theocritus of Syracuse (c.310–250 B.C.) whose bucolic poems were called idylls, and Virgil (70–19 B.C.) who modelled his *Eclogues* on the poems of the Greek writer were the founders of idyllic or pastoral poetry in Europe. The classical idyll presents as its subject-matter the simple life and society of shepherds against the background of a remote, serene landscape. The values and beauties of pastoral life soon came to be associated with the myth of a bygone golden age. Nostalgia for the lost simplicity and innocence of a rural existence, untouched by the corrupting effects of civilization, caused the revival of the idyllic tradition in 18th century German literature. While only a few authors, Geßner (1730–1788) and Voß (1751–1826) among them, wrote idylls in the strict meaning of the term, a large body of poetry, prose fiction and even drama appeared containing motifs, episodes and scenes of an idyllic character. Schiller provided the philosophical theory of the genre in *Über naive und sentimentalische Dichtung* (1795). → HIRTENDICHTUNG.

H.W.N.

ILLUSIONSBÜHNE

Type of stage which, by means of properties, wings and technical devices, simulates a specific setting in an attempt to create the illusion of reality. → GUCKKASTENBÜHNE.

ILLUSTRIERTENROMAN

Novel which appears in the form of serialized instalments in magazines. → FORTSETZUNGSROMAN.

IMITATION → MIMESIS

IMPRESSIONISMUS (impressionism) = Eindruckskunst

Term originally applied to a French school of painters of the late 19th century. Within German literary history it denotes a concept of writing predominant c.1890–1910 which developed as a counterbalance to the aims of → EXPRESSIONISMUS and → NATURALISMUS. Impressionists aimed to convince their audience of the value and merits of the momentary emotion, of the private sensual experience and the ephemeral nature of the moment and accordingly in their art they attempt to portray all the facets, shades and nuances of such perceptions. As a consequence they favour lyric poetry and the one act play as vehicles and → ONOMATOPOESIE, → SYNÄSTHESIE, → PARATAXE, → ERLEBTE REDE and → STREAM OF CONSCIOUSNESS as stylistic devices. In German literature *Impressionismus* is represented by Liliencron (1844–1909), Altenberg (1859–1919), Schnitzler (1862–1931), the young Hofmannsthal (1874–1929) et al. → MODERNE.

A.O.

IMPRESSUM

Note in a publication specifying publication details such as copyright, the place and the date of publication, the editor, publisher, number of editions, etc.

IMPRIMATUR (imprimatur) = Druckerlaubnis

Formula which means 'let it be printed'; the offical licence given by a censor of the Roman Catholic Church for a book to be published. Now also applies to the consent given by an author, after reading the final proofs, authorizing the publication of his work. → DAMNATUR.

INDEX LIBRORUM PROHIBITORUM (Index of Forbidden Books)

List of books which members of the Roman Catholic Church were forbidden to read. Abolished June 1966.

INDIREKTE REDE (indirect or reported speech)

The reported form of a speaker's original utterance (→ DIREKTE REDE), which requires appropriate changes in tenses, pronouns, etc. → ERLEBTE REDE.

INHALT

1. Subject-matter of a literary work. → GEHALT.

2. Table of contents: table in a book which lists the chapters or major divisions of a work.

INITIALE

The capital letter which commences a verse, paragraph, or chapter; sometimes elaborately decorated and illuminated. →MINIATUR.

INKUNABELN (incunabula) = Frühdrucke, = Wiegendrucke

The first books printed with movable type, esp. those printed before 1500.

INNERE EMIGRATION

Term used to designate the action of those literary men and women who, like their exiled colleagues, were opponents of the Nazi regime, but who for one reason or another remained in Germany. Yet it is infinitely more difficult to come to terms with the internal émigrés than with their external counterparts, who after all have the detail of their residence abroad in common. Who, under a system of ruthless control, can properly claim to have been a writer of the resistance? Ernst Jünger (1895–), who actively promoted fascism in the 1920s and published an allegorical novel in 1939, the symbolism of which has to be decoded before one can detect any signs of philosophical opposition in it? Or Gottfried Benn (1886–1956), who vociferously welcomed the Nazis and who fell into disgrace and disappeared in the German army not to be heard from again until after the war? Or Frank Thieß (1890–1977), who coined the term *Innere Emigration* and who attacked Thomas Mann (1875–1955) for not having shared the hard lot of those who stayed behind and whose shrill voice was silenced only after the discrediting discovery was made that he had lavished praise on the regime only a few years before? Or Werner Bergengruen (1892–1964), in whose historical novels it is hard to tell whether tyranny is portrayed negatively or favourably? The explanation given for such ambiguities is the watchful eye of the party under whose stern glance it was possible to express oneself only in 'slave language', a camouflaged writing 'between the lines', innocuous to the censor, understandable to the fellow oppressed. But the question remains whether it is the language of a true or of a rebellious slave.

Still, there are incontrovertible cases such as that of Ernst Wiechert (1887–1950) and Friedrich Percyval Reck-Malleczewen (1884–1945), who were thrown into concentration camps, Jochen Klepper (1903–1942), who committed suicide with his Jewish wife, Christian writers like Gertrud von Le Fort (1876–1971) and Reinhold Schneider (1903–1958), as well as lyricists like Rudolf Alexander Schröder (1878–1962) and Oskar Loerke (1884–1941), who obviously suffered deeply under National Socialism and reacted by withdrawing into the hermetic realms of religious writing and apolitical poetry. To do justice to the phenomenon it is therefore necessary to study every individual case carefully.

E.S.

INNERER MONOLOG (interior monologue) →STREAM OF CONSCIOUSNESS

INNERLICHKEIT

Quality of introspectiveness and subjectivity, often involving a rejection of the external world in favour of a concentration on one's own experiences and mental processes.

INREIM

Form of → BINNENREIM: occurs when a word within the metrical line rhymes with the last word of that line:

e.g.: Eine starke, schwarze Barke
       segelt trauervoll dahin . . . (Heine).

INSCHRIFT (inscription)

Words written or engraved (on paper, stone or wood) as an epigram, address or dedication to someone. →EPIGRAMM.

INSPIZIENT (stage-manager)

INSZENIERUNG (staging, production of a play)

INTENDANT

Artistic and administrative director of a → LANDES–, → STADT– or → STAATSTHEATER, who is employed by either the municipal authority or the regional or national government.

INTERLINEARGLOSSE →GLOSSE

INTERLUDES (interludes)

Short dramatic or musical pieces performed between the acts of the med. mystery and morality plays, or between the courses of a banquet; often of a comic and farcical nature.

INTERPRETATION

The study and exposition of literary texts. The term is occasionally still used as an alternative for the originally equivalent Graecism → HERMENEUTIK which in English (as hermeneutics) continues to be applied almost exclusively to the interpretation of biblical texts. Modern German distinguishes between *Hermeneutik* as the theory of interpretation and *Interpretation* as the practice of the 'art' of exposition, so that strictly speaking any theoretic statement about *Interpretation* is the concern of

Hermeneutik. A further relevant distinction is that between → LITERATUR-WISSENSCHAFT and *Literaturkritik* (→ KRITIK). The latter is much narrower in meaning than English literary criticism and close to *Interpretation*, referring primarily to the criticism of contemporary texts. All *Interpretation* conveys value judgements, implicitly positive in the case of texts of the established canon, explicitly positive or negative in the *Kritik* of recent literature.

The last one hundred years or so have seen the development of a range of interpretative approaches, from the extrinsic (*werktranszendent*) methods such as the 19th century → POSITIVISMUS, which aimed at understanding each work in terms of empirically knowable, external biographical data, to the intrinsic (→ WERKIMMANENT) methods, such as the phenomenological method of the 1920s to 1950s, which in theory rigorously excluded all extraneous factors and tried to explain each work on its own terms (→ NEW CRITICISM and *explication de texte*). The difference in approach is determined by the interpreter's philosophic conception of literature, e.g. either as the reflection of a particular empirical reality or of the spiritual totality of an age (e.g. *geistesgeschichtliche Methode* → GEISTESGESCHICHTE) or as a timeless, autonomous, aesthetic phenomenon. Other established methods are the existentialist, morphological, sociological, psycho-analytical, mythological, formalist and structuralist methods. Most interpretations are synthetic, combining elements of intrinsic and extrinsic methods. Precise, close reading is a prerequisite for every interpretation. One broad method of approach which underlies virtually all methods, whether the author is conscious of it or not, is that of the hermeneutic circle. (→ HERMENEUTISCHER ZIRKEL).

Since texts come to life only when read and reflected upon by individual readers, and since consciousness changes in time, all texts are in need of re-interpretation by each new generation. The level of accuracy and sophistication of an interpretation depends to a large extent on the range of experience (*Erfahrungshorizont*) and expectation (*Erwartungshorizont*) of each reader. It follows then that no single interpretation can be complete or perfect.

P.M.

INTERPUNKTION (punctuation) = Zeichensetzung

Insertion of punctuation marks (*Satzzeichen*) in a written passage, to divide it into units of speech.

IRONIE (irony)

The German word has on the whole the same application as the English equivalent irony. From the Greek *eironeia* (dissimulation) comes the basic notion, common to all types of irony, of the (comic or tragic) opposition between appearance and reality. It is customary to distinguish between (1) irony used as a rhetorical device (by a speaker/writer appearing to say one thing but really meaning another), and (2) situational irony or irony of events (in which a person's/character's actions or words prove to have an effect or meaning contrary to what he intends). 'Socratic irony' is a special type of (1), Socrates feigning naivety and ignorance in order to expose the weakness of his adversary's arguments.

In literature, (1) is encountered in the 'voice' of the poet or the prose narrator, as well as in dramatic dialogue; (2) is usually known as 'dramatic irony', the most famous example being Oedipus's curse, which unbeknown to him is a curse on himself. Dramatic irony, which is often referred to in German as *tragische Ironie* and may just as well occur in narrative literature, depends for its effect on the victim's unawareness of what he is saying or doing. → ROMANTISCHE IRONIE is a complex notion and a German specialty, and refers to the author's self-conscious intrusion into his work in order to expose its status as artifice and fiction. The term was coined by Friedrich Schlegel (1772–1829), who saw this highly ambivalent kind of irony (everything is ironized, including the ironist) as a key ingredient of modern literature.

P.T.

JAHRMARKTSSPIEL

Entertainment offered at fair grounds, usually in the form of → KASPER-LETHEATER, →PUPPENSPIEL or → SCHATTENSPIEL. .

JAMBUS (iambus) = Iambus

Metrical foot of two syllables, the first unstressed or short and the second stressed or long. (xx́). →METRIK.

JARGON (jargon)

Vocabulary or mode of speech which is peculiar to a particular trade, profession or group of people, and may be unintelligible to outsiders.

JENAER ROMANTIK → FRÜHROMANTIK

JEREMIADE (jeremiad)

Lamentation: speech or poem which is extremely sorrowful or complaining in mood, in the manner of the lamentations by the prophet Jeremiah in the O.T.

JESUITENDICHTUNG

The literature produced by members of the society of Jesus which reached its fullest development c.1550—1700. Although it was an international phenomenon, it exerted its greatest influence in the German-speaking countries, in the dramatic genre in particular. The large number of schools controlled by the Jesuits facilitated and fostered the production of plays, which were strongly didactic, and were used for the propagation of Catholic teachings at the time of the Counter-Reformation. The plays drew from classical and biblical sources, and also retained themes from the med. → MYSTERIENSPIELE. In the late Baroque, tragedy began to dominate, and historical events and figures increasingly formed the subject-matter. Because the plays were performed in Latin, the influence on the national literatures was limited. During performances German synopses were provided for the benefit of the audience. The Jesuits' main contribution to the development of German theatre can be seen in their innovative theatrical techniques: quick scene changes, sophisticated theatre machinery, lighting effects, etc. Music and dance were utilized to create an early →GESAMTKUNSTWERK.

JUGENDLITERATUR →KINDER– UND JUGENDLITERATUR

JUGENDSTIL (art nouveau)

Jugendstil was a conscious reaction to the blustering massiveness of the Bismarck years in the new Reich. In particular the overloaded neo-historical style — in architecture, drama, painting etc. — aroused contempt and ridicule in the generation which came of age towards the end of the 19th century. But *Jugendstil* was also a practical protest against mass production and industrial ugliness. It drew its inspiration as much from the spartan clarity of Japanese drawing as from the theories of the English social reformers, notably William Morris and John Ruskin. Morris's emphasis on the integrity of the individual designer-craftsman — and his own practical example — are important here. Thus *Jugendstil*, it should be emphasized, covered many art forms: Stefan George's elaborately cool and careful choice of words (e.g. *Die Spange*), as well as the type-face, paper and binding chosen for his work (e.g. the journal *Pan*, much of the work of the Bondi Verlag, etc.), is but one typical instance.

The journal *Jugend*, established in Munich (1896), was standard-bearer for the movement; the term *Jugendstil* itself may be said to originate with Otto Eckmann (1865–1902) whose markedly linear style was a notable and recurrent feature of *Jugend* in its earlier years.

Jugendstil was by no means limited to Germany and may meaningfully be compared with, e.g. the *Sezession* in Austria, *Art Nouveau*, or the 'Nineties Group' (Beardsley) in England; and it shared their later tendency to decorative complexity and excess (*Schlingpflanzenlinie*). The movement was at its height between approximately 1895 and 1910.

Although *Jugendstil* is applied to literature too the term is still very much under discussion and no satisfactory definition of literary *Jugendstil* has yet been offered. →MODERNE.

B.C.

KABARETT (cabaret) = Brettl, Kleinkunst, Überbrettl

Form of theatrical entertainment originally presented in a public house; comprising a number of songs and sketches performed in a fast-moving style, with a minimum of theatrical accessories. Traditionally highly critical of the establishment, *Kabarett* holds it up to ridicule, subjecting it to biting satire.

KALAUER

Pejorative term for a pun or play on words which is forced, artificial, or in bad taste.

KALENDER → KALENDERGESCHICHTE

KALENDERGESCHICHTE

Refers to a short, usually fictional prose text normally published in a popular almanac (*Kalender*). Until the mid-19th century these almanacs often constituted the only secular reading of the lower classes, and were also widely circulated amongst the middle classes. They were bought primarily for the useful information they contained; dates, times of the rising and setting of the sun and moon, market dates, astrological and medical advice, but from the 16th century onwards almanacs also included reading material intended primarily to educate and entertain their readers, who usually had only a minimum of formal education. Thus almanac stories are generally simple in style and often have a didactic moral undertone. While they often adopted formal elements from other traditional short literary forms such as the prose farce, anecdote, satire or chronicle, these were amalgamated into a distinctive form of their own, appropriate to the specific characteristics of their medium, the *Kalender*. The *Kalendergeschichten* were often related to the particular region where the almanac was published e.g. the almanac stories by Hebel (1760–1826), Auerbach (1812–1882) or Gotthelf (1797–1854), and the language coloured by the regional dialect. During the 19th century almanac stories, which had previously been published anonymously, were increasingly acknowledged as an artistic form and some authors republished their *Kalendergeschichten* in separate collections (e.g. Hebel, *Schatzkästlein des rheinischen Hausfreundes*, 1811). This partial emancipation of the *Kalendergeschichte* from its medium continued into the 20th century, when, with the decline of popular almanacs as a literary medium, almanac stories were also written for separate publication;   e.g. the *Kalendergeschichten* by Brecht (1898—1956) and Graf (1894—1967). →ALMANACH.

F.V.

KALLIOPE (Calliope)

Muse of rhetoric, eloquence and heroic poetry. →MUSEN.

KAMMERSPIELE

Small intimate theatre (300—800 seats) for the production of plays not suited to larger stages.

KANZLEISPRACHE

The German used by the chancelleries for legal records from the late 13th century when the vernacular started to replace Latin in this function. This, together with the invention of the printing press and the Reformation, provided the impetus for the standardization of written German. The Saxon chancellery, on whose *Kanzleisprache* Luther based the language of his Bible translation, used an East Central German variety, as did the imperial chancellery when it was in Prague. To an increasing extent this variety became the model for literary German, a tradition continued by Opitz (1597—1639), Leibniz (1646—1716), Goethe (1749—1832), and others. →DRUCKERSPRACHE.

M.C.

KAPITALE

Roman script consisting of capital letters only (→MAJUSKELN) used for manuscripts and inscriptions from the 4th to 6th century. Gradually superseded from the 5th century onwards by the more rounded →UNZIALE.

KAROLINGISCHE RENAISSANCE (Carolingian Renaissance)

The revival of interest in the Latin language and culture stimulated and encouraged by Charlemagne (768—814) who was the patron of a group of scholars (many of whom were Irish monks) at his court, who copied, collected and commented on a vast number of works of classical Roman literature.

KASPERLE, KASPERLETHEATER

Puppet theatre whose main character is a comic figure called *Kasperle*.

KASTALIA (Castalia)

A spring on Mount Parnassus (→ PARNASS) which was sacred to the Muses, and according to the ancient Greeks was a source of poetic inspiration. → HELIKON, →MUSEN.

KASTRIERTE AUSGABE (editio castigata, castrata, expurgata) → AUSGABE

KASUS

The literary presentation of a case and a set of rules against which it is measured, where a conclusion is not necessarily intended. → EINFACHE FORMEN.

KATASTROPHE (catastrophe, denouement)

Term which designates both the change which produces the unhappy solution of a drama (esp. tragedy), and the conclusion (→ LÖSUNG) itself.

KATHARSIS (catharsis)

According to Artistotle (384–322 B.C.), catharsis was the feeling of moral and emotional purification which tragedy should evoke in the audience. After experiencing emotions such as pity and fear (*Furcht und Mitleid*) the audience would feel emotionally refreshed and purged.

KAUDERWELSCH (gibberish, jargon)

Unintelligible or nonsensical speech, sometimes a medley of different languages or dialects.

KEHRREIM (refrain) = Refrain

Phrase, line or verse repeated at regular intervals in a strophic song or poem, often at the end of a stanza.

KELLERTHEATER → ZIMMERTHEATER

KETTENREIM = Äußerer Reim

Rhyme scheme: aba, bcb, cdc etc. → REIM.

KINDERLIEDER (children's songs)

Nursery rhymes, lullabies etc.

KINDER— UND JUGENDLITERATUR

Though generally known as *children's* literature in English, both terms refer to books written specifically for young readers and listeners to the age of about fifteen. Its relationship to adult literature is complex. Much of literature gives pleasure to readers of all ages and the origins of *Kinder— und Jugendliteratur* are to be found in the popular oral tradition. Some adult writing has been adapted for children and has thereby achieved a much wider readership e.g. Defoe's *Robinson Crusoe* adapted by J.W. Wyss, as *The Swiss Family Robinson* in 1712. Today *Kinder— und Jugendliteratur* also shares with all modern literature a partnership with the non-book media. The history of *Kinder— und Jugendliteratur* is however shorter than that of adult literature, since the 18th century is seen as its starting point. The Age of Reason and particularly the publication of Rousseaus's *Emile* (1762) marks the recognition of childhood as a legitimate, distinct stage in human development. The 19th century concentrated on books whose sole aim was to instruct and edify but there were some rare exceptions which appealed to the imagination, and these continue to delight and are revered as 'classics'. They include the fairy tales collected by the eminent linguists Jacob and Wilhelm Grimm and published as *Kinder— und Hausmärchen* (1812—15), which established the fairy/folk tale as a German institution and made it the favourite literary export; Wilhelm Busch's *Max und Moritz* (1865) which inspired Rudolf Dirk's early American comic *Katzenjammer Kids*; Dr. H. Hoffmann's *Struwwelpeter* (1845) and Karl May's Wild West series (65 volumes) which began with *Winnetou* in 1892.

Modern *Kinder— und Jugendliteratur* is characterized by a desire to teach children how to cope with reality rather than to avoid it. Erich Kästner's *Emil und die Detektive* (1929) is an early example of this modern realism. Since the 1960s the focus has been on the realistic children's 'problem' book set in a specific socio-political context. Theatre groups such as *Grips* in Berlin and publishers like Beltz and Gelberg show clearly their concern with social issues. Through translation, *Kinder— und Jugendliteratur* has become increasingly international and in the last twenty years has managed to attract some of the best writers and illustrators, including such authors as Isaac Bashevis Singer who commented in 1969: "While adult literature, especially fiction is deteriorating, the literature for children is growing in quality and stature".

M.N.

KITSCH (kitsch)

Originally used as a term for cheap art, then as a concept applied to all art which is not considered to be genuine, because it substitutes glossiness for beauty, hollow pathos for greatness, sensation for tragedy and sentimentality for sentiment.

Since the difference between beauty and glossiness is often difficult to determine, the exact line between *Kitsch* and genuine art is sometimes hard to find. The judgement whether or not a given work is *Kitsch* depends on the artistic ideal of a given period. The younger generation can reject as *Kitsch* what the older saw as a genuine art form (e.g. → JUGENDSTIL). In contrast to the genuine work of art, which concentrates on the representation of the given subject-matter and for this reason appears to be of a harsh and reserved nature, *Kitsch* intends to evoke a soothing and elevated state of feeling in the recipient. This intention determines its means of presentation. Thus the *Kitsch* narration prefers a lyrical vocabulary of emotional appeal, which is often repetitive and additive and fails to be coherently integrated into the work. This can be seen in the symbolism of the *Kitsch* work, which does not naturally emerge from the context of the work but rather appears to be superimposed from the outside. The black and white world view of the *Kitsch* work is presented through undifferentiated human types following the pattern of the fairy-tale, whose secularized and trivialized form the *Kitsch* work represents. Like the fairy-tale it describes a world in which evil is punished and good rewarded. In contrast to the fairy-tale it applies this view to its presentation of contemporary life, introducing the reader into an escapist world in which the confrontation with reality is avoided and those wishes denied to him in everyday existence are fulfilled. The untruthfulness of the *Kitsch* world and its artistic incongruity have been summed up by Broch (1886–1951) in his description of *Kitsch* as "evil in the value system of art". → TRIVIALLITERATUR.

E.K.

KLADDE

Rough draft, preliminary uncorrected notes; notebook.

KLAGELIED (lamentation)

Melancholy poem or song. → ELEGIE, → JEREMIADE.

KLANG (sound)

A wider concept than onomatopoeia, *Klang* refers to the overall acoustic impression, other than sentence melody and rhythm, created by a poem when read aloud. This can be the quality of the vowel and consonant sounds, felt as *dark, light*, hissing or liquid etc., the echo effect created by the repetition of certain sounds (rhyme, assonance, consonance, e.g. the *u* sound in Goethe's *Wandrers Nachtlied II*, 1780), the speed with which some sound groups have to be spoken as against others (e.g. the acceleration and deceleration in Rilke's *Das Karussell*, 1906), or a combination of these. – In the poetry of the German Romantics, *Klang* was often more important than meaning, resulting in chant-like poems reminiscent of magic spells (Brentano, 1778–1842, Tieck, 1773–1853). → LYRISCH.

A.V.

KLANGMALEREI → ONOMATOPOESIE

KLAPPENTEXT (blurb)

Note on the jacket of a book describing the text or author etc. → WASCHZETTEL.

KLASSIK (classicism) = Weimarer Klassik

Klassik means classicism in the abstract, literary excellence comparable with the best work of any civilization at its peak, and *deutsche Klassik* is classical German literature, first defined by Gervinus in the first comprehensive history of German literature (1835), as the work produced by Goethe and Schiller in the ten years of their close friendship and alliance (1795–1805). Modern scholars usually advance the opening date to 1788 (Goethe's return from Italy). Medievalists speak of an earlier classical period round about 1200 A.D.. 18th century German classicism is commonly regarded as a German Renaissance delayed by the Reformation, one in which, chiefly owing to Winckelmann, Greek influence prevailed over Latin.

The chief aims of German classicism were formal excellence and high seriousness of content. In verse, French forms like the alexandrine were banished, and replaced in drama, following the English tradition, by → BLANKVERS, or in *Hermann und Dorothea* (1797), Goethe's approach to the epic, by an adaptation of Greek hexameters, while in the satirical *Xenien* (1796) Greek distichs were imitated.

The general tone in both prose and verse avoided the dry moralism of the Enlightenment (→ AUFKLÄRUNG) and the rebellious exaggeration of the → STURM UND DRANG, but everywhere there are expressed reverence for and delight in the beauty and variety of what Goethe called 'the natural forms of human life' in all ages and places, supported by an unceasing search for the psychological insight and moral conviction resulting from prolonged experience of active life, especially among the middle class. Ralph Farrell rightly says that "one basic quality [of classicism] . . . is the reflection in literature of wholeness in life", and this "implies all-sidedness, a harmonious development of all sides of the self" and also "a harmony of the self with its world, with its society, however much it may find itself beset by problems and even though tragedy be recognized as an inevitable part of the human condition". Ideas and feelings of this kind about the typical human lot are the basis of poems as different as Schiller's *Der Spaziergang* (1795) and Goethe's *Alexis und Dora* (1796).

Goethe the naturalist became a serious scientist in optics and botany, and Schiller's aesthetic reflexions profoundly challenged current thought about the function of art in society. The chief concern of both writers was for the continued spread of the humane culture which had become a main feature of their age. In lines written soon after the Peace of Lunéville (1801), which destroyed the old German Reich, Schiller consoled himself with the thought that 'he who cultivates the spirit' is bound in the end to prevail. → GOETHE-ZEIT.

W.H.B.

KLASSIZISMUS

Name given to the stylistic character of those literary and artistic works which are obviously close imitations of Greek and Roman models, or e.g. of French or Italian poetry, art and drama similarly inspired. In Germany it is found at its crudest in Gottsched's *Kritische Dichtkunst* (1730), with its uncritical praise of French 'classical' drama and poetic theory, and its nonsensical interpretations of Aristotle's *Poetics*.

In art, Winckelmann's studies of Greek art were original and perceptive, an inspiration much praised by Goethe (1749–1832). Lessing (1729–1781) followed him up with sharp critical insight, and brought his impeccable scholarship and fine intelligence to bear on Greek, French and English drama and dramatic theory. These and several other classically grounded writers like Wieland (1733–1813), Johann Heinrich Voß (1751–1826) and above all Herder (1744–1803), made it easier for Goethe and Schiller (1759–1805) to become truly classical in an original way, and no longer just 'klassizistisch'.

W.H.B.

KLAUSEL

1.   Clause, proviso. →STÄNDEKLAUSEL.

2.   Clausula, cadence; the final verse of a stanza.

KLEINKUNST →KABARETT

KLIMAX (climax)

1.   Rhetorical figure in which a series of words, phrases or sentences is arranged in such a way that the forcefulness or expression is gradually increased. = Steigerung.

2.   In tragedy the highest point of the rising action (→ STEIGENDE HANDLUNG). →WENDEPUNKT.

KLIO = Clio

Muse of historiography and epic poetry. →MUSEN.

KNITTELVERS

Verse form which has four stresses per line, with rhyming couplets;
e.g.:   Hab nun, ach, die Philosophei,
          Medizin und Juristerei,
          Und leider auch die Theologie
          Durchaus studiert mit heißer Müh. (Goethe: *Urfaust*).

KODEX →CODEX

KOLLAGE →COLLAGE

KOLLATION (collation)

Critical comparison of versions of a text in order to establish variants etc.

KOLPORTAGEROMAN

Cheap and sensational story of no literary merit. → GROSCHENHEFTE, →HINTERTREPPENROMAN, →TRIVIALLITERATUR.

KOMIK

Komik can be used, with or without the definite article, to mean *comedy* or *the comic* in their widest sense, denoting one of the basic literary modes, not restricted to comic drama. With *das Komische* as an alternative, it is often found in conjunction with and in opposition to → TRAGIK or *das Tragische*. The meaning of *Komik* in this abstract sense is sometimes obscure and if it is to be used at all, as clear as possible a preliminary definition should be given. The term is used with greater precision to mean the comic element in a literary work, e.g. *Komik* in Goethe's *Faust*, or in the sense of comic effect and the means by which comic effects are produced, e.g. *Die Komik der Unzulänglich-keit* (comedy of inadequacy) or →SITUATIONSKOMIK (comedy of situation). Although some critics attempt to differentiate *Komik* from → HUMOR, the term can often be best rendered by *humour*, e.g. *Sprachkomik* (verbal humour), *unfreiwillige Komik* (unconscious humour). *Humour* may also be the best translation when *Komik* is preceded by the indefinite article, e.g. *eine kindliche Komik* (a childish kind of humour), or when the reference is to a writer other than a comic dramatist, e.g. 'Heine war ein Meister der satirischen Komik' (Heine was a master of satirical humour).

Komik has other meanings, some of which may be unclear unless attention is paid to the context in which the word appears, e.g. it can mean the technique of writing comedy, or a style of comic acting. In contrast to these specialized uses, *Komik* will sometimes be found in the index to a reference work or literary history as an all-embracing term, covering every possible aspect of comedy and humorous writing.

C.P.M.

KOMISCHE FIGUR = komische Person, = lustige Person

Stock comic figure which originated in the Greek → MIMUS whose sole function was to entertain the audience. Comic effects were achieved by improvised jokes, *lazzi*, etc., rather than by action in the play itself. The *komische Figur* was a constant feature in the development of Western theatre; its culmination can be seen in the multitude of comic types found in the →COMMEDIA DELL'ARTE. Shakespeare (1564—1616) even used the comic figure in his serious dramas, e.g. the Fool in *King Lear*, but here the figure is fully integrated into the action and no longer entertains the audience directly. The comic figure has survived to the present day. Examples through the ages include → HANS-WURST, → PICKELHERING, → KASPERLE, → STABERL, and the modern clown.

KOMISCHE PERSON → KOMISCHE FIGUR

KOMISCHES EPOS

Form of epic poetry which parodies the heroic epic poem (→ EPOS) by using its elevated style, but treating an insignificant subject or person.

KOMMERSBUCH

Collection of student songs, associated with *Studentenverbindungen* and *Burschenschaften* of the → BIEDERMEIER era, but continuing to be published throughout the 19th century. The earliest example dates from 1781.

KOMMISSIONSBUCHHANDEL

Wholesale book store which acts on behalf of a number of publishers and sells to retailers only.

KOMÖDIANTEN → ENGLISCHE KOMÖDIANTEN

KOMÖDIE (comedy)

Komödie is used either as a generic term for comic drama or to describe an example of the genre. Distinctions were once made between *Kömodie* and → LUSTSPIEL, the former sometimes being used for satirical comedies informed by wit rather than humour, but because of disagreement about the difference and because boundaries between the various dramatic genres have become indistinct, *Komödie* and *Lustspiel* are now generally regarded as interchangeable terms; in reference works either term may be found as a heading covering comic plays of all kinds. There are, however, special cases in which *Lustspiel* would be an incongruous substitute, e.g. in → TRAGIKOMÖDIE or in *die ernste Komödie*, a form of comedy, common in German literature, with a serious basis concealed by superficial humour. *Komödie* also has conventional uses, e.g. when the subject is Greek comedy (*die attische Komödie*) or in the translated title of Shakespeare's *Comedy of Errors* (*Die Komödie der Irrungen*).

Komödie is a component of many words describing types of comic drama. Some of these, such as *Sittenkomödie* (→ SITTENSTÜCK) (comedy of manners) or *Typenkomödie* (comedy of types), are standard terms with direct equivalents in other languages; others are peculiar to German, e.g. *Bauernkomödie* (comedy of peasant life), *Verlachkomödie* (comedy ridiculing vices or foibles), or to particular plays, e.g. *Diebskomödie*, the subtitle of Gerhart Hauptmann's *Der Biberpelz* (1893), which has a thief as its heroine. Some derivatives of *Komödie* go back to a time when the word was loosely used with the meaning of *theatre*, e.g. *Komödiant* (actor, often in a derogatory sense) or *Komödie spielen* (play-act, or 'put on an act'). *Komödie* has other, wider meanings only remotely connected with drama, as in the translation of the title of Dante's *Divina Commedia* (*Die göttliche Komödie*).

C.P.M.

KOMPARATISTIK → VERGLEICHENDE LITERATURWISSENSCHAFT

KOMPARSE = Statist

An extra in a film or stage production with a non-speaking part. Normally associated with scenes where these actors are referred to collectively as the *Komparserie*.

KONTAMINATION

1. In textual criticism refers to the situation where several manuscripts have been combined to produce a new copy, which renders it difficult to ascertain the exact tradition.

2. In literary criticism the fusion by an author of a number of works or sources to create a new work in his name.

3. In linguistics the combination by a speaker of two words of similar meaning; e.g. *vorwiegend* from *vorherrschend* und *überwiegend*.

KONTRAFAKTUR

Changing of a secular song into a religious song, by modification of the words, but not the melody.

KONTUR (outline)

The presentation and description of characters and events in a literary work, so that they are quite distinct and clearly recognizable.

KONVERSATIONSLEXIKON (general encyclopaedia)

Book or set of books containing articles on all branches of knowledge, contemporary issues, etc., arranged in alphabetical order.

KONVERSATIONSSTÜCK (comedy of manners)

Light comic piece set in high society, characterized by brilliant and witty dialogue.

KONZEPT

Preliminary draft or rough copy of a speech or text.

KONZETTI (conceits) = Conceits

Extremely elaborate metaphors, plays on words or analogies which are a feature of most European literatures of the Baroque. They were seen as an important form of literary embellishment.

KORREKTUR

Checking and correction of proofs. →AUTORKORREKTUR, →BÜRSTEN-ABZUG, →FAHNENKORREKTUR, →HAUSKORREKTUR.

KORRESPONDENZ

1. Correspondence, exchange of letters.
2. The relationship and interdependence of the part to the whole; e.g. of a line to a stanza, of a stanza to the whole poem.
3. News service: agency which provides the press with news, information and pictures.

KOTHURN (cothurnus)

Extremely thick-soled boot worn by the principal actors in the ancient Greek tragedies.

KRAFTGENIE →GENIEZEIT

KREUZREIM = gekreuzter Reim

Rhyme scheme in which the alternate verse lines rhyme: abab cdcd etc. →REIM.

KREUZZUGSDICHTUNG

Epic and lyric poetry of the 12th and 13th centuries which treated the crusades. Frequent themes are the conflict between love and the crusades, the contrast between the pagans and the Christians, the destruction of the pagans, and subsequently, pleas to God to have mercy on the pagans.

KRIMI →KRIMINALROMAN

KRIMINALROMAN

In popular usage the term, often shortened to *Krimi*, refers to all novels dealing with crime and its detection, provided the novel is regarded as trivial. *Kriminalromane* are usually printed in cheap paperback editions and are not considered part of the cultural tradition because no 'lasting value' is ascribed to them. Hence, Dostoevski's *Crime and Punishment* is not considered a

Kriminalroman.

In West Germany, *Kriminalromane* are read more widely than any other kind of literary genre. In 1971 the Jerry Cotton series alone sold 300,000 copies per week. According to a conservative estimate each copy was read by about six persons on average. This means that close to eight million people read a copy of this series every month.

Literary critics took little notice of the *Kriminalroman* until the discussion of socio-literary problems in the 1960s directed their attention to →TRIVIAL-LITERATUR in general and to the *Kriminalroman* in particular. Since then investigations have appeared in ever increasing numbers. Attempts at defining the *Kriminalroman* first led to a distinction between *Verbrechensliteratur* which deals with general philosophical problems, such as the causes of crime, or the motivation and the conflicts of the criminal, and *Kriminalliteratur* which concentrates on the plot-related, merely entertaining aspects of solving a particular case, of identifying, capturing and convicting the criminal.

Although this distinction is arbitrary, it provides a welcome means of drawing a line between works like Aischylos's *Oresteia* and the oeuvre of Agatha Christie, without raising the intractable question of 'literary value'. Attempts have also been made at distinguishing between the → DETEKTIVROMAN which concentrates on resolving a mysterious case through analytical reasoning, and the *Kriminalroman* which describes, in a chronologically presented sequence of highly dramatic episodes, how the criminal is identified and hunted down. Although this distinction is somewhat theoretical, since novels normally comprise elements of both categories, it has been found useful for purposes of classification and analysis. But since German readers do not distinguish between *Detektivroman* and *Kriminalroman* and prefer to use the latter term for both categories, literary critics are now more or less agreed that the English term *Thriller* should be used for the second category and that *Kriminalroman* should be the generic term for both the *Detektivroman* and the *Thriller*. → TRIVIAL-LITERATUR.

H.W.

KRIPPENSPIEL → WEIHNACHTSSPIEL

KRITIK (literary criticism) = Literaturkritik

An intellectual activity which concerns itself with the evaluation of literary texts. In practice it concentrates on new publications and aims to inform the general public about developments on the book market. The findings are generally published in daily, weekly or monthly newspapers or magazines thus providing a service to the reading public and also exercising considerable influence on the market. *Literaturkritik* does not adhere strictly to scholarly criteria and does allow for subjective judgements but, depending on the calibre of the critic, can reach a very high standard.

In the case of a strictly scholarly evaluation it is preferable to refer to it as → WERTUNG which is part of → LITERATURWISSENSCHAFT. N.B.: Within the Anglo-Saxon tradition the distinction between *Literaturwissenschaft* and *Literaturkritik* is not as developed as it is in the German tradition. The English term *literary criticism* is therefore used for both these activities.

A.O.

KRITISCHE AUSGABE (critical edition) → **AUSGABE**

KRITISCHER APPARAT (critical apparatus) → **APPARAT**

KUDRUNSTROPHE

Verse form used for the med. epic poem *Kudrun*. Variation of the → NIBE-LUNGENSTROPHE in that it has a falling cadence in the third and fourth → LANGVERS and an additional stress in the fourth.

KÜCHENLATEIN (dog-Latin) = Mönchslatein

Frequently ungrammatical and incorrect form of Latin.

KÜNSTE = Sieben freie Künste → **ARTES LIBERALES**

KULINARISCHES THEATER → **ARISTOTELISCHES DRAMA**

KULISSEN (wings)

Movable painted walls placed at the side and back of the stage to form part of the scenery and to conceal the off-stage area from the audience.

KULTISMUS → **SCHWULST**

KUNSTMÄRCHEN

A → MÄRCHEN is a story which is neither determined by the limitations of the real world (history) nor by the conventionally accepted conditions of a created world (fiction). In a *Märchen* the miraculous (*das Wunderbare*) is depicted in the same matter-of-fact way as reality. In contrast to the *Volksmärchen*, the *Kunstmärchen* (a) is not transmitted orally but in written form; (b) its author is known; (c) although using the techniques and motifs of a *Volksmärchen*, it is a conscious work of art in which the artist's personality and his literary period are readily identifiable. Based upon fairy-tale elements in med. writing, the *Kunstmärchen* came into existence during the French Rococo period from where it spread into other European literatures. Employing irony, satire and allegory it aims to provide a witty and frequently moralizing form of entertainment. It reached its culmination point in German literature with Romantic writers; e.g. Novalis (1772–1801), Brentano (1778–1842), Tieck (1773–1853), Hoffmann (1776–1822), Chamisso (1781–1838), Eichendorff (1788–1857). For these poets, the secrets and truths of life reveal themselves essentially in poetry, i.e. in the world of imagination where no limitations to reality exist; consequently, for them the *Märchen* is the purest expression of poetry. The *Kunstmärchen* remained important in Realism; e.g. Mörike (1804–1875), Storm (1817–1888), and, after the interlude of Naturalism, has gained a new prominence in 20th century writing.

U.B.

KUNSTPROSA

Prose which is artistically constructed, with attention given to choice of language and rhythm, as opposed to ordinary prose such as that of everyday conversation.

KURRENTSCHRIFT (Gothic script)

KURSIV (italicized print)

Sloping type which can be easily distinguished from normal upright type and is thus frequently used to emphasize a particular word or sentence.

KURZGESCHICHTE

The term *Kurzgeschichte* is a loan translation from the English *short story*, but its meaning is nevertheless somewhat more restricted than the English term. This is due in part to the fact that German already had a common term (→NOVELLE) for medium length fiction, i.e., the kind of length represented by many of the short stories of W. Somerset Maugham (1874–1965); and in part also to the fact that a specific type of short story was the occasion for the borrowing from English, that associated with names such as O. Henry (1862–1910) and Guy de Maupassant (1850–1893): the brief (one to ten thousand words) often pointed story which has a distinct twist in its ending. The German term *Kurzgeschichte*, therefore, refers narrowly to this type, while the English *short story* refers more broadly to fiction of clearly less than novel length, i.e. including *Novelle* length, for which the term 'long short story ', is sometimes used. No parallel expression is possible in German. Until about 1920–30, the English term *short story* itself was used in German, but by 1930 the loan translation was in common use. The form has been extensively used by the younger, post World War II generation of writers (e.g., Aichinger, Böll, Lenz). While in the 19th century the *Novelle* was the most popular short fiction genre in Germany, it seems now to have been displaced by the *Kurzgeschichte*.

J.M.E.

KURZVERS = Kurzzeile

1. Metrical line normally comprising eight syllables.
2. Half of a →LANGVERS, 2 x 4/4 metre XXXX XXXX. = Halbzeile.

KURZZEILE →**KURZVERS**

LAIENSPIEL

Dramatic performance by people who are not professional actors.

LANDESTHEATER

Theatre subsidized and administered by a federal state (*Bundesland*). In some states it is called a → STAATSTHEATER. An important function of the *Landestheater* is to take productions to regions which do not have an established theatre.

LANGVERS = Langzeile

Metrical line of 4 x 4/4 metre; XXXX XXXX XXXX XXXX. The first half of the line is referred to as the → ANVERS, the second as the → ABVERS. The *Langvers* is the most common metrical line of Germanic heroic and MHG epic poetry. → KURZVERS.

LANGZEILE → LANGVERS

LATEINSCHRIFT

Roman script as opposed to → KURRENTSCHRIFT.

LAUT

The single sound as opposed to → KLANG, the overall acoustic impression.

LAUTSCHRIFT (phonetic script)

Script in which each character represents a single unit of sound. → BILDER-SCHRIFT, → SILBENSCHRIFT.

LEBENDES BILD → TABLEAU VIVANT

LEDERAUSGABE (leather-bound edition) → AUSGABE

LEGENDE = Heiligenleben

Like the English legend, the German term *Legende* used in ordinary speech can mean 'untrue story', even 'lie'.

When referring to a literary genre, however, the German term is more restricted and more specific than the English. *Legende* in this context means a narrative of the life of a saint, a prophet, a holy person, a martyr etc. or an event in such a person's life, usually a miracle. Although most med. collections contain *Legenden* of Christian saints (e.g. *Legenda aurea* c.1270), there are also *Legenden* of oriental and Buddhist holy persons. The *Legende* has itself become the source for other literary works and traces of it can be found in plays, narratives and lyric poetry throughout history. (e.g. Goethe, *Der Gott und die Bajadere*, 1797; Keller, *Sieben Legenden*, 1872). In the 20th century the *Legende* is treated psychologically (e.g. Hesse, *Siddhartha*, 1922) and ironically (e.g. Thomas Mann, *Der Erwählte*, 1951). → EINFACHE FORMEN, → HEILI-GENLEBEN.

A.O.

LEHRDICHTUNG, LEHRGEDICHT, LEHRSTÜCK = Didaktik

Didactic or informative works intended in antiquity for non-literate audiences, in modern times to inculcate moral or political standpoints. Formerly it was not considered to be 'true' literature because it was not purely imaginative, but this view is now less accepted. Traditionally in verse, it has also included legend, fable, satire, epigram and drama. In classical antiquity written in hexameters, *Lehrdichtung* described subjects like agriculture (Hesiod, c.7th century B.C., Virgil, 70—19 B.C.), science (Lucretius, c.99—55 B.C.) and poetics (Horace, 65—8 B.C.). Med. and Reformation writers used *Lehrdichtung* for religious exposition and social criticism (Dante, *The Divine Comedy*, c.1307—1321; Freidank, *Bescheidenheit*, c.1215—1230; Brant, *Das Narrenschiff*, 1494); while 17th and 18th century Neoclassicism revived witty, urbane *Lehrdichtung* in Boileau and Pope. The German Enlightenment (→ AUFKLÄRUNG) enjoyed both moralizing and educational *Lehrdichtung* (Brockes, *Irdisches Vergnügen in Gott*, 1721—1748; Haller, *Die Alpen*, 1732; Gellert, *Fabeln*, 1746—1748). Rare in classical and Romantic German writing (an exception is Goethe's *Metamorphose der Pflanzen*, 1790), *Lehrdichtung* has since been used for political purposes, as in Heine's *Deutschland, Ein Wintermärchen* (1844) or Brecht's *Lehrstücke* (1929—1934). In recent years it has manifested itself in protest songs or the works of Socialist Realism (→ SOZIALISTISCHER REALISMUS).

M.St.

LEICH (lay)

Med. lyric poem of varying length and with free verse; *Leich* can also refer to a melody without a text.

LEINENAUSGABE

Book which is bound in cloth. → AUSGABE.

LEITARTIKEL (editorial, leader)

Leading article in a newspaper or journal, usually written by the editor.

LEITFADEN (textbook, guide, manual)

Book which explains the basic principles of a subject in a concise and easily comprehensive manner.

LEITMOTIV (leitmotiv)

Originally a musical term, later applied to literature also. In opera, particularly the 'music drama' of Richard Wagner (1813—1883), a *Leitmotiv* is a short recognizable musical theme which is identified in that drama with a particular person, object, situation, or feeling. The *Leitmotiv* has three main functions within the music drama. First, it enhances the text being sung, in its simplest form occurring in the orchestra when the singer alludes to the person or object with which it is associated. Secondly, it can remind the audience of events which occurred earlier in the opera: it can revive memories and past emotions. Thirdly, it provides, by skilful juxtaposition of *Leitmotiv* and text, an orchestral commentary on the action on the stage. It can give the thoughts of the characters on the stage, and, perhaps more importantly, it can give the audience information of which the characters are unaware, thus providing a powerful means to achieve dramatic irony. The *Leitmotiv* technique in opera was further developed by Richard Strauss and Humperdinck, among others.

In *literature*, particularly in the works of Thomas Mann (1875—1955), the *Leitmotiv* involves verbal repetition — the repetition of words, phrases or whole sentences in different contexts, thus attaining various associations. In his writing there is a development from the repetition of characterizing phrases, as in the earlier works, to the repetition of whole scenes with slight variations. The *Leitmotiv* in literature is essentially a structural device which enables parts of a larger work to be linked through association, resulting in a more thoroughly integrated whole. Although Mann was an ardent admirer of Wagner's music and had a thorough knowledge of the thematic structure of his music dramas, one must not assume that his use of the *Leitmotiv* is due solely to his love of opera. Many authors before and since have used a similar technique, perhaps the most notable example being Fontane (1819—1898), and Mann himself claims that the use of the *literary Leitmotiv* can be traced back as far as Homer. →MOTIV.

J.N.—B.

LEKTOR

1. University teacher engaged to teach introductory and practical courses in a subject; e.g. a person who teaches his native language at a foreign university.

2. Reader: literary editor employed by a publishing house who reads and

assesses works offered for publication and works in close collaboration with the authors.

LEMMA

In textual criticism (→ TEXTKRITIK) the headings in the critical apparatus (→ APPARAT) giving references to the relevant passages in the author's work.

LESART (variant) = Variante

Different version of a text or part of it arising either from conscious revision by the author or from contamination by copyists or printers. → TEXTKRITIK.

LESEBUCH

Book featuring textual arrangements of works of literature for educational purposes; may be in the form of an anthology, or a reader made up of selected works by given authors.

LESEFRÜCHTE

1. Information or knowledge acquired through reading.

2. Florilegia: selections of passages from various authors; quotations.

LESER

The function of the reader in the literary process has become an important object of study with the reaction against criticism which regarded the text as existing apart from both author and reader, and against study of the text as the product of the author alone. Justification of literature and its study as necessary parts of a social system could be given by anchoring the works in an historical sequence of recipients (readers). The shifts in attitude and interest in the sequence could form a more proper basis for literary history and for aesthetic judgement than that provided for by the concepts of *timelessness* and *classicism* which arose from earlier schools, and which did not include the modern reader/ critic in the historical sequence.

Such a swing from the aesthetics of production (i.e. from the author) to those of reception necessarily gives rise to questions of distribution of books, of psychology and of social history, which are beyond the scope of the literary scholar. His field remains the literary text, and many theories have arisen which attempt to account for the text-reader relationship. The *implied* reader (term coined by Wolfgang Iser, *Der implizite Leser*, 1972), gives a place to both author and reader: the author can use all the means of literary expression to give a series of shifting perspectives to the happenings and persons of the work, and to challenge the reader's own attitudes and experiences in relation to them. The imagination of the reader is further activated by indefiniteness, *empty spots* in the structure of the text. The resultant *actualisation* or *concretion* is also worthy of study (demoscopic research). No reader ever fully realizes all the possibilities extant in the text structure. Other constructs (contemporary reader, ideal reader, intended, imaginary or conceptual reader) are theoretical attempts to assess reader function in and influence on, the text. They are means to particular critical ends.

The persona of the reader (i.e. 'dear reader') is one of the means of directing the imagination of the real reader. This is a frequent device in 18th century novels, but more modern authors tend to discard the persona as a distinct entity in favour of a strategy of perspective linked to characters within the plot.

Literature, although written by an author in a particular period, can outlive both the author and the period, but only because of the imaginative activity of the reader, recreating the structures of word and form given by the text. → REZEPTION.

E.P.

LESERING (book club) → **BUCHGEMEINSCHAFT**

LIED

Originally, a form of lyric poetry consisting of regular rhymed verses. Because of this regularity, the *Lied* lent itself to musical composition, with the result that the term has come to mean a poem set to music, and intended to be sung.

LIEDERHANDSCHRIFT = Sammelhandschrift

Collection of med. manuscripts of poetry, often extensively illustrated and illuminated. → MINIATUR.

LITERARHISTORIE → LITERATURGESCHICHTE

LITERARISCHE FÄLSCHUNGEN → FÄLSCHUNGEN

LITERAT

Frequently pejorative term for a writer.

LITERATUR

1. In the widest sense of the term, *Literatur*, like its English equivalent, means everything in 'letters', i.e. everything written (= *Schrifttum*). This very general meaning does not observe possible distinctions between different types of written material, and is therefore inadequate for the purpose of defining literature as the subject-matter of literary studies.

2. In a more specific sense, *Literatur* refers to that body of texts which is

132

primarily composed of language operating at the level of connotation; that is to say language as employed in a work of literature does not just use words and phrases in their lexical meaning (denotation) directly referring to external phenomena (e.g. the statement 'beware of falling rocks' refers directly to the impending danger of falling rocks and becomes totally redundant if there is no danger of falling rocks) but rather creates a world of its own. In such a text words and phrases are interdependent in more than just the normal grammatical sense; through the full use of aesthetic and stylistic possibilities of language they derive their actual meaning from their context.

This is why, in the ballad *Der Fischer* by Goethe (1749–1832), in the line "Das Wasser rauscht, das Wasser schwoll", it is impossible to replace the word 'Wasser' by the chemical symbol H_2O, because this symbol functions on the level of denotation only. H_2O may sometimes be substituted for the word 'water' but only when this word is used in its lexical meaning, i.e. if it is required to communicate "a colourless transparent tasteless odourless compound of oxygen and hydrogen in liquid state". In Goethe's poem, however, *Wasser* is the dangerous dark element from which life originated, the element of mermaids, a symbol of danger and constant temptation to man.

Within this body of texts there is a wide variety in quality ranging from artistically inferior texts (→ TRIVIALLITERATUR) to those which are the most satisfying aesthetically (→ DICHTUNG). *Literatur* therefore does not imply a value judgement, it merely distinguishes those texts making use of a specific function of language from all other texts. → FIKTION, → WIRK-LICHKEIT.

A.O.

LITERATURARCHIV → ARCHIV

LITERATURFEHDEN (literary controversies)

LITERATURGESCHICHTE (literary history, history of literature)
= Literarhistorie

Historians of literature gather and describe a given corpus of literary works. Their histories of literature present an ordered and full account of the preserved writings of a nation or of an age. Besides the facts of literature, a synoptic view of the origins, scope and transformations of the writings within that corpus is often included in such literary histories.

The historian of literature may proceed from clearly defined criteria, such as:

chronological consideration (e.g. Which works are written when?)
national character (e.g. How does nationality determine the character of the works of literature?)

historical and social change (e.g. How did the industrial revolution affect the production of literature?)

Change of styles and the development of the literary genres may also be recorded by the historian of literature, as well as the biographical data of the writers and poets.

Modern literary histories arose with the Italian Renaissance. However, not until the second half of the 19th century, and with the advent of positivism, (→ POSITIVISMUS) did the historians of literature (Wilhelm Scherer being the most notable among German scholars) show the determining force of heredity, environment and ascertainable physical causes upon the production of literature. Historical, bibliographical and biographical research and the objective description of a corpus of literature are a non-critical (i.e. non-aesthetic) scholarly task. → LITERATURWISSENSCHAFT.

Works of literature of an age or of a particular language are not merely a collection of the disparate writing of individuals; the historian of literature tries to discern and establish the place of individual works within an overall development.

R.P.

LITERATURKALENDER

Literary almanac which provides bibliographical and biographical information about living authors. → ALMANACH, → KALENDERGESCHICHTE.

LITERATURKRITIK → KRITIK

LITERATURPSYCHOLOGIE (psychology of literature)

Literary scholarship makes use of psychological knowledge and techniques and subordinates these to its own methods. Most literary theories emphasize the independent nature of the literary work and stress the limitations of the author's intention and of his conscious insight into the essence of his work. Psychoanalysis, however, offers methods which go beyond the accepted limitations of the conscious mind and reveal certain associations in the unconscious mind. The most important problem areas of literary scholarship in which psychological insights and methods can be utilized are: author biography; the literary creative process; psychological analysis of the work: that is, psychology as it relates to the psychological difficulties or development of the literary figures, language, style, symbolism; the psychology of reading and of the public, which is significant for the reception of literature. The question of authors' abnormal states of mind, resulting from drugs, neurosis, etc. — as in the case of Trakl (1887—1914), Kafka (1883—1924) and pop-artists — may also belong to the realm of literary psychology. → LITERATURWISSENSCHAFT.

L.Z.W.

LITERATURSOZIOLOGIE (sociology of literature)

Sociology of literature is, in the strictest sense of the word, a branch of sociology concerned with empirical investigations of the social conditions underlying the production and distribution of literature, as well as its measurable impact on the development of social groups. It involves examination of the social position of writers, readers, printers, publishers and booksellers, the mechanisms governing the book market, printing techniques, literary institutions, censorship, etc. This branch of *Literatursoziologie* is not highly developed in Germany.

Literatursoziologie also means the investigation of literature as a social phenomenon from a theoretical point of view, closely related to aesthetics and the sociology of knowledge (*Wissenssoziologie*). It looks at the writer and historian as representative of a certain social class, layer or group in a given historical period, as a basis for the understanding of the work of literature, and also uses the work of literature to gain a deeper understanding of the problems of a social system. This method has been developed mainly in Marxist literary criticism: its beginnings are found in Mehring's works, and its most important representative, as far as German literature is concerned, is Lukács. The term is basically used in this context in the GDR. In the 1960s the theorists of the Frankfurt School and especially Adorno's interpretation of the autonomous work of art as a protest against the inhumanity and injustice of society have had a very great impact in West Germany.

In its broadest sense the term tends to confound 'social' and 'sociological' and is generally used to denote any approach that looks at literature primarily in its social and historical context in opposition to → WERKIMMANENT, or structuralist approaches. This usage has always been widespread in the FRG, rather disparagingly in the post-war period and with approval over the last fifteen years as a result of the strong demand of the student generation of the late sixties for a more 'socially relevant' treatment of literature. → LITERA-TURWISSENSCHAFT.

L.B.

LITERATURSPRACHE → SCHRIFTSPRACHE

LITERATURWISSENSCHAFT

A collective term for a number of highly diversified and specialized academic disciplines which concern themselves with the study of literature in all its aspects. As distinct from the more subjective *Literaturkritik* (→ KRITIK), *Literaturwissenschaft* has to fulfil the requirements of a *Wissenschaft*, i.e. it has to provide means and methods for a systematic and objective inquiry into its subject. The development of a theory of literature and new methods and also the constant critical analysis of existing methods and approaches are part of *Literaturwissenschaft*. But it also encompasses more practical aspects of the scholarly pursuit of literature such as → INTERPRETATION, → LITERATUR-GESCHICHTE, → LITERATURPSYCHOLOGIE, → LITERATURSOZIOLOGIE, → METRIK, → REZEPTION, → STILISTIK, → TEXTKRITIK, etc.

A.O.

LITTERATURE ENGAGEE → ENGAGIERTE LITERATUR

LIZENZAUSGABE

Edition of a work printed under licence to another publisher. → AUSGABE.

LOCUS COMMUNIS (commonplace) = Gemeinplatz

Platitude, trite remark.

LÖSUNG (dénouement)

The conclusion and solution of a dramatic conflict. → KATASTROPHE.

LÜGENDICHTUNG

Popular literary genre originated by Lucian (c.120–180) which relates fantastic, improbable, or highly exaggerated events. A recurring feature is the character of the braggart (e.g. miles gloriosus, Bramarbas, Baron von Münchhausen, Cyrano de Bergerac). → MÜNCHHAUSENIADE.

LUSTIGE PERSON → KOMISCHE FIGUR

LUSTSPIEL

Term originally coined to replace the Greek derived → KOMÖDIE, like → SCHAUSPIEL for → DRAMA, and *Trauerspiel* for → TRAGÖDIE. Later attempts were made to differentiate these pairs. While either *Lustspiel* or *Komödie* is used to refer to comic drama as a genre, *Lustspiel* in its narrow sense denotes plays informed by → HUMOR rather than → KOMIK, i.e. *Lustspiele* accept the world as it is and display a serene understanding of human frailty. Their milieu is usually bourgeois or upper-class, therefore the term *Konversationslustspiel* is often used. The distinction between *Lustspiel* and *Komödie*, neat in theory, is problematic in practice. Few plays belong to one genre alone, e.g. Grillparzer's *Lustspiel, Weh' dem, der lügt* (1840), has elements of low comedy (the half-witted Teuton Galomir). Other languages have no equivalent distinction, nor do all German scholars recognize the above categories or agree on which plays should be assigned to each. Scholars generally speak of Shakespeare's *Lustspiele* and Molière's *Komödien*, but both *romantische Komödie* or *romantisches Lustspiel* can be found referring to the same plays. While the *Lustspiel* is considered the superior achievement, a number of superficial plays e.g. those of Bauernfeld (1802–1890), or Kotzebue (1761–1819) would also

136

belong to this category. *Lustspiel* is thus best used for a group of subdued comedies, treating philosophical and moral questions, e.g. Lessing, *Minna von Barnhelm* (1767), Hofmannsthal, *Der Schwierige* (1921). → WEINERLICHES LUSTSPIEL.

F.W.

LYRIK (lyric poetry)

Term of Greek origin: 'what can be sung to the *lyre*'. Broadly speaking, poetry as against mere verse. No neat definition can be given, particularly as the attempt, made above all in German criticism, to base such a definition on what Staiger had termed → LYRISCH, has now generally been abandoned. Following Benn's *Probleme der Lyrik* (1951), the intellectual element and calculated craftsmanship have been seen as equally legitimate aspects of *Lyrik*.

The term would then include (a) poetry of emotive subjectivity, spontaneity, immediacy and musicality (Staiger's *lyrisch*), as well as (b) *Gesellschaftslyrik*, composed for and in accordance with the rules prevalent in a given society such as that of the Minnesingers or of the Baroque court poets, (c) →GEDAN-KENLYRIK, which reflects on philosophical, theological and aesthetic problems such as the vindication of God e.g. Haller (1708—1777), the concept of Beauty or of the Ideal e.g. Schiller (1759—1805), and (d) the mannerist, *l'art pour l'art* and hermetic traditions e.g. Kuhlmann (1651—1689) George (1868—1933), Celan (1920—1970).

Characteristic features common to all forms of *Lyrik* are verse, rhythm and imagery — but not necessarily stanza division and rhyme — as well as brevity, concentration on the essential, contraction of complex thought to a point of density, which purposely suggests a variety of associations and hence interpretations. The latter has become a prominent characteristic of modern *Lyrik* which uses special techniques (→CHIFFRE) to create it. →GATTUNGEN.

A.V.

LYRISCH

In Emil Staiger's definition (*Grundbegriffe der Poetik*, 1946), a state of momentary fusion (of *Erinnerung* in the sense of 'being within or taking inside') of the self with the world around, which can be present in poetry, drama or narrative literature, but in German literature, it finds its purest expression in the poetry of Goethe (1749—1832) and of the Romantics. Its immediacy of feeling manifests itself in a heightened musicality, the identity of word and → KLANG, at the expense of reflection and logical development or argument. Hence the predominance of short paratactic phrases, simple language, the modulation of rhythm according to mood rather than metre and the frequent use of the present tense. The *lyrische* element is often concentrated in the refrain which serves to strike again the same note of intimacy, while the remainder of the poem may be more reflective or descriptive. Staiger observes a similar change from *lyrisch* to reflective in the last line of Goethe's *Wandrers*

Nachtlied II (1780). →DRAMATISCH, →EPISCH.

A.V.

LYRISCHES ICH (lyrical I, persona)

The persona who speaks as 'I' in a lyric poem but is not identical with the poet (empirical I).

MÄNNLICHER REIM (masculine rhyme) = einsilbiger Reim, = stumpfer Reim

Rhyme which ends on a stressed or long syllable.

MÄR → MÄRE

MÄRCHEN

The term has two meanings in German: (1) In a broad sense the word signifies a folk-tale (*Volksmärchen*), i.e. any popular story transmitted by oral tradition, e.g. fable, joke, anecdote, animal tale, religious tale, or fairy-tale. (2) In its strict sense the term *Märchen* refers to the last category, the fairy-tale. The word does not exclusively designate a story about fairies but rather one involving magic and enchantment. The traditional fairy-tale is set in an unrealistic world and often depicts a lowly hero or heroine who overcomes obstacles and adversaries usually by magical means and who finally marries a prince or princess and inherits a kingdom. The fairy-tale is simple in its structure, being made up of a series of motifs and episodes which may recur not only in other stories of the same culture but also in tales of other cultures. The term *Volksmärchen* signifying a popular narrative of unknown origins which has been transmitted orally and often altered in the telling is to be distinguished from the → KUNSTMÄRCHEN, a story written by an individual author in self-conscious imitation of the popular form. → EINFACHE FORMEN.

M.S.

MÄRE = Mär

In the M.A. the term designated any prose or verse narrative. Later, in the 13th century, it came to mean a fictional or untrue story. → MÄRCHEN.

MAGAZIN (magazine)

A periodical publication, frequently illustrated, with an assortment of articles by various authors on topics of contemporary interest.

MAGISCHER REALISMUS (magic realism)

The term originates with painting: it was first introduced by Franz Roh in 1924, when he called upon the artists of the period to show their works in an exhibition at Mannheim, Germany, entitled → NEUE SACHLICHKEIT. He encouraged a new art form committed to a realistic and sober perception of life. Specifically, he ruled out the impressionist and expressionist modes of painting and banished the sensualists and surrealists of the time.

In his book *Nach-Expressionismus. Magischer Realismus* (1925), Franz Roh established the term 'magic', if by negative connotations only. It was not in any way to be related to religious feelings; it was not to be 'mysterious' either. It implied, however, techniques of singling out details of a subject and, by a process of enlargement, alienating them from their normal context (cf. the collages of Max Ernst or some cityscapes by de Chirico).

In stark contrast to the Expressionists, the new art sought freedom from sentimentality, demanded close observation in lieu of ecstasy, and concentrated on the mundane (machines, city streets, close-up portraits, bars and bordellos). It replaced the cosmic dreams and apocalyptic visions of the previous generation with analytical, sober accuracy: the here and now which meets the eye was blown up and studied in detail. Thus, the isolated and precise detail becomes magical, leading a life of its own. Elements of this magic realism can be found in the literature of the period, also; e.g. in Benn (1886–1956), Kafka (1883–1924) and the early Brecht (1898–1956), et al. Broch (1886–1951) wrote of the new art form: "Hypertrophy is bound to occur eventually in any circumscribed order. The day comes when the order is forcibly broken asunder and the perceptive faculty once more takes its bearing directly from reality. The feeling for the whole is lost, but life gains a new and clearer horizon."

In its extreme isolation, the created object may – as in the poetry of Wilhelm Lehmann (1882–1968) or the early Krolow (1915–) – live in complete separation from the human sphere. Its magic thus becomes inscrutable.

R.P.

MAJUSKELN (majuscules) = Versalien

Capital letters as opposed to small letters. →MINUSKELN.

MANIER

1. Stylistic trait which is peculiar to, or characteristic of a particular writer.

2. Uncritical and sometimes laboured imitation by an author of another author's style, or of literary conventions and traditions.

MANIERISMUS (mannerism)

The concept is based on the Italian term *maniera*, which was taken over from the French *manière* of 13th and 14th century courtly literature and denotes the desirable qualities of style and grace in human deportment, art and architecture. But Vasari uses it as early as 1550 to characterize the style of the period of Raphael, Leonardo and Michelangelo. Luigi Lanzi's coinage of *manierismo* (1789) reflects the negative classicist criticism of anti-naturalistic developments towards deformation and exaggeration in the late Renaissance, a criticism already expressed by Diderot in 1767 as a consequence of his insistence on naturalness. Mannerism had developed a theory of art which rejected the classicist theory of the imitation of nature by insisting on the importance of inventive imagination, originality, intellectual wit and calculated design in order to surprise with the creation of the new and unexpected. Mannerism gained acceptance in literature in the 16th and 17th centuries in movements such as Euphuism, Gongorism, Marinism (→ SCHWULST) Préciosité (→ PREZIOSITÄT) and in metaphysical poetry and literary rhetoric generally. The treatises by Pellegrini (1639), Gracian (1642) and Tesauro (1655) on imagination, ingenuity and the power of language provide not only a theory of mannerist practice but also a link to Aristotelian rhetoric and topics. The influence of mannerism is still noticeable in the debates on the 'Ancients and Moderns' and on the 'miraculous' in French and German literature. Goethe's short treatise *Einfache Nachahmung der Natur, Manier, Stil* (1789) attempts a synthesis of the dialectic. Recent research (Ernst Robert Curtius, Gustav René Hocke et al.) has gone beyond the stylistic analysis of individual writers and defined the dialectic of classicism and mannerism as a constant factor in European art and literature, which was already visible in the Atticism—Asianism debate of the 3rd century B.C.; the dialectic has immediate application in literary periodization. A danger, however, lies in the possible loss of the historic significance of the term.

W.V.

MANTEL– UND DEGENSTÜCK

Type of comedy of Spanish origin, so-called because of the cloaks and swords worn by the principal male characters. Characterized by gallantry, adventure and romance, the play centres around various complicated intrigues, which are eventually resolved happily. The characters' major motivation is honour, either personal or familial. This constitutes an important theme in the play.

MARGINALIEN (marginalia) = Randglossen

Explanatory notes written into the margin of a text. →GLOSSE.

MARINISMUS →SCHWULST

MASKE (mask)

1. Facial covering worn by actors for a particular theatrical effect.
2. The conscious but passive acceptance of a → BILDNIS. → ROLLENSPIEL.

MAUERSCHAU → TEICHOSKOPIE

MEHRDEUTIGKEIT → DOPPELSINN

MEISTERGESANG → MEISTERSANG

MEISTERSANG

The sociological definition restricts *Meistersang* to the pursuit and exercise of the craft of singing and composition by artisan fraternities or guilds in towns in the 15th and 16th centuries, but its origins can be traced to developments in the 13th and 14th centuries among *Spruch* poets such as Frauenlob and Mügeln, whom the *Meistersinger* themselves looked upon as their inspiration. The now usual narrower view defines *Meistersang* simply as the strictly regulated production and performance of songs by resident craftsmen in organized *Singschulen*. The schools had their own statutes, and the production of songs was likewise governed by a code of laws known as a → TABULATUR. According to a precedent established in Nuremberg by Hans Folz (c.1440–1513), to achieve the title of *Meister* a candidate had to compose a new strophe and melody, which would be performed to (usually four) judges (→ MERKER) for their assessment. The work would be expected to conform to metrical and compositional rules laid down in the *Tabulatur*. *Meistersang* spread from the Rhine to south Germany, Austria and Bohemia. Originally organized by the church, the essentially lay members later proved receptive to Luther's Reformation.

R.F.

MEISTERSANGSTROPHE = Altdeutsche Strophe, = Minnesangstrophe

The tripartite verse form of the *Meistersinger* and *Minnesinger*. The first two parts, the → AUFGESANG, were rhymed verses of equal length and similar rhyme scheme, also known as → STOLLEN, the third part, the → ABGESANG, differed in both length and rhyme scheme. There was no restriction on the number of lines to a verse as long as this pattern was followed.

MEISTERSINGERBÜHNE → HANS–SACHS–BÜHNE

MELODRAMA (melodrama)

1. An oration or declamation accompanied by music. A dramatic form which can be traced back to pre-Aeschylean tragedy and which became re-established as a popular form of theatre in the 1770s in France.

2. A sensational drama with a crude plot, which, by full use of theatrical effects and music, generates alternately horror and relief.

MELPOMENE

Muse of tragedy. → MUSEN.

MEMOIREN (memoirs) = Denkwürdigkeiten, = Erinnerungen

An author's description of his participation in events, mainly of an historical or political nature, often with the intention of justifying his actions. The distinction between *Memoiren* and the autobiography is not always clear, but *Memoiren* tend to be more subjective and meditative. Further, they often present the author's life as he would have seen it, rather than being an accurate account of his actions; e.g. Goethe's *Dichtung und Wahrheit* (1811 ff.).

MEMORABILE

A 'primary form' (→ EINFACHE FORMEN), in which all the facts necessary for the explanation and motivation of a memorable event are related. The *Memorabile* emphasizes the uniqueness and completeness of the happening, in contrast to the unresolved, generalizing nature of the → KASUS.

MERKER

1. Stock character in the early → MINNESANG, portrayed as a malevolent and jealous figure who constantly attempts to thwart the romance of the lovers.
2. Person who judged the performance of the *Meistersinger* in their competitions. → MEISTERSANG.

MERKVERS → DENKVERS

MESSBUCH → MISSALE

MESSIADE

Poem about the life of Christ, the Messiah.

METAPHER (metaphor)

Figure of speech which transfers a word from a context to which it originally or usually belongs to a context to which it does not originally or usually belong: "der Mond, das Auge der Nacht" (Huchel). Modern German criticism therefore defines a metaphor as 'a word in a co-determining context' (Weinrich) rather than, as traditional rhetorics did, as an abbreviated comparison. A metaphor blends two originally separate spheres together to form a new identity; the more juxtaposed these spheres (bold metaphor = *kühne Metapher*), the greater the 'arousal jag' (Berlyne). A comparison (→ VERGLEICH) stresses the non-identity of these spheres: 'der Mond ist wie ein Auge'.

The use of metaphors is more prominent in some periods than in others. In German Baroque literature they have a largely ornamental function and aim at a surprising effect (e.g. *Korallenmund*). With Goethe (1749–1832) and the German Romantics they are often used to animate or anthropomorphize nature (→ PERSONIFIKATION): "wie *lacht* die Flur" (Goethe) and to suggest a universal harmony; Expressionism uses metaphors to portray the world, felt to be hostile, as demonic or grotesque: "die Kometen mit den Feuer*nasen*" (Heym). Since Mallarmé (1842–1898) the *absolute Metapher* has become a characteristic of much modern poetry; no longer rationally understandable it creates a reality which exists on the level of language alone: "schwarze Milch der Frühe" (Celan). Because of it being over-used in the 1950s and 1960s the *Genitivmetapher*, of which this is an example, has been condemned as "petty cash of surrealism" (Holthusen).

A.V.

METONYMIE (metonymy)

Figure of speech in which the term for one thing is applied to another, with which it is closely associated; e.g.: im Shakespeare lesen. → PARS PRO TOTO, → SYNEKDOCHE.

METRIK (prosody, versification, metrics) = Verskunst

In a wider sense the study of the structural elements of verse (metre, rhythm) and its arrangement (rhyme, strophe, stanza). In a narrower sense referring only to formal aspects of metre and verse sequence. Metre in German verse (→ METRUM) is determined by the relationship between accented and unaccented syllables. The following traditional terms are accepted to describe metre: Foot (→ FUSS) as the smallest metrical unit consisting of one accented syllable (→ HEBUNG, symbol: x̄) and one or two unaccented syllables (→ SENKUNG, Symbol: x); → JAMBUS (iamb) xx̄; → TROCHÄUS (trochee) x̄x; → ANAPÄST (anapaest) xxx̄; → DAKTYLUS (dactyl) x̄xx. A *Verszeile* (metrical line) consists of a series of feet (usually 3–5; less commonly 6–8); thus one speaks of e.g. a *vierfüßiger Jambus* (xx̄ xx̄ xx̄ xx̄). A verse ending with an accented syllable is called *männlich* (masculine), and with an unaccented syllable *weiblich* (feminine). In Germanic verse the accented syllables should coincide with the naturally stressed syllables of the words. Verse rhythm (→ RHYTHMUS) is a combination of two principles: the abstract metrical 'regular' order and the concrete 'irregular' order of the natural flow of language. Verse rhythm consists in the individual modification of the underlying regular metrical continuum through the distribution of varying degrees of stress and pitch, speed of utterance and pauses.

Metrical lines of identical or different structure combine to form many types of stanzas. (→ STROPHE).

H.H.

METRON → METRUM

METRUM (metre) = Metron

1. The rhythmic pattern in poetry, which arises from the distribution of stressed or long and unstressed or short syllables into approximately equal units. = Versmaß.

2. Versfuß → FUSS.

MIME (actor)

MIMESIS (mimesis) = Imitation, = Nachahmung

Greek for imitation. In the history of literary theory the term is used to indicate the concept, derived from the *Poetics* of Aristotle (384—322 B.C.) and the *Republic* of Plato (428—348 B.C.), that poetry is essentially an imitation of nature. This view was discarded by the Romantics (→ ROMANTIK), but the term *Mimesis* was given new importance in the mid-20th century by Erich Auerbach's *Mimesis* (1946) and by the discussion of the problem of realism. → FIKTION, → LITERATUR, → WIRKLICHKEIT.

E.W.H.

MIMIK

The art of mime (→ PANTOMIME), i.e. the imitation of a person or action by the use of facial expressions and gestures without speech.

MIMUS = Planipes

Historical term for a primitive form of theatre which originated in pre-Christian Greece and Sicily. It was a crude form of entertainment aimed at a wide audience using mime, and later, dialogue, and was often integrated into theatre festivals to provide comic relief.

MINIATUR (miniature) = Buchmalerei

Originally denoted the med. practice of illuminating manuscripts. However, *Miniatur* now also applies to any picture or portrait painted or printed on a reduced scale.

MINNE

The MHG term for love. Its original wide range of meanings is contracted during the MHG period to denote love between the sexes and, by the end of the MHG period, sensuality or lust. In MHG the term is also used specifically for the convention of courtly love. The earliest manifestations of this convention are found in the courts of Provence, c.1100, from where it spreads, during the 12th century, to northern French and German-speaking courts. Courtly love finds its literary expression in the courtly epic and particularly in the lyric of the → MINNESANG. It is characterized by the knight's untiring and faithful service to his chosen lady (→ FRAUENDIENST), whom he regards as far superior to himself in every respect, who is almost always married to another and therefore must remain anonymous. While the knight's implied aim is often consummation of the relationship, the stated aim is to receive a 'reward' from the lady — perhaps a token of her affection or even just an acknowledgement of his services. Since the lady is the knight's moral (and sometimes social) superior, and since there are frequently external obstacles such as husbands or their spies (→MERKER), rewards are rarely attained and unfulfilled longing is therefore the predominant emotion expressed by the courtly lover. An important aspect of the convention is the premise that the service of a good lady, while painful, is in itself valuable, since it ennobles the knight and spurs him on to deeds of chivalry.

P.Oe.

MINNESANG

MHG tradition of the love lyric, celebrating particularly (but not exclusively) courtly love. The lyrics are designed to be sung by the poet for the entertainment of the court, although in the case of most songs only the text has survived, while the melody has been lost. The poets were all members of the nobility, they ranged from emperors (Henry VI) to itinerant singers whose livelihood depended on their art. Literary and thematic antecedents for the *Minnesang*, particularly for its French forerunner, the songs of the Troubadours, may be found in the love lyric of the Arab courts in Spain, but the MHG tradition also uses elements of folk poetry, classical and med. Latin poetry and religious poetry.

The earliest poems of the *Minnesang* appear c.1150—1175 in the Danube region of German-speaking Europe. A second and independent stream of tradition, taking its inspiration from the Provençal lyric and concerned exclusively with courtly love, arises mainly in the regions along the Rhine and flourishes c.1170—1190. In the first two decades of the 13th century the *Minnesang* spreads over the whole of German speaking Europe. It reaches its peak and fulfilment in the work of Walther von der Vogelweide (c.1168—1228), and then begins to decline into formalism.

P.Oe.

MINNESANGSTROPHE →MEISTERSANGSTROPHE

MINUSKELN (minuscules)

Small letters, as opposed to capitals. →MAJUSKELN.

MISCHSPIEL → TRAGIKOMÖDIE

MISSALE (missal) = Meßbuch

Book containing liturgical services for the whole year.

MITLEID UND FURCHT (pity and fear) → KATHARSIS

MITTENREIM

Form of internal rhyme in which the end of a verse line rhymes with the middle of the preceding or following line.

MODELL (model)

In scientific usage, the model is a schematic representation of an object's structure, showing the interaction and function of its parts, and serving to facilitate the scientific examination of complex or intangible phenomena. The term was adopted by Brecht in 1948 to characterize his specific use of the traditional didactic parable as a means of realizing his concept of epic theatre (→ EPISCHES THEATER). The new theatre was to be instrumental in bringing about revolutionary change in social consciousness by exposing the structure of society as a whole, by revealing the laws governing its processes and thereby enabling the recipient to understand his social environment and to control it. The new function required new means of presentation. Brecht, who defined reality in purely empirical terms, rejected the symbolic form of presentation as meaningless. The traditional function of the symbol, which, according to Coleridge "partakes of the reality it renders intelligible", has, in Brecht's view, lost its validity: the visible phenomenon has long since ceased to be capable of imparting knowledge about the workings of the whole; the symbolic form of presentation can only reproduce phenomena, it cannot render the interaction of the complex social whole intelligible. The allegorical form is even less capable of revealing the structure of the real social situation: the allegory uses the material of the real world, which has no real value in its own right, to convey a fixed meaning, which is determined by the particular structure of ideas within the allegory as a whole. The allegorical presentation is intentionally artificial and today, in the absence of a binding world-view, the underlying structure of ideas is either arbitrary or inaccessible or both. The didactic parable, on the other hand, which had fallen into disuse since the Enlightenment (e.g. Lessing's *Parable of the Ring* in *Nathan der Weise*, 1779), had the formal characteristics Brecht required: the bipartite structure, consisting of the parable-context depicting the real situation, and the parable-story, the simplified analogous representation of that situation; the epic presentation, i.e. the presence of a narrator, who presents the view of reality (of which he is part) from the ideological standpoint he represents; and the didactic intention, which implies the practical application of the knowledge imparted. Brecht took up the form and renewed it. He changed the relationship between parable-context and parable-story into a dialectical relationship, i.e. the real situation is confronted not only by its simplified, but at the same time by its alienated representation. The principles and method determining the reduction and abstraction of the social processes are not those of the autonomous artist, but the Marxist principles and method of social analysis. Thus Brecht equates the ideological standpoint with scientific method. He termed the new form a *Modell*, thereby emphasizing the scientific method and purpose: the dialectical relationship between the theoretical model and the practice of social reality.

After Brecht, i.e. when freed from the conditions of Brecht's epic theatre, the form and function of the parabolic model underwent radical changes e.g. Frisch (1911–), Dürrenmatt (1921–), Martin Walser (1927–). The parable lost its practical, political purpose; the first part of the bipartite form, the objective portrayal of the real situation, was dropped and the aesthetic part, the abstract representation of the real situation, remained. This reduced form of the parable retained the name *Modell*. Various attempts have been made to distinguish between the parable and the model – e.g. the parable condenses and alienates actual events, the model sketches a sociological constellation, which may or may not have a practical basis or application – but the definition now largely depends on the way in which the form is used. Max Frisch, for example, characterizes his *Biedermann und die Brandstifter* (1958) as a didactic play without a didactic purpose, i.e. an anti-parable, whereas he refers to *Andorra* (1961) as an approximation to the model: but elsewhere he expressly states that both plays are parables. Frisch's objection to the parable's insistence on a fixed meaning, on commitment to a particular ideological standpoint, points to one distinction: the model is comparatively open to experimentation. However, the aesthetically closed form of the model is also restrictive, if not dogmatic, as Frisch implies in the playing through of the various other possibilities in his *Biografie* (1967).

On the whole, the post-Brecht model, no longer constrained to reflect the Marxist theory and method of social analysis, has become a means of analysing behavioural patterns and social norms and values, rather than the laws governing the social processes. The emphasis is on the question or problem, not on a dogmatic solution. The attempt to effect political change has become an attempt to influence moral attitudes. The development of the form since Brecht appears to be leading to its dissolution. →PARABEL.

P.L.

MODERNE

Term coined by Eugen Wolff (*Die 'Moderne' zur Revolution und Reform der Literatur*, 1887) to denote new tendencies in literature, which at the time were represented by the movement of → NATURALISMUS. The term came into wider circulation through Hermann Bahr (*Zur Kritik der Moderne*, 1890) who was also co-editor of the journal *Die Moderne* (1890 ff). The term was never very precise. Bahr himself used it initially to refer to *Naturalismus* but the journal was not restricted to contributions from 'naturalists' and only one year later, Bahr (*Die Überwindung des Naturalismus*, 1891) used the term to refer to all new developments surpassing the art of *Naturalismus*. (→IMPRESSIONISMUS, → EXPRESSIONISMUS, → JUGENDSTIL, → SYMBOLISMUS). The term is now commonly applied to a generation of Austrian writers – e.g. Andrian (1875–1951), Altenberg (1859–1919), Beer-Hofmann (1866–1945), Hofmannsthal (1874–1929), Schnitzler (1862–1931) – who at the turn of the century rejected the predominant positivistic and deterministic philosophy and created a new art form based on the importance of impressions and subjective experiences and portrayed a world consisting of a web of nuances, sensuous sensations and stimuli to which the human imagination and also the nervous system responded. The impression and the dream took the place of 'reality'.

A.O.

MODEWÖRTER

Words or phrases which become fashionable for a limited period, but subsequently disappear from popular usage.

MÖNCHSLATEIN → KÜCHENLATEIN

MONTAGE

The conscious application of film techniques to literature; e.g.: the use of flashbacks and fade-outs in order to create rapidly changing impressions.

Not to be confused with →COLLAGE.

MORALISCHE WOCHENSCHRIFTEN

18th century periodicals which originated in Puritan England, frequently in the form of a collection of stories, essays and dialogues which sought to instruct the public on matters such as etiquette, morals, etc.

MORITAT → BÄNKELSANG

MORPHOLOGIE (morphology) = Formenlehre

The study of word-forms. Many words in a language like German are simple, e.g. *Mann*, but many others are analysable into a number of *morphs*, e.g. *Mann-es*, *männ-lich*, each designating some meaning or function. All those morphs which share the same function (e.g. plural: $\overset{(..)}{-}er$, $\overset{(..)}{-}e$, $-en$, $-s$) form a class called a *morpheme*.

The use of morphological devices (like the plural suffixes) to provide the different forms of the same lexical word is called *inflection*, and involves, in German, tense, mood, person and number distinctions in the verb, and case and number in the noun, etc. Tense, number, case etc. are thus said to be the *inflectional categories* of German.

The other major area of morphology is *word formation*. This is an account of the formation of complex word stems from simpler elements, by *derivation* (*Ableitung*); e.g. *männ-lich*, *Frei-heit*, *zer-brechen*, and by *compounding* (*Zusammensetzung*), e.g. *Hoch-haus*, *Bahn-hof*, *Rot-haut*.

Morphs, like *Mann*, which can stand alone are called *free*, while those which occur only in association with other morphs, like −es, −lich, Umlaut as a plural sign, are bound. In German, most bound morphs are *affixes*, sub-classified as *prefixes*, e.t. *ge*−, *ver*−, *un*−, and *suffixes*, e.g. −*ung*, −*er*, −*lich*.

R.H.

MOTIV

1. Psychological: In the sense of English *motive*, that which causes or influences an action, e.g. of a person (the writer), of a character or of a whole dramatic process.

2. Literary: (*motif*) a structural component of the content/subject-matter complex and characterized by the following: (a) It is a self-contained unity, as it can exist outside a specific context (can be handed down). (b) It fulfils a necessary function in relation to the overriding thematic context or dramatic process; to be distinguished from other traits or images with only an additive function (ornament, atmosphere etc.) (c) It is a phenomenon which recurs traditionally or intrinsically within a work. (d) It is an occurrence or action rather than an object, state, concept or topic. (A thunderstorm can be a *Motiv* in so far as it takes place, the misanthrope in so far as he hates, the city in so far as it is human activity but not if it is an agglomeration of houses.) In the Tristan and Isolde context a *Motiv* would be the drinking of the love potion; the →THEMA: love; a →SYMBOL: the cup; the →STOFF: the Tristan and Isolde story; a →TOPOS: the cliché-like topic of the *Liebestod*. The concept →LEITMOTIV, transferred from music (Richard Wagner, 1813−1883) to literature has a wider application than *Motiv* as it is used not only for recurring motifs but also for words and phrases which recur (often in variations) in different parts of a work (e.g. quotations from *Faust* in Thomas Mann's *Zauberberg*, 1924). This means that *Leitmotive* are normally not proper motifs but rather structural or stylistic elements.

   According to their function within a given work there may be distinguished a central motif (*Hauptmotiv*), subordinate motifs (*Nebenmotive*) and make-weight motifs (→FÜLLMOTIV).

H.H.

MÜNCHHAUSENIADE

Story relating the fantastic deeds of Baron von Münchhausen (1720−1797). The best-known form of →LÜGENDICHTUNG.

MUNDARTDICHTUNG →DIALEKTDICHTUNG

MUSEN (Muses)

The sister-goddesses (daughters of Zeus and Mnemosyne) who presided over learning and the arts in general, and poetry and music in particular. (→ERATO,

→ EUTERPE, → KALLIOPE, → KLIO, → MELPOMENE, → POLYHYMNIA, → TERPSICHORE, → THALIA, → URANIA). Since Hesiod and Homer their number has been fixed at nine; Hesiod also was the first to name them. → HELIKON, → HIPPOKRENE, → KASTALIA, and → PARNASS are associated with the Muses, and with poetic and artistic creativity and inspiration.

MUSENALMANACH

Annual collection of hitherto unpublished poetry, by several authors who frequently write anonymously or under pseudonyms.

MYSTERIENSPIELE (mystery or miracle plays)

Form of med. religious drama, widespread throughout Europe. Originally mystery plays were dramatizations of short sections of the Latin liturgical service, later they became complete plays which were written in the vernacular and produced by the trade guilds outside the church. Originally there was a clear distinction between mystery and miracle plays on the basis of their subject-matter. The term mystery play was applied to a drama based on biblical stories, and the term miracle play applied to a drama in which a divine miracle played a part. The miracle play most frequently treated the life of a saint, but as it also used biblical material, the two terms came to be interchangeable. → BIBLISCHES DRAMA.

MYSTIK (mysticism)

Belief in the spiritual apprehension of truths beyond the limits of rational understanding. In a religious context it means an individual's direct spiritual contact with a deity without the medium of a priest.

German *Mystik* reached high points during the M.A., the → BAROCK, →STURM UND DRANG, and the →ROMANTIK.

MYTHOLOGIE (mythology)

The study of myths or, more frequently in literary contexts, a collective term for the entire corpus of myths or for the myths of a particular society (e.g. Greek mythology, Teutonic mythology). The mythology employed by modern writers usually belongs to an earlier culture (e.g. the predilection of German writers for Greek, Roman and Nordic mythology) although modern usage also allows, as a wider meaning, any system of codes or signs predominating in a society (Barthes's *Mythologies*, 1957). The function of mythology in earlier societies was to reinforce social codes by ritual, to offer symbolic explanations for otherwise inexplicable phenomena and to define man's place in the cosmogony. The narratives of mythology, which tend to be products of folk culture rather than of a single author, concern the exploits of gods, heroes and animals. Psychoanalytical, Formalist and Structuralist approaches have variously revealed the extent to which mythology's truths occur in elaborate symbolic, encoded forms. In literature, earlier mythology can be used to reassert or reinterpret archetypal truths (as is often the case in mythological drama), to offer a scheme of imagery (e.g. the ornamental mythological epithets in Baroque poetry) or to provide an illuminating pattern of symbolic correspondences (e.g. the juxtaposition of mythology and modernity in Joyce's *Ulysses*, 1922, and Thomas Mann's *Der Tod in Venedig*, 1912). Often various mythologies are synthesized in modern works, where the mythological material used does not necessarily still enjoy the force of myth. →MYTHOS.

J.J.W.

MYTHOS (myth) = Mythus

Often an ill-defined concept, especially in literary criticism. Although its various connotations frequently become blurred, it tends to be used in one of the following senses: (i) a myth from an earlier culture, only known through a subsequent literary version, (ii) a modern work which enjoys a comparable status among contemporary readers, (iii) an archetypal pattern (e.g. the myth of the birth of the hero), (iv) a plot or narrative scheme (the original Aristotelian meaning), (v) an evident fiction or poetic truth, as opposed to *Logos*, in this sense often with pejorative overtones (especially in rationalist contexts). Meanings (iv) and (v) are relatively rare. Most of the problems associated with the concept concern the first three meanings. Since in modern versions earlier myths do not necessarily retain their original 'mythical' quality — which is a product of certain archetypal plot-configurations and types of character, as well as a generic sense of time and space — the use of *Mythos* can blur an important distinction between the use of myth and mythical quality. Moreover, the attempted 'return to myth' in much modern writing betrays a comparable lack of differentiation between myth as material and the mythical quality. In its second sense, *Mythos* can refer to modern works, such as Kafka's *Das Schloß* (1926), which have attained the status of modern myths, but here *Mythos* becomes little more than a measure of a work's reception; it seldom leads to connections being established between such a status and any actual mythical properties it may display. Recent 'myth criticism' has been concerned with the detection of archetypal patterns in literature and their relation to mythical structures. Archetypal patterns are, however present in much non-mythical literature, and it is symptomatic of the reverence in which myth is held and the consequent inflationary use of myth-oriented terminology that features of literature are so readily attributed to a nebulous *Mythos* concept.

J.J.W.

MYTHUS →MYTHOS

NACHAHMUNG →MIMESIS

NACHDICHTUNG

Free translation or adaptation of a literary work.

NACHDRUCK

1. Emphasis, stress.
2. Pirated edition: unauthorized reproduction of a literary work. = Raubdruck.

NACHLASS (literary estate)

Unpublished works, notes, etc. left by a writer or composer at his death.

NACHSCHRIFT

1. Postscript.
2. Unauthorized copy of a manuscript or text taken with the intention of illicit reproduction.

NACHSPIEL

Short one-act piece played at the end of a theatrical performance. Frequently highly comic, it was quite separate from the drama which preceded it.

NACHTRAG (addendum)

Supplementary addition to a work, postscript.

NACHTSTÜCK

Short prose narrative form used by E.T.A. Hoffmann (1776–1822) in particular. The content rather than the form characterizes the *Nachtstück*, which probes the sinister side of human existence, exploring facets such as insanity, physical deformities, the supernatural, and the criminal mind.

NAIV UND SENTIMENTALISCH

In an attempt to explain the basic difference between himself and Goethe, Schiller in his essay *Über naive und sentimentalische Dichtung* (1795) made this distinction and developed it into a typology of literature.

The *naive* writer is fully integrated into his environment, is at one with nature, does not experience a distance between himself and the world around him and can therefore reproduce nature directly without having to reflect upon it or being conscious of it. This immediate reproduction of reality, according to Schiller, is the realist approach of the *naive* writer. Examples of such writers given by Schiller are Homer, Shakespeare and Goethe. The *sentimentalische* writer, however, is always aware of a distance between himself and nature and experiences this as a loss. He therefore constantly strives to regain this lost sense of unity with nature. He develops and presents concepts and notions which he hopes will achieve this aim. This, according to Schiller, is the idealistic approach of the *sentimentalische* writer. The genre typical of this type of approach are the → SATIRE, the → ELEGIE and the → IDYLLE. An example of such a writer would be Schiller himself. The two modes of presentation are not mutually exclusive. Indeed, it has been the aim of → KLASSIK to combine them.

The terms are therefore descriptive rather than qualitative.

A.O.

NAMEN, SPRECHENDE → SPRECHENDE NAMEN

NARRATOR → ERZÄHLER

NARRENLITERATUR (folly literature)

Type of didactic literature which developed from the 15th to the 17th centuries, which uses humour and satire to attack and expose human weaknesses and social injustice. The best-known and most influential example is Brant's *Narrenschiff* (1494), in which fools represent various sins and weaknesses, with the result that sin and foolishness appear synonymous.

NATIONALEPOS

Form of heroic epic, which, dealing with a significant legendary or historical episode in the development of a nation, has come to be accepted as a primary expression of the national mythology. *Nationalepos* is therefore a term to be applied only to a heroic epic of national significance, usually in verse, from a remote period of a national literature. Examples are: for England *Beowulf*, for Germany the *Nibelungenlied*, for Greece the *Iliad*, for Rome the *Aeneid* and for India the *Râmâyana* and the *Mahâbhârata*.

E.W.H.

NATIONALHYMNE (national anthem) → HYMNE

NATIONALLITERATUR

The literature of a nation or people.

NATIONALTHEATER

The concept of a *Nationaltheater* in Germany originated during the 18th century and was inspired by the French model. Its aim was to bring together the finest dramatic talents of the nation and to present drama which was specifically national. Despite several attempts to found such an institution, the idea was never successfully realized, due to the lack of a genuinely national dramatic literature, and the fact that Germany was not united.

NATURALISMUS (naturalism)

A literary movement of the late 19th century which recognized the social problems of capitalism and the industrial age as well as the dependence of human development on hereditary (*Vererbung*) and environmental factors (*Milieu*). Attempts were made to establish art as a scientific experiment, based on universal, scientific laws.

German *Naturalismus* began with Julius and Heinrich Hart's *Kritische Waffengänge* (1882–84) and the periodical *Die Gesellschaft* (ed. Conrad, 1885–1902). It reached its climax with the early works of Holz (1863–1929) and Hauptmann (1862–1946). Literary models were the novels and theoretical writings of Zola (1840–1902) and the plays of Ibsen (1828–1906) and Tolstoy (1828–1910).

At the time the terms *Realismus* and *Naturalismus* were interchangeable, though application varied. Although the representation of scientifically established truth was regarded as the primary task of literature, this did not exclude further aims and purposes: "The new poetry will consist of blending Realism and Romanticism so that the naturalistic truth of dry and expressionless photography merges with the artistic liveliness of ideal composition" (Michael Georg Conrad). Similar views were held by Bölsche (*Die naturwissenschaftlichen Grundlagen der Poesie*, 1887). Holz developed the most elaborate theory of Naturalist art, condensed in the formula $Kunst = Natur - x$, in which x represented the material limitations of any artistic reproduction. *Natur*, however, meant for Holz not only external but also internal psychological reality so that the purpose of his art became the analysis of modern man in general. *Naturalismus* thus merged with other literary tendencies and movements ($\rightarrow$ JUGENDSTIL, $\rightarrow$ EXPRESSIONISMUS).

In German literature *Naturalismus* had its major successes on the stage (Hauptmann, Holz, Schlaf 1862–1941, Halbe 1865–1944, Sudermann 1857–1928), sponsored by theatre companies such as the $\rightarrow$ FREIE BÜHNE (founded in 1889) in Berlin. In the plays a critical view of middle class and working class reality was current. Unnatural stage devices such as the monologue were abandoned. Dialect and sociolect were introduced as means of characterization, and tightly structured dramatic conflicts gave way to epic elements which stressed the historical relativity of all action. *Naturalismus* quickly exhausted its possibilities. "Naturalism is either an interval to allow the old art to revive or an interval in which to prepare for the new; either way it is only an entr'acte" (Bahr, 1891).

G.S.

NATUREINGANG

The description of nature which often forms the introduction to a love-song, thus combining the themes of nature and love.

NATURTHEATER (open-air theatre) = Freilichttheater

NEBENHANDLUNG (subplot)

Plot which is complete in itself yet remains secondary to the main plot. →HANDLUNG.

NEBENMOTIV →MOTIV

NEBENROLLE (minor role) →ROLLE

NEMESIS (Nemesis)

Greek goddess of retribution, who meted out punishment to erring mortals.

NEUDRUCK (reprint, reimpression of a work)

NEUE SACHLICHKEIT

Term with no exact equivalent in English, as it implies not only the idea of a 'new objectivity' but also a new sobriety and matter-of-factness (Jost Hermand). Coined in 1923 with reference to a proposed art exhibition, the term is used loosely to describe art and literature, and indeed the general outlook in Germany during the 1920s. In contrast to the visionary, ecstatic and revolutionary concepts of → EXPRESSIONISMUS, *Neue Sachlichkeit* reflected the more stable political and economic conditions in the Weimar Republic (→ WEIMARER REPUBLIK) after the currency reform (1924) and the end of inflation up to the death of Stresemann (1878–1929). A unique element of *Neue Sachlichkeit* was the interest in all expressions of contemporary culture, including boxing, technology and the Americanization of all spheres of life. It contained however two fundamental weaknesses: first, its commitment to stability led to a conservative bourgeois stance, which explains why the Nazis accepted *Neue Sachlichkeit* and rejected Expressionism; secondly, it could only embrace radicals and liberals until the political crisis beginning in 1930 forced writers to take sides. The term is of importance because it was widely used at the time rather than for any value it might have in helping to define a period of literature.

E.W.H.

NEUHUMANISMUS → HUMANISMUS

NEUKLASSIK (Neoclassicism)

A movement towards the revival and recovery of ancient classical traditions in German literature. The movement had its origins in the work of Nietzsche (1844–1900) and developed around the turn of the century with the emergence of Stefan George (1868–1933) and his circle as a reaction to the dominant trends in art towards the end of the 19th century: Impressionism (→ IMPRES-SIONISMUS), Naturalism (→ NATURALISMUS) and the art of the 'decadents' (→ DEKADENZDICHTUNG, → ÄSTHETIZISMUS). Neuklassik sought to restore the spirit and styles of the ancient models.

Being to a large extent imitative, it produced little or nothing of value; it served as the starting point of much academic discourse regarding the discipline of language, value and function of form, and considerations of genre and versification (e.g. Paul Ernst, *Weg zur Form*, 1906; Wilhelm von Scholz, *Gedanken zum Drama*, 1904). Even the George circle's *Blätter für die Kunst* (1892–1919) had only limited influence.

To restore, for example, the concept and form of Greek tragedy remained at best a theoretical exercise in an age void of tragic heroes in the Greek sense. Nevertheless the return to Greek mythology in the dramas of Hugo von Hofmannsthal (1874–1929) introduced an important trend in 20th century European literature.

In English letters, Neoclassicism is a movement for the revival in poetry of the styles and outlook of Greek and Roman classical writers. It is an earlier movement than Weimar Classicism (→ KLASSIK) and predates German *Neuklassik* by more than 300 years (Renaissance to the 18th century). It included such poets as Dryden (1631–1700), Pope (1688–1744), Swift (1667–1745), Addison (1672–1719) and Johnson (1709–1784).

R.P.

NEUPHILOLOGIE

The study of modern languages and literatures, as distinct from Latin and Greek. → ALTPHILOLOGIE, → PHILOLOGIE.

NEUROMANTIK

An unusually amorphous term, in its wider application it can include musical giants (Wagner, Richard Strauss) and lesser lights (Pfitzner) who, in the wake of *true* Romantics (Schubert, Weber, Beethoven to a degree), worked out, developed and hugely extended their legacy. In the other arts it may be used to define for example those huge representational, historical canvasses or Gothic railway stations, Romanesque insurance palaces and Florentine banks which characterized the → GRÜNDERZEIT (after 1870–71) and the few decades on either side (e.g. *Neuschwanstein* in Upper Bavaria, the *Hamburger Rathaus*, the *Votivkirche* in Vienna, *St. Pancras* in London).

In the more specifically literary sense, while it can denote gargantuan, historical *Epigonen* such as the best-selling Felix Dahn, *Der Kampf um Rom* (1876) and the 'gothick' *Goldschnittlyrik* of von Scheffel (1826–1886), it is most often applied – the term appears in this context as early as 1906 – to the deliberate counter-attack on the → NATURALISMUS of the 1890s (Hauptmann, Sudermann, Halbe, Holz and Schlaf, the → FREIE BÜHNE) – on its sordid super-realism and emphasis on the perverse, reverse side of life. Thus *Neuromantik* stresses delicacy, suggestion, mood, beauty for its own sake, nostalgic evocation of times past. The links and confusion with → IMPRESSIONISMUS are apparent at once. While major figures such as George (1868–1933), Hesse (1877–1962), Hofmannsthal (1874–1929) and Rilke (1875–1926) notably in respect of their earlier work, also at times Hauptmann (1862–1946), have been grouped under *Neuromantik*, the term is obviously too wide to be really useful. In practice it generally refers nowadays to those writers around the turn of the last century (c.1890–1910) who stress the magical, miraculous, archaic and/or present a moodful, idealized, stylized and sometimes scented picture of the past. Hofmannsthal's lyrical dramas and some novels of Ricarda Huch (1864–1947) seem to be textbook examples. One cannot really limit *Neuromantik* in any real time sense. It is more accurately an ever-recurrent tendency rather than a school or movement.

B.C.

NEW CRITICISM

John Crowe Ransom's book, *The New Criticism*, appeared in 1941. The term was in use in England and the U.S.A. in the 1930s. It was at first applied to a group of American critics, but is now also used to describe a method of literary criticism, which was in vogue in German scholarship in the 1950s and 1960s, but which is now not so dominant.

Although the new critics had their differences, there was a common basic approach, which is called in German → WERKIMMANENT. *New Criticism* directs its attention to the literary text alone (intrinsic aspects), eschewing biographical and historical evidence and considerations of the author's intentions (extrinsic aspects). This concern with the text alone is semantically based, as *New Criticism* stresses the uniqueness of the nature of literary discourse, which is to be examined in the meanings and relations of words, symbols and images. For this reason *New Criticism* is not greatly concerned with genres, nor with thematic questions, but predominantly with *structure* and *texture*. Likewise the form of a work is seen not in terms of plot structure but as a *structure of meanings*. In practice *New Criticism* concentrates on the interpretation of a text as an aesthetic structure (→ INTERPRETATION), a method known earlier in French studies as 'explication de texte'. The major English exponent of *New Criticism* was I.A. Richards (*Principles of Literary Criticism*, 1924, and *Practical Criticism*, 1929). The foremost representatives of the German variant of *New Criticism* (*werkimmanente Interpretation*) were Wolfgang Kayser and Emil Staiger.

E.W.H.

NIBELUNGENSTROPHE

The most important stanza form in med. German heroic poetry; also found in lyric poetry. The stanza consists of four → LANGZEILEN, the first three contain six stressed syllables and the fourth has seven. The rhyme scheme normally comprises rhyming couplets.

NICHTARISTOTELISCHES DRAMA → EPISCHES THEATER

NOMINALSTIL (substantival style) = substantivischer Stil

Style characterized by the frequent use of nouns and substantival constructions.

NOVELA PICARESCA → SCHELMENROMAN

NOVELLE

The term *Novelle* has far more currency in German than its English counterpart *novella*, and refers to an important genre much cultivated in the German-speaking countries in the 19th and early 20th centuries, but its precise meaning is a matter of debate. What is not disputed is that it entered the German language at about the turn of the 18th and 19th centuries, derived from the Italian *novella* ('something new or newsworthy') which also gave English its word *novel*. A succession of great writers of the 19th century; e.g., Kleist (1777–1811), Keller (1819–1890), Stifter (1805–1868), Meyer (1825–1898), Storm (1817–1888) wrote much important realistic fiction of medium length, somewhere between a short story and a novel, and the word *Novelle* gradually became attached to this genre of intermediate length fiction. It continued to flourish until the early 20th century, when it gradually became displaced by the shorter → KURZGESCHICHTE as the most productive fictional mode of less than novel length. Because of its length, characters and situations in the *Novelle* are more rounded out than those of the *Kurzgeschichte*, but not developed in the extensive way characteristic of the novel. In addition to this common ground there is also a strong and long-standing tradition of treating the *Novelle* as a genre with much more specific characteristics. Discussion in this mode has always centered on a number of classic statements by Goethe (1749–1832) (on an unusual, but real event), Tieck (1773–1853) (on a clear turning-point in the plot), and Heyse (1830–1914) (on symbolism and a sharp outline), and generally sees the *Novelle* as a form which is essentially a highly artistic one, with great attention to formal composition. On this view, it is a concentration on artistry which distinguishes *Novelle* from →ERZÄHLUNG. Both this attitude to the definition of the *Novelle*, and that which regards it more simply as a story of medium length, continue to be well-represented. → FALKENTHEORIE, →WENDEPUNKT.

J.M.E.

OBERBÜHNE

The upper floor of a double-floored stage, used esp. in Shakespearean plays.

OBJEKTIVISMUS

In Marxist terminology a pejorative term for the view that phenomena can be perceived objectively, i.e. independently of the political and social opinions of the person perceiving.

ODE (ode)

Form of lyric poetry, which treats elevated themes, using elaborate language. There are no strict formal requirements, but German odes are usually written in unrhymed stanzas. The *Ode* frequently makes a direct address to its subject, often in the *Du* form. The tone is less spontaneous and more restrained than that of the → HYMNE, which it closely resembles, esp. in its subject-matter; e.g. truth, friendship, joy, love, the father-land etc.

OFFENE FORM (open form) = atektonisch → GESCHLOSSENE FORM

OFFIZIN (printing office)

ONOMATOPOESIE (onomatopoeia, echoism) = Klangmalerei,
= Schallnachahmung, = Tonmalerei

Rhetorical figure: words whose sounds reinforce and echo their meaning, or the formation of such words;
e.g.: Und außen horch! gings trapp, trapp, trapp. (Bürger, *Lenore*) → KLANG.

ORDENSDICHTUNG

A broad term which is applied to the literature developed by religious orders. → DEUTSCHORDENSDICHTUNG, → JESUITENDICHTUNG.

The monastic orders performed a valuable task in cultivating Latin literature and recording popular literature in the vernacular.

ORIGINALAUSGABE → AUSGABE

ORIGINALGENIE → GENIEZEIT

ORTSKOLORIT (local colour)

The detailed representation in literature of the speech, dress, customs, etc. of a particular region.

OSSIANISCHE DICHTUNG

Literature inspired by Macpherson's collection of poems, published in 1760, which he claimed was a translation of poems by the Gaelic bard (→ BARDE) Ossian. In fact, it was Macpherson's own work. However, its publication had great impact on the → STURM UND DRANG movement. Characteristic features were descriptions of harsh landscapes, winter scenes, autumn storms etc., befitting the prevailing tone of lamentation and melancholy.

OSTERSPIEL

The oldest form of liturgical drama in the M.A. The *Osterspiel*, originally performed in church, with the events surrounding Christ's resurrection as the subject-matter, represents the important transition from the Latin trope (→ TROPUS) to the vernacular → PASSIONSSPIEL in that it still contains elements of the liturgy but includes freely composed scenes. By the end of the 14th century *Osterspiele* had been superseded by the passion plays and → MYSTERIENSPIELE, which were performed outside the church. → GEIST-LICHES DRAMA.

OXYMORON (oxymoron)

Figure of speech in which two incongruous or contradictory elements are juxtaposed; e.g.: *Helldunkel, alter Knabe.* → CONTRADICTIO IN ADJECTO, → PARADOXON.

PAARREIM

The rhyming of two consecutive verse lines to form a → REIMPAAR.

PANTALONE (Pantalone)

Stock character from the → COMMEDIA DELL'ARTE: the stereotyped foolish husband.

PANTOMIME (mime)

Form of dramatic entertainment in which the characters act without speech, conveying thoughts and emotions by facial expressions and gestures, which are often highly exaggerated, frequently with musical accompaniment. →MIME.
N.B. Not to be confused with the English pantomime.

PANTRAGISMUS

Highly pessimistic attitude: notion that the world is governed by tragedy, that every action is predestined to failure; exemplified in the dramas of Hebbel (1813–1863).

PARABEL (parable)

Short fictitious narrative about an ordinary situation, which illustrates a moral precept or a general truth about human nature, as the narrator draws a sustained analogy between the material in the story and the lesson he is attempting to impart. →GLEICHNIS, →MODELL.

PARADIGMA →EXEMPEL

PARADOXON (paradox)

Statement which although apparently contradictory or absurd, is in fact valid, e.g.: ". . . einer der rechtschaffensten zugleich und entsetzlichsten Menschen seiner Zeit." (Kleist, *Michael Kohlhaas*). →OXYMORON.

PARALIPOMENA

Material not included in the body of a literary work, and appended as a supplement.

163

PARALLELDRUCK (parallel text)

Publication which provides two (or more) versions of the same text on opposite pages.

PARALLELISMUS (parallelism) = Gleichlauf

Figure of speech: the recurrence of similar syntactical patterns.

PARATAXE (parataxis) = Beiordnung

The juxtaposition of main clauses. →HYPOTAXE.

PARENTHESE (parenthesis) = Schaltsatz

A word, phrase or clause inserted into a sentence which is grammatically complete without it; usually indicated by the use of brackets, dashes or commas around it.

PARERGON (parergon)

Secondary or auxilary work, separate from the main body of a literary work.

PARNASS (Parnassus)

Mountain in Greece which was reputed to be the home of Apollo and the Muses. It is therefore associated with poetry and literary creation. →KASTALIA, →MUSEN.

PARODIE (parody)

The German term has the same connotations as parody in English and in both languages the same distinction is made between parody and travesty (→ TRAVESTIE). Parody is the imitation, with more or less ridiculing or deflating intent, of the form, style and mannerisms of a literary type or genre, or of a particular author, and the substitution of a trivial or comic content for a sublime or serious one. Thus Alexander Pope adopts and exaggerates the characteristics of the heroic epic in his *The Rape of the Lock* (1712), which describes the theft of a snippet of hair.

Though some parodists — perhaps all — have an affinity with what they parody, theirs is an aggressive technique, which ridicules the verbal pretensions and mannerisms of the target.

Looked at in an historical dimension, parody has the function of demolishing anachronistic or exhausted forms. Sometimes this leads to the creation of major new forms; Cervantes's *Don Quijote* (1605 ff), for example, can be seen as not simply a parody of the chivalric romance, but as the first novel.

P.T.

PARS PRO TOTO

Figure of speech (a kind of → SYNEKDOCHE) in which a part of something is used to express the whole; e.g.: 20 Köpfe instead of 20 Personen. (→METONYMIE).

PASSION (Passion); PASSIONSSPIEL (passion play)

The Passion means the sufferings of Christ on the Cross, esp. as recorded in the Gospels. The passion play was a med. drama on this theme, which developed from the → OSTERSPIEL. Frequently, the production of passion plays entailed considerable expense, and they lasted several days. They enjoyed great popularity, and were performed from the late 14th to the early 16th century. The present Oberammergau *Passionsspiel* has been substantially altered and the text bears little resemblance to the original.→GEISTLICHES DRAMA.

PATHETISCH (with pathos) →PATHOS

PATHOS (pathos)

Pathos in English is that quality in a work which evokes pity and sadness in the reader/spectator, and is more likely to occur in sentimental and melodramatic works, rather than tragedy. In German, however, *Pathos* is closer to Aristotle's (384–322 B.C.) usage, meaning an intense experience of emotion and suffering, which results from the (invariably wrong) decision the tragic hero makes. *Pathos* is thus an essential element in tragedy. For Emil Staiger (*Grundbegriffe der Poetik*, 1946) *Pathos* is one of the constituents of the quality → DRAMATISCH. *Pathos* in this context denotes the urge to convince and presupposes a resistance which has to be overcome. It is advocating what should be the case and opposing the status quo. →PROBLEM.

N.B. Pathetisch = with pathos; NOT pathetic.

A.O.

PAWLATSCHENTHEATER

Form of → WANDERBÜHNE unique to the Viennese popular tradition. *Pawlatschen* were simple wooden stages frequently incorporating the cart used by the players. These stages were hastily erected for partly improvised performances in courtyards and market-places.

PEGASOS (Pegasus)

In Greek mythology a winged horse which sprang from the blood of Medusa after Perseus had slain her. Bellerophon tamed Pegasus with a special bridle given to him by Athena. The two then fought and killed the Chimaera. Because of his association with → HELIKON and → HIPPOKRENE, Pegasus is taken by some authors to be a symbol of poetic inspiration.

PENTAMETER (pentameter)

Metrical line consisting of five feet, usually dactyls or spondees. →METRIK.

PERIODE (period)

1. Segment of time, epoch.
2. Full-stop: point which marks the end of a sentence.
3. Complex sentence comprising a series of different clauses.

PERIPETIE (peripeteia, peripety)

In tragedy, the hero's sudden change of fortune, usually a change from prosperity to ruin, which is one of the basic elements of the tragic plot. →ANAGNORISIS, →HAMARTIA, →WENDEPUNKT.

PERIPHRASE (periphrasis, circumlocution)

Use of many words to express something which might be conveyed in a few; often employed for purposes of euphemism.

PERSONALES ERZÄHLEN →AUKTORIALES ERZÄHLEN

PERSONENVERZEICHNIS →DRAMATIS PERSONAE

PERSONIFIKATION (personification, pathetic fallacy)

Figure of speech in which inanimate objects or abstract qualities are invested with human attributes and abilities.

PERSPEKTIVE

1. Perspective. In theatre and painting the creation of the visual impression of depth and dimension.
2. The point of view from which events are narrated (→ERZÄHLER) or from which the world is described. The application of the term is usually confined to narrative works and refers to the type of narrator, e.g. first-person narrator, omniscient narrator etc. = *Erzählhaltung,* = *Erzählperspektive,* = *Erzählsituation.*
3. In the GDR the optimistic view of the socialist future which is often mandatory for the writer of socialist realism. → SOZIALISTISCHER REALISMUS.

E.W.H.

PHANTASMAGORIE (phantasmagoria)

The creation on stage of the illusion of ghosts, phantasms, or dreamlike visions, by means of technical devices for theatrical purposes.

PHILOLOGIE

The study of a people or culture mainly by means of its language and literature. Philology is concerned specifically with the editing, classification, commenting and interpretation of texts. Its two major branches, linguistics and literary criticism, are supported by the study of textual criticism, palaeography, grammar, stylistics, rhetoric, metrics and poetics. (→ METRIK, →POETIK, → RHETORIK, → STILISTIK, → TEXTKRITIK).

As an academic discipline, philology has a long history. Its origins can be traced to the ancient Greeks, particularly to the famous library at Alexandria which became the centre of a renowned school in the 4th century B.C. Its activities included the codification and editing of literary texts as well as the writing of glosses to these texts. The Greeks strongly influenced the Roman philologists, while the med. European and Byzantine scholars built on the legacy of Rome. The → RENAISSANCE, with its interest in classical antiquity and its literary heritage, gave a new impetus to the discipline, which was further intensified by the invention of the printing press, and which was sustained into the 18th century. In the 19th century, the methods which had been developed and tested in the study of Greek and Latin texts were beginning to be applied to vernacular literatures. The leading figures in this process in the area of German language and literature were the brothers Grimm and Carl Lachmann. They thus laid the foundations of a new branch of philology, → GERMANISTIK, which has become an academic discipline in its own right. → ALTPHILOLOGIE, → NEUPHILOLOGIE.

P.Oe.

PHONETIK (phonetics)

Phonetics is the study of the sounds used in human language. Any utterance can be regarded as a sequence of discrete sounds, *segments*, whose properties are studied primarily in three ways. *Articulatory* phonetics aims at a description of these segmental speech sounds on the basis of their production. *Acoustic* phonetics is concerned with them as patterns of air vibrations. A third approach, *auditory* phonetics, looks at the reception of sound by the hearer.

Each distinct sound, *phone*, can be given a unique description by stating the activity of the vocal organs in its production. For *vowels*, in which air, set in vibration by the vocal chords, passes through the mouth without any obstruction, one refers to the *position* (*front, central, back*) and *height* (on a *high* to *low* scale) of the highest point of the tongue, and to the lips (*rounded* or *spread*), and for *consonants*, to the type of obstruction, whether complete (*stops*), partial (*fricatives*), complete but with open nasal passage (*nasals*), etc., and to the place where this occurs, e.g. at the lips (*bilabials*) etc.

The International Phonetic Alphabet provides a symbol for every phone, e.g. [k] as in *sk*ill, [ʒ] as in lei*s*ure, etc.

PHONOLOGIE (phonology)

Phonology as part of General Linguistics aims at discovering generalizations about the way all human languages make use of sound, and a statement of the sound system of a language is called its phonology. This will include a list of the phones (→ PHONETIK) used by speakers of that language, and a classification of these into *phonemes*, distinctive classes of phones; for in any given language not every phonetic distinction is relevant. For instance, there are two 'l' sounds in English, the 'light' [l] and the 'dark' [l^w] , but, although phonetically different, they never function distinctively in English, because [l] is used only when a vowel follows, and [l^w] only when no vowel follows, as in *l*eaf and fee*l*. These two phones thus make up one phoneme, /l/, are its *allophones*, and are in *complementary distribution*, in that where one occurs the other cannot. The phonology of a language will also include *phonological rules*, which are statements of the sort just made about the distribution of [l] and [l^w] in English, as well as statements of other regularities of a language's sound system, such as *Auslautverhärtung* in German, the rule that stem-final /b/, /d/, /g/ are pronounced as the corresponding voiceless sounds [p] , [t] , [k] at the end of a word, cf. Ra*d* v. Ra*d*es.

R.H.

PICKELHERING

Stock comic figure of English origin. → ENGLISCHE KOMÖDIANTEN.

PIERROT

Stock pantomine figure of the clown, usually dressed in a white costume and with a whitened face.

PIETISMUS (pietism)

Pietism was a reform movement in the Protestant church and religion, which flourished in Germany — although there were similar contemporary movements in other European countries, e.g. Puritanism in England — between about 1670, when Philipp Jakob Spener (1635–1705) founded the 'Collegia pietatis' in Frankfurt am Main, and about 1740, when with the accession of Frederick the Great the Pietists lost their hitherto dominant influence in the Prussian education system.

Instead of the rigid dogmatic intellectualism of orthodox Protestantism Pietism emphasized the importance of individual and subjective aspects of religious experience. It emphasized feeling as opposed to doctrinal understanding (e.g. Goethe's *Faust I*: "Gefühl ist alles;/Name ist Schall und Rauch,/Umnebelnd Himmelsglut''), and the personal relationship of the individual to God. This led to the celebration of Christ as friend, brother, lover and husband of the soul. Pietism was on the one hand an active reform movement, insisting on the primacy of good works and on the practical regeneration of social ethics, and on the other hand a passive and mystical flight from the world into contemplation. The literary products of the Pietists (hymns, religious poetry, diaries, confessions and → ERBAUUNGSLITERATUR) are not as important as the influence the movement had on literature later in the 18th century. The Pietists, through their constant practice in the observation and analysis of (religious) emotions, contributed greatly to the refinement and intensification of feeling, and to the development of a language adequate to express it; e.g. Goethe's *Werther* (1774) and Klopstock's *Messias* (1748). The flowering of subjectivism in 18th century German literature (→ STURM UND DRANG, → ROMANTIK) cannot be fully appreciated without an understanding of Pietism. The Pietist cult of friendship as love (→ EMPFINDSAMKEIT), the greater importance given to woman as *schöne Seele*, and the new sensitivity in the experience of nature were all to play an important part in German literature.

The effect of Pietism on the German language was to replace Latin by German in religious writing and in education, to overcome the complex sentence structures of the → BAROCK writers in a search for a clear and simple syntax, to introduce a dynamic element into the language with a preference for verbs of motion, especially using prefixes (*ein, hinein, durch, entgegen, hinab, hinauf, aufwärts*, etc.), and to develop the expression of abstract ideas by the use of verb-substantives ending in *−ung, −heit* and *−keit*. The predominant use of water metaphors (*Quelle, Brunnen, Strom, Fluß, Wassersturz, Wasserfall*, etc.) was taken over and developed by later writers, especially Goethe. Pietism also influenced 18th century German literature, in that many writers were educated in Pietist institutions.

E.W.H.

PIKARISCHER ROMAN → SCHELMENROMAN

PLAGIAT (plagiarism)

The appropriation of another person's writings or ideas and representation of them as one's own.

PLANIPES → MIMUS

PLATTDEUTSCHE DICHTUNG

Literature written in Low-German dialect. → DIALEKTDICHTUNG.

PLEONASMUS (pleonasm)

Redundancy of expression: the use of more words than are necessary to express an idea or situation, so that a superfluity results; sometimes this may be a deliberate stylistic device.

POEME EN PROSE → PROSAGEDICHT

POESIE → DICHTUNG

POETA DOCTUS

Highly educated and cultured author who writes for an equally well-educated public.

POETIK (poetics) = Dichtungslehre

An academic discipline which concerns itself with questions of literary genres, literary forms and modes of presentation as well as with a general theory of literature. *Poetik* is therefore an integral and central part of → LITERATUR-WISSENSCHAFT.

The published account of such views and theories is also referred to as *Poetik*.

The oldest surviving *Poetiken* are the fragments on tragedy and epic poetry by Aristotle (384–322 B.C.) and the *Epistula ad pisones* (known as *De arte poetica*) by Horace (65–8 B.C.). Since then every period or cultural movement has produced its own *Poetik* according to its particular notion of literature. There are in principle two types of *Poetiken*: prescriptive ones, which establish rules and regulations for the writing of literature and judge literature according to these rules; and descriptive ones, which by means of analysis and comparison of individual literary works aim to arrive at a description and characterization of a genre. Modern *Poetiken* are generally descriptive. → GATTUNGEN.

A.O.

POETISCHER REALISMUS → REALISMUS

POINTE

The pungent and unexpected twist in a joke, aphorism or anecdote: the gist or essential meaning.

POLICHINELLE → PULCINELLA

POLITISCHE DICHTUNG

Writing which reflects either directly or indirectly in its content political or social concerns, usually, but not always, associated with the desire to bring about change. It thus comprises a broad category which may also embrace the terms → TENDENZDICHTUNG and → ENGAGIERTE LITERATUR. Disagreement exists as to the exact nature of *politische Dichtung*, and at least three types may be distinguished: (1) the author produces political propaganda, either of an affirmatory or critical kind, and suppresses his own personality; (2) the author writes on behalf of a particular ideology, but retains his artistic autonomy; (3) the author expresses his personal reaction to a given political situation. A distinction can also be made between works of *politische Dichtung* which are specifically intended to have a political impact and those which acquire a political significance only in the course of time. Although *politische Dichtung* embodies a strong and enduring tradition in German literature, which may be traced back at least as far as Walther von der Vogelweide's *Spruchdichtung* (1198—1227), only comparatively recently has it achieved literary respectability. There has always been the suspicion, particularly in the case of lyric poetry, that literature which articulates a political message impairs its own aesthetic worth, since ambiguity and artistic innovation, which are considered necessary components of a literary work, must invariably be limited. Conversely, it has been argued that to couch a political message in literary terms impairs its political effectiveness. Another school of thought, however, maintains that the category is superfluous anyway, since all writing is inherently political. Some favoured forms of *politische Dichtung* are the ballad (Brecht, *Von der Kindesmörderin Marie Farrar*, 1922), the satirical novel (Heinrich Mann, *Der Untertan*, 1918) and the documentary drama (Weiss, *Die Ermittlung*, 1965). → BALLADE, → DOKUMENTARTHEATER.

W.S.S.

POLYHYMNIA

Muse of dance and music. →MUSEN.

POSITIVER HELD

Term current in Soviet and early GDR discussions about Socialist Realism (→ SOZIALISTISCHER REALISMUS) but superseded in the GDR in the mid-1960s by the term *sozialistisches Menschenbild*. Initially, the *positive Held* was to be an uncomplicated as well as an exemplary and selfless character. Unlike the hero (→ HELD), he was not tormented by self-doubts. Nor did he question the social/political system to which he subordinated all personal concerns in unflagging devotion to the revolutionary transformation of society. With increasing adherence to the heritage of bourgeois classical literature in these societies came also the recognition that the *positive Held* remained a lifeless, cardboard figure. Far from inducing identification/emulation in the reader, he rather undermined the entertaining as well as the edifying intentions of Socialist Realism. Hence the demise of the *positive Held* in favour of more differentiated and complex literary figures.

B.E.

POSITIVISMUS (positivism)

Positivism was the predominant method in German literary criticism

(→ LITERATURGESCHICHTE, → LITERATURWISSENSCHAFT) during the second half of the 19th century. The positivists preferred to deal in data and facts only and rejected metaphysics and speculation of any sort. Positivism in literary criticism was the attempt to adopt the method of the sciences for the study of literature. For this reason the activities of these scholars were somewhat restricted. On the one hand they had to secure the facts which meant producing reliable editions, biographies, lexica and the tracing and recording of literary sources, on the other hand the aim was the writing of a history of literature based on this information. The most representative literary historian was Wilhelm Scherer (*Geschichte der deutschen Literatur*, 1883) who attempted to explain German literature and its development in terms of the writer's background (milieu, heritage) his upbringing (education) and his personal experiences. The emphasis was on the genesis of the literary text rather than on aesthetic considerations.

Although positivism as a means of studying literature was superseded at the turn of the century in favour of greater emphasis on →INTERPRETATION, the remaining merit of this method is to be seen in its contribution to the documentation and recording of sources, texts and data which form the basis for *Literaturwissenschaft* as practised today.

A.O.

POSSE

Derived from the med. → FASTNACHTSPIEL, also known as *Possenspiel*, the term is now restricted to the 19th century comedies influenced by the → COMMEDIA DELL'ARTE and the French *vaudeville*. *Posse* is low comedy, in local dialect, akin to farce and burlesque. The schematic plots provide occasions for song and dance. The *Posse* can be satirical, especially in the so-called → COUPLET. Theatrical success often depended on the skill of the individual actors, for whom these plays were especially written. The *Lokalposse* and *Sittenstück* aimed at a pseudo-realistic portrayal of (petty) bourgeois life. The main centres of this urban entertainment were Berlin and Vienna. Raimund (1790–1836) transcended the genre, and Nestroy (1801–1862) gave it literary merit. The *Posse* finally gave way to the Viennese *Operette*, yet the influence of Nestroy's *Possen* can be felt in Horváth (1901–1938), Brecht (1898–1956) and Dürrenmatt (1921–). →ZAUBERSTÜCK.

F.W.

POSTILLE

Devotional book which contains explanations of biblical texts. Also known as *Hauspostille*, which was a collection of biblical quotations intended to be read to the family. The term *Postille* is now applied to any literary work which is aimed at a particular group.

PRÄFIGURATION (prefiguration)

Usually a literary work, or an element from a work, employed for symbolic effect in a subsequent piece of literature, e.g. the use of Shakespeare's *Romeo and Juliet* (1595?) in Keller's *Romeo und Julia auf dem Dorfe* (1856) or Dante's Beatrice in Hesse's *Demian* (1919). Other sources — paintings, games, films, even earlier parts of the same text — can also serve as prefigurations, provided they signal a pre-existent pattern against which the events and characters of a work are to be interpreted. The term derives from figural Bible exegesis and denotes a scheme whereby the persons and events of the O.T. were interpreted as prophecies of the N.T. and its history of salvation. In its modern, generally secularized use 'prefiguration' has lost this prophetic connotation; it no longer suggests the subservient, predictive role of the earlier text nor does it imply that the post-figuration will necessarily fulfil all the expectations initially aroused by such a scheme of symbolic correspondences. Prefigurations can be either explicit or covert. They can have a variety of functions: adding a heroic aura to a modern realistic plot, exploiting satirically contrasts between the contemporary world and that of the prefiguration, playing with the reader's expectations or introducing a sense of patterned fatalism into a work. → VORAUSDEUTUNG.

J.J.W.

PRÄGNANZ

Brevity of expression, succinct and pithy.

PRÄSENZBIBLIOTHEK

A library where books may be consulted, or read on the premises, but not borrowed.

PREISLIED

In old Germanic poetry, a poem in praise of some august personage, usually on an occasion such as a military victory or a death.

PREZIOSITÄT

1. Preciosity: refinement of language, ideas or style which is so excessive that it appears affected and self-conscious.

2. *Préciosité*: French literary movement of the 17th century which developed in the salons of influential aristocratic women who dubbed themselves 'les précieuses'. One leading *Précieuse* was the Marquise de Rambouillet (1588–1665), whose salon in the Hôtel de Rambouillet (1618–1650) was frequented by the major writers, thinkers, and members of the nobility of the period. The *Précieuses* sought to elevate and refine the French language, in order to make it a fit vehicle for literary expression. They deplored

coarseness and bluntness, and aimed at purity and delicacy of expression, manners and style. This fastidiousness led to some abuses and extravagances, which Molière satirized in *Les Précieuses ridicules* (1659). However, in his preface he stated emphatically that ". . . les plus excellentes choses sont sujettes à être copiées par de mauvais singes. . .", pointing out that he was poking fun at the excesses, and not at *préciosité* itself.

F.K.

PRIMÄRLITERATUR

Creative literary works, as distinct from works about them. → SEKUN-DÄRLITERATUR.

PROBE (rehearsal) → GENERALPROBE

PROBLEM, PROBLEMATIK

1. Question, usually of an intellectual or spiritual nature, which is put forward for discussion and solution.

2. For Emil Staiger (*Grundbegriffe der Poetik*, 1946) *Problem* is one of the constituents of the quality → DRAMATISCH. *Problem* in this context means the envisaged aim which is to be achieved by literary means. For this reason the problematic style is end-oriented, i.e. everything is employed for the purpose of reaching the conclusion (in a drama) or the point (in an aphorism or a joke). → PATHOS.

A.O.

PRODESSE ET DELECTARE

Quotation from Horace's *Ars poetica*, which states that the dual function of poetry is to provide both aesthetic pleasure and moral guidance.

PROLEGOMENA

Introductory or preliminary discourse of a literary work.

PROLETARIERDICHTUNG → ARBEITERDICHTUNG

PROLETKULT

Russian abbreviation for proletarian culture. Organization founded in Russia in 1917 with the goal of fostering and developing a specific culture of, and by, the proletariat. In 1923, after a period of great cultural activity, it was dissolved, because its leader, Bogdanov, wanted it to be independent of party political lines.

PROSA (prose) = ungebundene Rede

As Monsieur Jourdain was instructed in Molière's *Le Bourgeois gentilhomme*

II, 4 (1670): "tout ce qui n'est point prose est vers; et tout ce qui n'est point vers est prose". Prose is ordinary language in speech or writing, free from the regular rhythms and rhymes of verse. The adjective *prosaisch*, like *prosaic*, carries more than a suggestion of pejorative meaning, indicating a degree of dullness or the absence of inspiration. In literary criticism however *Prosa* is contrasted with *Poesie*, and as *Kunstprosa* (→EPIK) prose can become a vehicle for imaginative and emotional as well as intellectual and informative discourse. In general, prose appeals to the intellect, and poetry to the imagination, and in this sense the devices of poetry are unsuitable for the purpose and function of prose. Attempts have been made to use prose in the same way as verse, e.g. Baudelaire in his *Petits Poèmes en prose* (1869) or Peter Altenberg (1859—1919), but more usually authors writing in prose, wishing to achieve the effects of verse, have tended to include verse in a prose-work. German prose writing was, with some exceptions, undistinguished before Lessing (1729—1781). His critical essays and polemics owe much to his wide acquaintance with French and other writers of the European Enlightenment (→ AUFKLÄRUNG). Lessing's prose is a model of lucidity, cogency of argument, vigour and unambiguousness, and these qualities are normally the aims of prose as opposed to the aims of poetry. A generation later, with Goethe, German prose acquired new parameters, corresponding to Goethe's very wide-ranging human sympathies and intellectual interests, his imaginative power and encyclopaedic reading. During the 19th century prose displaced verse as the vehicle for drama.

J.M.L.

PROSAGEDICHT (prose poem, poème en prose) = Poème en prose

Short prose form which through its choice of language and rhythm approaches poetry in its suggestive and lyrical qualities, but can be differentiated from it because of its lack of metrical lines, rhyme and verse division. → LYRIK, → LYRISCH.

PROSODIE (prosody)

The study of versification, incorporating such elements as sound, metre, rhythm, stanza form etc.

PROSPEKT

1. Backdrop, the wall at the rear of a stage set which is painted to create the illusion of a specific place.

2. Prospectus: descriptive account of the main points of a forthcoming literary work or commercial enterprise.

PROTOKOLL (minutes of proceedings, report of a meeting)

PROZESSIONSSPIEL → FRONLEICHNAMSSPIEL

PSEUDONYM (nom de plume, pen-name, pseudonym)

Assumed name under which an author or artist is known. e.g.: Novalis = Friedrich von Hardenberg.

PUBLIZIST (journalist)

Person who writes on current political and social issues.

PULCINELLA = Polichinelle

Stock male character from the →COMMEDIA DELL'ARTE.

PUNCH

Comic figure modelled on → PULCINELLA. → COMMEDIA DELL'ARTE.

PUPPENSPIEL (puppet or marionette show)

Both the performance of a play by puppets (*Handpuppen*) or marionettes and the actual puppet or marionette theatre are referred to as *Puppenspiel*. It was a very popular form of entertainment, esp. in the 16th and 17th centuries.

The *Puppenspiel* is particularly significant in the history of German literature, since it was when as a boy in Frankfurt Goethe (1749–1832) saw a *Puppenspiel* performance of *Dr. Faustus*, that he first became acquainted with the Faust legend. This experience contributed to his life-long preoccupation with the theme.

A.O.

PURGIERTE AUSGABE (bowdlerized edition) →AUSGABE

PURISMUS (purism) = Reinheit der Sprache

Purity of language became something of a fetish in 17th century Germany. It was connected with the rising tide of literature written in the vernacular, and reflected a new-found pride in its ability to convey complex and subtle ideas. The most important aim was to stamp out the use of dialect, French and incorrect Latin mixed in with the German. These and other rules were contained in the poetic theories which prescribed the correct way of writing. Literary societies (→ SPRACHGESELLSCHAFTEN) played a major role in spreading purism throughout the German-speaking world. Some writers took it to extremes by coining new words to replace those that were based on a foreign language, even if they were commonly used. Although such excesses provoked ridicule and opposition, the trend continued strongly during most of the 18th century. In later times puristic tendencies were increasingly connected with narrow-minded nationalism.

E.Kr.

QUADRIVIUM → ARTES LIBERALES

QUANTITÄT (quantity) = Silbenlänge

The duration of time necessary to pronounce a syllable. → QUANTITIE-RENDE DICHTUNG, → SILBENMASS.

QUANTITIERENDE DICHTUNG (quantitative verse)

Verse in which → QUANTITÄT determines the metrical pattern as opposed to → AKZENTUIERENDE DICHTUNG. → AKZENT.

QUARTETT → VIERZEILER

QUELLE (source) = Vorbild, = Vorlage

The source from which an author derives his plot material; e.g. a myth, a biography, a diary, an historical account, a book by another writer, etc.

QUELLENANGABE

1. Citing or acknowledgement of sources consulted in a literary work or in a work of literary criticism.

2. Bibliography.

QUELLENKUNDE

The study of historical sources, e.g. letters, manuscripts, etc.

QUODLIBET

Collection of apparently arbitrarily selected poems; medley.

RÄTSEL (riddle) = Enigma

Puzzle in which several elements of a familiar object, place or situation are named, the object being to guess the whole. However, as these elements are presented in an unexpected arrangement, the solution requires some ingenuity. The answer is usually pungent and witty, and as well as being humorous may point to some basic truth. The various types of *Rätsel* include arithmetic and visual riddles (→ REBUS). The *Rätsel* is considered to be one of the oldest → EINFACHE FORMEN in literature, as it is closely associated with the oracular pronouncements in Greek mythology.

RAHMENERZÄHLUNG

Form of fiction which has been adopted by writers of many nationalities since classical times. The procedure involves embracing one or more narratives (→ BINNENERZÄHLUNG) within another narrative. A *cyclic* framework brackets stories of similar content or tendency within a framework of common relevance. A single tale may also be presented within a framework calculated to enhance its probability. A well-known example of the cyclic framework is Gottfried Keller's series of *Züricher Novellen* (1878), all concerned with personalities from the history of Zurich. This series, which is didactic in tendency, provides notable examples of persons worthy of imitation or instances of human folly to be avoided by the young man (Jacques) for whose benefit the *Novellen* are related by his godfather. In Keller's *Sinngedicht* (1882) all the stories including the framework tale are concerned with relationships between the sexes; in this case the internal stories are arranged in contrasting pairs so that the respective attitudes of the sexes are given balanced expression. Meyer's *Der Heilige* (1879) forms an impressive example of a single framework story in which the fortunes of important and influential persons are related by a comparatively simple man whom chance has brought into their sphere of life. In Theodor Storm's *Der Schimmelreiter* (1888) the inherently improbable events of a ghost story are distanced and given enhanced probability by a double framework (grand-mother's chest with yellowing manuscript, the narration of the local schoolmaster to the traveller who records his meeting with the schoolmaster at the beginning). The *Rahmenerzählung* technique was widely used by 19th century writers of *Novellen* but it is also used by writers of novels and a similar device is sometimes used by dramatists. e.g.: Grillparzer in *Der Traum ein Leben*

1840). →NOVELLE.

J.M.L.

RANDGLOSSEN →MARGINALIEN

RAUBDRUCK (pirated edition) →NACHDRUCK

RAUMBÜHNE (apron stage)

A stage which projects into the auditorium so that the audience can be seated around it on three sides.

REALENZYKLOPÄDIE →REALLEXIKON

REALISMUS (realism)

Term used (1) to designate the style of a literary work and (2) to denote a literary period. = Bürgerlicher Realismus, = poetischer Realismus.

(1) *Realismus* denotes a style which attempts to render empirical reality in a balanced and personal way which contrasts both with Naturalism (→NATU-RALISMUS) and its predilection for the sordid and unpleasant and with the idealism of Classicism (→ KLASSIK) and the fantastic forms of Romanticism (→ ROMANTIK). Engels defined *Realismus* as the faithful rendering of typical people in typical circumstances, a concept which became the basis for Socialist Realism (→ SOZIALISTISCHER REALISMUS). Historically speaking *Realismus* is a style appearing in the later stages of the development of a culture.

(2) As a term for a literary period *Realismus* is used for the time between 1830 and 1880 (*bürgerlicher Realismus, poetischer Realismus*). It is the period of growing industrialization and the emergence of large political and social movements. The preferred literary forms of the period are the novel and the → NOVELLE. Due to the later emergence of these social changes, *Realismus* in Germany differs from that in France and Britain. In contrast to the French attitude of disillusion (Flaubert, *Madame Bovary,* 1857) and the didactic and moralistic attitude of the British realists (Dickens, *Pickwick Papers,* 1837), German *Realismus* attempts to reconcile the rendering of contemporary reality with the traditional concept of humanism, stressing the description of seemingly simple things in the → BIEDERMEIER, emphasizing their symbolic relevance (Gotthelf, *Die schwarze Spinne,* 1842; Stifter, *Bunte Steine,* 1853). In the work of Gottfried Keller the attempt is made to link the new realities of the day with the concept of democracy and a non-transcendental faith (*Der grüne Heinrich,* 1854). With Raabe, Meyer, Storm and Fontane (*Effi Briest,* 1894) *Realismus* turns to a more psychological analysis of reality. From its beginnings with the contributions of Büchner (*Lenz,* 1839) and Grabbe (*Napoleon oder Die hundert Tage,* 1831), through to those of Fontane, *Realismus* in Germany expresses the apprehension of a threat to a meaningful existence by the newly emerging social

and cultural forces. Towards the end of the 19th century *Realismus* was superseded by Naturalism, the Neo-romantic movement (→ NEUROMANTIK) and Symbolism (→SYMBOLISMUS).

E.K.

REALLEXIKON = Realenzyklopädie, = Sachwörterbuch

Dictionary or encyclopaedia which explains the terminology and principles of a single discipline as distinct from general lexica.

REBUS (rebus)

Type of riddle (→RÄTSEL) in which pictures etc. suggest words or syllables of words.

RECHTSCHREIBUNG (orthography)

Correct spelling.

REDAKTEUR = Schriftleiter

Sub-editor of a magazine or newspaper: person responsible for a particular section, e.g. sports, arts, cookery etc. The editor, responsible for the whole publication, is the *Chefredakteur*.

REDE (speech) → **DIREKTE REDE**, → **ERLEBTE REDE**, → **INDIREKTE REDE**

REDEFIGUR →**RHETORISCHE FIGUR**

REDEKUNST →**RHETORIK**

REDENSART

Expression which through constant use has become hackneyed and meaningless, so that it is used as a trite formula.

REFERAT

Report or paper written or presented orally, usually involving detailed research on a specialized subject.

REFRAIN →**KEHRREIM**

REGIE (direction, production of a play)

REGISSEUR (director) = Spielleiter

REICHER REIM = erweiterter Reim

Form of expanded and repeated rhyme derived from oriental poetry;
e.g.:   Waldung, sie schwankt heran,
Felsen, sie lasten dran,
Wurzeln, sie klammern an,
Stamm dicht an Stamm hinan. (Goethe, *Faust II*). → REIM.

REIGENLIED, REIHEN

Med. song comprising a narrative section interspersed with stanzas of a
round dance.

REIHUNG

Accumulation of words or phrases, esp. without connecting words.

REIM (rhyme)

Similarity or identity of sound, (esp. in poetry). When accented vowels and
any sounds following are identical, they constitute a rhyme. Rhyme may occur
at the end of the verse line, internally i.e. within the line, and initially.
Äußerer Reim → KETTENREIM, → ALLITERATION, → ANFANGS-
REIM, Anreim → ALLITERATION, → BINNENREIM, → DREIREIM, einsil-
biger Reim → MÄNNLICHER REIM, → ENDREIM, → ENDSILBENREIM,
erweiterter Reim → REICHER REIM, → GEBROCHENER REIM, gekreuzter
Reim → KREUZREIM, → GESPALTENER REIM, → GRAMMATISCHER REIM,
Haufenreim → REIMHÄUFUNG, → IDENTISCHER REIM, → INREIM,
→ KEHRREIM (not a rhyme!), → KETTENREIM, → KREUZREIM, → MÄNN-
LICHER REIM, → MITTENREIM, → PAARREIM, → REICHER REIM,
→ REIMHÄUFUNG, → REIMPAAR, → REINER REIM, → RÜHRENDER REIM,
→ SCHLAGREIM, → SCHWEIFREIM, Stabreim (→ ALLITERATION), stumpfer
Reim → MÄNNLICHER REIM, → UNREINER REIM, → VERSCHRÄNKTER
REIM, → WEIBLICHER REIM, → ZÄSURREIM, Zwischenreim → SCHWEIF-
REIM.

REIMBRECHUNG (broken rhyme)

Occurs when two consecutive verse lines which rhyme together are not
syntactically connected, the first verse line following a previous syntactical
pattern and the second commencing a new one.

REIMFOLGE (rhyme scheme)

REIMFORMEL

Rhyming words which have gradually become clichés; e.g.: Herz - Schmerz.

REIMHÄUFUNG = Haufenreim

Repetition of the same rhyme in more than two consecutive verse lines. →ANAPHER.

REIMPAAR (rhyming couplets) →**PAARREIM**

REINER REIM (perfect rhyme)

Occurs when the rhyming sounds (vowel and following consonant) are exactly matched. →RÜHRENDER REIM.

REINHEIT DER SPRACHE →**PURISMUS**

REISSER

Box-office success, sensational novel or film; pejorative term for a literary or artistic work which, although financially successful, has no artistic merit.

REMITTENDE (returned copy)

Publication which has not been sold and is returned to the publisher.

RENAISSANCE (Renaissance)

In a general sense the term signifies any reawakening of past cultural phenomena, e.g. the reappearance of styles in fashion or architecture. More specifically the term applies to developments in painting, sculpture, architecture and literature between the late M.A. and the modern world (1350–1600). After the Turkish conquest of Constantinople (1453) many scholars fled to Italy where they stimulated interest in the writings of ancient poets, philosophers, historians, and rhetoricians. They greatly expanded the study of Latin and Greek literature. Their admiration for the classical past and a belief in the strong individual as conceived in classical culture merged with a more general longing for spiritual rejuvenation in Western Europe to produce such eminent works as those of Petrarch, Ariosto, Tasso, Michelangelo, Raphael and Leonardo da Vinci (Italy), Lope de Vega and Cervantes (Spain), Rabelais, Montaigne and Ronsard (France). *Renaissance* ideas came to England only in the 16th century and did not exert their greatest influence until the Elizabethan and Jacobean periods. It is difficult to apply this term in German literature: here Humanist and *Renaissance* concepts were soon overshadowed by Luther's reformation with its emphasis on the importance of the individual in religious matters. In the sphere of science Copernicus published his hypothesis picturing a heliocentric universe in 1543, thereby questioning the Ptolemaic cosmos of med. astronomy and astrology. The verification of his theories by Kepler and Galileo reinforced the belief in the principles and methods of the new science.

V.K.

REPERTORIUM

1. Register, index.
2. Compendium: thorough and systematic presentation of a subject, which becomes a standard text-book or reference work.

REPLIK

1. Reply, rejoinder.
2. Replica (of a work of art).

REPORTAGE (factual reporting)

Normally the media (television, radio and newspapers) relate in *Reportage*-form the material selected for publication to the viewing or reading public. In this context the term *Reportage* denotes a non-literary prose style. When used in literary criticism, the term signifies the adoption in a literary text of a non-literary prose style to report events or the results of research and investigation.

In recent years some sociological and psychological investigations have set up models for journalistic reports presenting to the reading public verifiable and objective documentation but in narrative form, so that fact and fiction can no longer be clearly distinguished. Examples of *Reportage* ranging from objective to novelistic can be found in current German literature; e.g. Erika Runge, *Bottroper Protokolle* (1968), Böll, *Die verlorene Ehre der Katharina Blum* (1974), Alice Schwarzer, *Der kleine Unterschied und seine großen Folgen* (1975), Walraff, *Der Aufmacher. Der Mann, der bei 'Bild' Hans Esser war* (1977).

Reportage thus can become a literary device and may be employed for aesthetic purposes.

R.P.

REPRISE

Revival of a play or film which has not been performed for some time.

REQUISITEN (stage properties)

Articles necessary for the staging of a play (excluding costumes and scenery).

RESTAURATIONSZEIT

Period following the fall of Napoleon and the restoration of pre-Napoleonic conditions. In German literary history also known as → BIEDERMEIER.

RETARDATION, RETARDIERENDES MOMENT

Retardation is the dramatic device of delaying plot developments so that tension and suspense are heightened. *Retardierendes Moment* is the point when *Retardation* occurs.

REVOLUTIONSDICHTUNG → POLITISCHE DICHTUNG

REZENSION (review) = Besprechung
Critical report in a newspaper or magazine about a book, play, film etc.

REZENSIONSEXEMPLAR (review copy)
Copy of a book which the publisher provides for the reviewer.

REZEPTION

The reception of a work of art by a reader, listener or spectator. A recently developed approach to literature, *Rezeptionsästhetik*, specifically analyses the relationship between literature and its recipients (→ LESER) and ascribes to the reader an active part in the actualization of the work of art. As no reader ever fully realizes all the possibilities extant in a text, *Rezeptionsästhetik* aims to produce an historical account of all receptions as far as they can be documented. → ÄSTHETIK.

A.O.

RHETORIK (rhetoric)

Since Aristotle (384–322 B.C.) rhetoric possesses both a philosophic and a literary realm: it is a body of teachings on the art of inventing persuasive argumentation and on speaking (*Redekunst*) and writing well. After dominating school and university curricula for 2000 years, the two aspects have been declared obsolete: argumentative theory because of the development of modern analytic science, literary theory because of the emphasis on poetic genius in the 17th and 18th centuries. However, the recent interest in the human foundations of knowledge, science, law and society shown by hermeneutics (→ HERMENEU-TIK) and the study of imagination and communications have stimulated much new research into both realms of rhetoric. Since Aristotle the basic argumentative realm of rhetoric is treated under the heading of → TOPIK. As an artistic method, rhetoric is divided into five parts: 1. invention: how to find the subject-matter of any speech or writing; 2. disposition: how to give order to the material; 3. elocution: how to find suitable expressions; 4. memory: how to memorize the speech; 5. action: how to present it in public. Of these, invention and elocution became the subject of detailed elaboration. Invention deals specifically with the techniques of persuasive strategy and is investigated in five sub-parts: 1. proem: how to begin a speech or writing; 2. narration: how to present a case; 3. probation/argumentation: how to argue the case and prove the argument (the detailed treatment of topics belongs here); 4. refutation: how to refute the argumentation of the opposition; 5. epilogue: how to conclude the speech or writing. Elocution details the rules of grammatical correctness, intellectual and linguistic clarity, aptness of expression and suitable ornamentation within the system of the figures of speech. Although this division was clearly based on the analysis of judicial speech, historically the first and most important genus in the development of rhetoric, the prescriptions were consequently adapted to the other two genera of deliberative speech and the speech of praise or eulogy; their adaptation marks the area of transition of rhetoric into literature. Today, the system of classical prescriptive rhetoric has become an indispensable instrument in the historical and critical analysis of literature in theory and practice.

W.V.

RHETORISCHE FIGUR (figure of speech) = Gedankenfigur, = Redefigur, = Sinnfigur

Arrangement of language contrived for a particular rhetorical effect, which adheres to recognizable models; e.g.: → PARS PRO TOTO, → PLEONASMUS etc.

RHYTHMUS (rhythm) = Sprachrhythmus

Recurring movement (beat) in spoken language, determined by various relations of accented and unaccented or long and short syllables. Rhythm has a natural basis in the word and sentence stress of a language. For instance, words in Germanic languages (e.g. German, English) have their stress on the first or root syllables, while key content words are stressed within a sentence. In poetry, the metrical structures (→ METRIK) are based largely on the natural rhythm of the language used. However, there will sometimes be a deviation from this for stylistic reasons. The rhythm of a text will sometimes imitate heart beat, the billowing of waves, the galloping of a horse, and other natural processes. → FREIE RHYTHMEN.

M.C.

RITTERDICHTUNG → HÖFISCHE DICHTUNG

RITTERSPIEGEL → SPIEGEL

ROBINSONADE

Form of → ABENTEUERROMAN, which took its name from Defoe's *Robinson Crusoe* (1719), although some examples date from the M.A. Predominant themes are exile and isolation on an uninhabited island, and the hero's adventures during his struggle for survival.

ROKOKO (Rococo)

Style which developed from the Baroque (→ BAROCK) and flourished in Europe in the 18th century. It is light, lively, sometimes frivolous and reflects the values of the Enlightenment; i.e. in contrast to the Baroque and its metaphysical strivings it turns to the realms of earthly existence. *Rokoko* is the form of art cherished by the 18th century lower nobility and middle class. It is perfectly balanced, harmonious and playful. Ornamentations and decorations in architecture, furniture and painting lose their voluminous appearance typical of the Baroque and become rather delicate instead. As happened in the case of Baroque the term *Rokoko* was eventually transferred from architecture and sculpture to the art forms of literature and music (e.g. Mozart). Anacreontic poetry (→ ANAKREONTIK) with its themes of wine and love, its dallying, frivolous atmosphere within the framework of a delightful nature scenery is a most popular literary art form of 18th century society. The reader does not expect a true expression and reflection of nature, indeed he is enjoying the refinement and delicacy of an artificial setting. Anacreontic poetry originates in 16th century France continuing in an unbroken line to the 18th century with the 'poésie fugitive' of Piron (1689–1773) and Gresset (1709–1777). It was taken up in England e.g. Prior (1664–1721), Waller (1606–1687), Gay (1685–1732) and in Germany e.g. Gleim (1719–1803), Uz (1720–1796), Götz (1721–1781). A favoured short form of epic poetry is the fable e.g. Gellert (1715–1769), Hagedorn (1708–1754). Wieland proves himself a master of larger epic works (*Oberon*, 1780), while Beaumarchais with his *Mariage de Figaro* (1785) and Lessing with *Minna von Barnhelm* (1767) produce outstanding examples of comedy. Common to all these art forms are clarity and transparency of expression and an optimistic belief in the values of an enlightened society.

V.K.

ROLLE (role)

Though it is common to speak of roles in a drama as major (*Hauptrolle*) or supporting (*Nebenrolle*) — a practice satirized by Shakespeare in his presentation of the mechanicals in *A Midsummer Night's Dream* — it is well to remember the maxim that there are no small parts, only small actors. The actor's role includes not only the words assigned him by the author but also such details as physical traits, attitude of other characters, past as well as present behaviour. Some theorists of the drama (Brecht) emphasize the need to distinguish between role and performer; others (Stanislavski and the American adherents of the Method) stress the need for the performer to draw on his inner life and experiences to fill out the role. Casting actors in roles suited to their personalities is normal practice in the performance media (deriving from the former practice of employing specific physical types for specific repertoire roles → SOUBRETTE, character actor, romantic lead, etc.), but equally common and often more rewarding is the idea of casting against type.

M.M.

ROLLENGEDICHT

Lyric poem written in the form of a first-person monologue, in which a person who is usually named in the title expresses feelings and ideas, which are not necessarily those of the poet.

ROLLENSPIEL (role-playing)

Term taken over from the theatre, where it referred to the dramaturgical device of theatrical self-consciousness, and taken up by sociologists (in U.S.A. Ralph Linton, *The Study of Man*, 1936 and in Germany, Ralf Dahrendorf, *Homo sociologicus*, 1958) to denote a mode of behaviour expected of any individual occupying a certain position or belonging to a certain group. The role is thus normally determined by forces beyond the individual, when for example society forms a stereotyped image (→ BILDNIS) of an individual. The role may be determined by social pressures, political systems or by the demands of individual relationships. Awareness by the individual of the *Bildnis* may lead to the conscious or unconscious adoption of the role associated with it. Role-playing is sometimes seen as fundamental to the human condition. Max Frisch (1911–) maintains "everyone who expresses himself is playing a role", and shows in *Andorra* (1961) how a *Bildnis* may compel an individual to play the associated role. Some definitions of role-playing are so all-embracing that almost all social behaviour could be described as role-playing. The role then becomes very similar to C.G. Jung's (1875–1961) concept of the 'persona': "the role which a person plays; the mask he puts on not only for others but for himself". Role-playing is seen by some as a negation of individual freedom, in that the demands of the role may deny all possibility of spontaneity; but role-playing may also be seen as a new kind of freedom, in that the individual may choose to experiment with different roles (as in Max Frisch, *Mein Name sei Gantenbein*, 1964). The sociological interest in role-playing was taken up by writers, who made it a dominant theme in their work (the dramas and novels of Max Frisch; Grass, *Die Blechtrommel*, 1959; Johnson, *Das dritte Buch über Achim*, 1961; Böll, *Ansichten eines Clowns*, 1963; Peter Härtling, *Niembsch*, 1964, etc.). For the student of literature it is the conscious act of role-playing, when the character is aware of the role, which is of most interest, as this is the more favoured theme in modern literature. Conscious role-playing is usually made explicit in the work of literature (e.g. *Mein Name sei Gantenbein*), but the concept of *Rollenspiel* can be fruitfully applied to assist interpretation in works where role-playing is not explicitly shown to be a conscious activity of a character (e.g. *Das dritte Buch über Achim*).

E.W.H.

ROMAN (novel)

Neither the German nor the English term has proved capable of close definition. Whereas *novel* (like the German → NOVELLE) is derived from Latin *novus*, the German *Roman* was originally used in 12th century France to denote any work written in the native language (lingua romana) as opposed to Latin (lingua latina). Later it was used only of works in prose, and in this sense it was taken over in German in the 17th century. The impossibility of defining the term *novel* or *Roman* is well illustrated by E.M. Forster's resigned attempt: "any fictitious prose work over 50,000 words. . ." (*Aspects of the Novel*, 1927) and Thomas Mann's ironic: "Ein Roman ist, was der Romanschreiber schreibt". Failing a definition, attempts have been made (a) to distinguish the novel from other literary forms, such as the epic and the *Novelle*, and (b) to draw up typologies or subcategories of the novel. As regards (a) the distinction between novel and *Novelle* presents few difficulties if one starts from the essential characteristics of the *Novelle*. The distinction between novel and epic has been best described by Wolfgang Kayser: "Narration of the total world (in an elevated style) was called an epic; narration of the private world in a private style is called a novel." (*Das sprachliche Kunstwerk*, 1948). The emphasis on the individual and the private in the novel is a necessary consequence of the loss of faith in the concept of a harmonious world. As regards typologies, the most unhelpful is that which purports to classify novels according to theme, e.g. *Abenteuer—, Bauern—, Künstler—, Ritter—* und *Räuberroman* etc. Such classifications tell us little and are in the case of many novels quite inapplicable. Establishment of subcategories of the → ZEITROMAN have been somewhat more helpful, i.e. utopian novel, historical novel, novel of city life etc. The most prevalent type-classification in the history and theory of the German novel, and the most characteristic for the German tradition, is that which includes the → ENTWICKLUNGS— and the → BILDUNGSROMAN. Recent scholarship has been more concerned with typologies based not on theme but on form, e.g. narrative perspective, type of narration etc. →EPOS.

E.W.H.

ROMAN A CLEF → SCHLÜSSELROMAN

ROMANTIK

In English the term *romantick* was first used in 1650 to refer to *romances*, originally Provençal verse or prose narratives in the *Romanic* vernacular. The English *romantic* and German *romantisch* became popular in the 18th century as adjectives meaning 'as in romances', i.e. adventurous, fantastic, sentimental. Popular usage has retained this typological meaning up to the present day.

Romantisch also assumed a historical meaning, denoting the age of *romances*, especially the M.A., but generally also modern Christian tradition in contrast to classical antiquity. August Wilhelm Schlegel's *Vorlesungen über schöne Literatur und Kunst* (1801—1804) contained the first comprehensive history of this romantic tradition which includes med. literature as well as the works of Dante, Petrarch, Ariosto, Tasso, Boccaccio, Cervantes, Shakespeare, Calderon and Goethe (translation of Shakespeare by August Wilhelm Schlegel 1797 ff., Cervantes by Tieck 1799 ff., Ariosto and Calderon by Gries 1801 ff.) *Romantik* and *Romantiker* were first used in the writings of Friedrich von

Hardenberg (Novalis) between 1798 and 1800. The terms related to a philosophical and aesthetic interpretation of *romantisch*, which supplemented the historical meaning, and gave *romantisch* futuristic and utopian qualities. In Friedrich Schlegel's definition (1798) literature as *romantische Poesie* was to become a 'progressive universal' art with a political and religious mission: it was supposed to penetrate life and establish peace as well as social harmony.

Romantik is now commonly applied to those German writers and artists whose creative work began after 1789 but not later than 1815, i.e. between the French Revolution and the end of the Napoleonic Wars (Jean Paul, Hölderlin, Novalis, Friedrich Schlegel, Tieck, Brentano, Fouqué, Kleist, Eichendorff etc.). In German literature, however, there has never been a *romantische Schule* with common aims, purposes and aesthetic principles (→ FRÜHROMANTIK, → HEIDELBERGER ROMANTIK). Concepts of *Romantik* in other European literatures often differ considerably from the various German concepts subsumed under this term.

G.S.

ROMANTISCHE IRONIE (romantic irony)

Term coined by Friedrich Schlegel (1772–1829) and his circle of early Romantic theorists and writers to designate the author's self-conscious intrusion into his work in order to expose its status as artifice and fiction. Schlegel regarded this highly ambivalent form of irony – everything may be ironized, including the ironist – as a feature of all great literature and predicted that in modern (i.e. post-Romantic) literature it would be a key ingredient. Romantic irony breaks artistic illusion, revealing the author's manipulative hand at work e.g. Laurence Sterne in *Tristram Shandy* (1760–1767). On the philosophical level, the Romantic ironist ironically notes the limitations of existence, of the universe, and of himself, but paradoxically rises above them in his art.

In modern German literature, Thomas Mann (1875–1955) is perhaps the author whose work most brilliantly and consistently makes use of Romantic irony (including self-irony).

The term was not much used in English until recently. → IRONIE.

P.T.

ROMANZE

Form of epic poetry which originated in 15th century Spain, which mainly portrayed popular heroes and their gallant and chivalric exploits. The *Romanze* was introduced into Germany in 1756 and became a popular genre with the Romantics. However, early exponents such as Goethe (1749–1832), Schiller (1759–1805) and Bürger (1747–1794) never clearly distinguished it from the → BALLADE so that the two terms became interchangeable.

ROTATIONSDRUCK (rotary press printing)

RÜCKBLENDE (flashback)

Scene inserted into a play, film or novel, presenting a time sequence of events which have occurred in the past.

RÜHRENDER REIM

Occurs when both the vowel sounds and the preceding consonants of the rhyming words are identical. → REINER REIM.

RÜHRENDES LUSTSPIEL → RÜHRSTÜCK, → WEINERLICHES LUSTSPIEL

RÜHRSTÜCK (sentimental play)

Type of → BÜRGERLICHES TRAUERSPIEL prevalent during the → AUF-KLÄRUNG which is sometimes confused with → RÜHRENDES LUSTSPIEL.

The *Rührstück* is basically a tragedy but is modified in such a way that through a display of sometimes incredible and excessive virtues on the part of the protagonist the tragic conflict is avoided and in the end the villain receives mild punishment while the virtuous are generously rewarded. This type of play was designed to move the audience to tears (hence its name) and was very popular during the latter half of the 18th century. Exponents of this genre in Germany were Kotzebue (1761–1819) and Iffland (1759–1814).

A.O.

RUNEN (runes)

Letters or characters of the earliest Teutonic alphabet, formed from the Greek and Roman alphabet, but modified to facilitate carving in wood or stone.

SACHBUCH

In a general sense, any book which contains factual information; but more specifically, a work which popularizes scientific knowledge. → FACHBUCH.

SACHLICHKEIT, NEUE → NEUE SACHLICHKEIT

SACHWÖRTERBUCH → REALLEXIKON

SÄMTLICHE WERKE → GESAMTAUSGABE

SÄNGER

1. Minstrel or troubadour who sang or recited epic and lyric poetry in the M.A.
2. Term used by Brecht (1898–1956) to designate the narrator in epic theatre. → EPISCHES THEATER.

SAGA (saga)

Med. Icelandic or Norse prose narrative, relating heroic events, or chronicling a family's history.

SAGE

Short prose narrative which contains a germ of truth, but as part of an oral tradition has become embroidered and enlarged. Like the → MÄRCHEN, the *Sage* frequently relates supernatural occurrences, but differs from the *Märchen* in that the *Sage* is intended to be believed. The *Sage* is usually localized, e.g. vampire tales, and often cites dates and historical figures and events. → EINFACHE FORMEN.

SALON (salon)

Social and intellectual gathering held in a private house. → PREZIOSITÄT.

SAMMELBAND (anthology)

Book which consists of a collection of works by various authors.

SAMMELHANDSCHRIFT → LIEDERHANDSCHRIFT

SATIRE (satire)

The exposure to ridicule and/or condemnation of specific or general vices, abuses or stupidity.

As with English 'satire', the German term may express a range of intensity of attack, from the amused derision of a Horace (65–8 B.C.) to the savage denunciation of a Juvenal (c.60–127), a Swift (1667–1745) or a Karl Kraus (1874–1936). Satire is distinguished from the merely comic by its critical, unmasking or derisive nature, and from mere denunciation or invective by its comic element, in the form of the ridiculous. The butt of a satire is thus simultaneously ludicrous and contemptible, though the emphasis may vary.

German writers on satire tend to play down the enjoyment of satire (by the satirist and the reader) more than their Anglo-Saxon counterparts and highlight satire's moral and didactic function. Satirists are seen either as playful humourists who gently mock men's foibles (the Horatian kind) or as outraged moralists who bitterly attack men's viciousness (the Juvenalian kind). This corresponds to Schiller's influential distinction (*Über naive und sentimentalische Dichtung*, 1795; → NAIV UND SENTIMENTALISCH) between *scherzhafte Satire* and *strafende Satire*.

P.T.

SATYRSPIEL (satyric drama)

Burlesque play with a chorus of satyrs, which formed part of the Greek → TETRALOGIE.

SATZAKZENT → AKZENT

SATZGEFÜGE → HYPOTAXE

SATZLEHRE → SYNTAX

SATZSPIEGEL

Size of the printed surface of a page.

SATZZEICHEN (punctuation mark) → INTERPUNKTION

SCARAMUZ (Scaramouche)

Stock character from the → COMMEDIA DELL'ARTE. A braggart, usually dressed in black, who replaced the earlier *Capitano*.

SCENARIO (scenario)

Outline or sketch of a drama, providing details of the scenes, characters, and setting.

SCHACHTELUNG → HYPOTAXE

SCHÄFERDICHTUNG → HIRTENDICHTUNG

SCHÄFERROMAN → HIRTENDICHTUNG

SCHÄFERSPIEL → HIRTENDICHTUNG

SCHALLANALYSE (sound analysis)

The investigation of the sounds and resonance of speech. This method of analysis was developed by Eduard Sievers in the 1920s. He posited that there is only one way of rendering vocally the sound and rhythm of a text, and developed the idea that all people can be divided into a small number of voice-types which remain a personal constant. He applied this technique to textual criticism in order to ascertain the authenticity of certain works, e.g. the Bible, Shakespeare etc. His method never attracted a wide following because few scholars were equipped with his extraordinary sensitivity to sound.

SCHALLNACHAHMUNG → ONOMATOPOESIE

SCHALTSATZ → PARENTHESE

SCHATTENSPIEL (shadow play)

Play in which the characters or puppets act behind a screen and thus appear as shadows to the audience.

SCHAUERROMAN (Gothic novel)

Type of fiction popular in the early 19th century, which was characterized by an atmosphere of gloom and mystery. The setting is often a deserted castle where macabre and melodramatic events occur, intended both to excite and horrify the reader.

SCHAUSPIEL

1. General term denoting any kind of play.
2. A serious play, structurally close to tragedy, in which the catastrophe is averted by a timely discovery by the hero; e.g.: Goethe, *Iphigenie* (1787).

SCHAUSPIELER (actor)

SCHAUSPIELFÜHRER (companion to the theatre)

Book listing the plots of better known plays.

SCHAUSPIELKUNST (dramatic art; dramaturgy)

SCHELMENROMAN (picaresque novel) = novela picaresca, = pikaresker Roman, = pikarischer Roman

Originated in Spain in the second half of the 16th century (anon., *Lazarillo de Tormes*, 1554; Alemán, *Vida del Picaro Guzmán de Alfarache*, 1599; Cervantes, *Novelas ejemplares*, 1613) and which reached Germany in translation early in the 17th century. The *picaro* is an outsider figure, part swindler and trickster, part scamp and scallywag. Usually of obscure or lowly birth, he sees society from below and through a variety of experiences in a multiplicity of localities, characters and episodes. As the function of the picaresque hero is the satirical exposure of society, his individual development is not of paramount concern (unlike the hero of the → BILDUNGSROMAN). His cleverness (Felix Krull) can often be hidden behind a real or assumed naivety (Schweik, Don Camillo). The structure of the novel, based on a sequence of episodes, shows that it is a form of adventure novel, but with a social-critical purpose. The picaresque novel may contain elements of the pastoral novel and of the romance of chivalry (→ ROMANZE), but is distinguished from these by the perspective – the picaresque hero is not Don Quixote but Sancho Panza! – and by the element of social criticism.

E.W.H.

SCHERZSPIEL

Baroque term for comedy.

SCHICKSALSTRAGÖDIE (fate tragedy)

Schicksalstragödie occurs as a literary phenomenon in the latter half of the 18th century and the first three decades of the 19th: from then on, its interest is purely historical. The 18th century's attempts to redefine the spirit and effects of Greek tragedy, notably Lessing's, drew new attention to the question of man's relationship to the gods, to time, causality and fate; Lessing in particular stresses man's freedom and responsibility, which is part of his general concern with character and individuality in drama. Thus the century's two most important renewals of the spirit of classical tragedy, Goethe's *Iphigenie auf Tauris* (1787) and Schiller's *Die Braut von Messina* (1803), underline' man's right of determination and decision, in the face of inscrutable 'divine' forces. There is another strand in the same period, however, which is more concerned with the links between chance or fate and the unwitting commission of crime. From a few tentative beginnings, such as the Englishman Lillo's *The Fatal Curiosity* (1736) to Karl Philipp Moritz's *Blunt* (1781) or the young Tieck's *Karl von Berneck* (1793), the mode attains great popularity up to the 1820s. Yet here, too, we can distinguish two sides: plays urgently concerned with man's seeming impotence in the face of circumstances, events, coincidences or fatal requisites, and his search for moral freedom and responsibility: Kleist's first play *Die Familie Schroffenstein* (1803), might be mentioned here, but above all Zacharias Werner's *Der 24. Februar* (1815) in its explicit attempt to raise man to full dignity above any fatality or curse placed on him by inexplicable forces. Other practitioners of the mode were, however, more conscious of its capacities for theatrical entertainment (Müllner, 1774–1829, Houwald, 1778–1845); Grillparzer's play, *Die Ahnfrau* (1817), does not escape the same charge, and this play is the last serious attempt by a major author to use the mode, amidst widespread criticism of what already seemed a debased form.

R.C.P.

SCHIMPFSPIEL

16th century type of farce, which was strongly influenced by the Dutch farces and the → COMMEDIA DELL'ARTE. The characters were usually lower or middle class figures who were frequently the butt of the jokes. Examples of the *Schimpfspiel* can be found in the → FASTNACHTSPIELE of Hans Sachs (1494–1576) and in the comedies of Gryphius (1616–1664).

SCHLAGER

Popular song or tune; (film, theatre, book) smash hit, box-office success.

SCHLAGREIM

Type of rhyme in which the rhyming words follow each other in the same line. → REIM.

SCHLAGWORT

1. Catchword, slogan; commonly used word or phrase.

2. Caption citing the contents of a book; e.g.: *Schlagwortkatalog* in a library.

3. Entry in a dictionary, lexicon etc. = Stichwort.

SCHLÜSSELROMAN (roman à clef) = Roman à clef

Novel which features actual people under fictitious names, and historically authentic events, which the reader is expected to identify.

SCHLÜSSELWÖRTER

Words which are invested with a particular allegorical significance by an author, so that they simultaneously convey the allegorical as well as their normal meaning.

SCHMÄHSCHRIFT

Writing which attacks a literary or political opponent in a highly subjective and personal manner.

SCHMIERE

Contemptuous term for an artistically inferior theatre group.

SCHMÖKER

Old book, esp. light fiction of little literary value.

SCHMUTZLITERATUR → SCHUNDLITERATUR

SCHNADAHÜPFL = Gstanzl

Bavarian or Austrian song, often humorous and gently satirical, with four-line verses in three-four time.

SCHNITT → ZÄSUR

SCHNULZE

A popular song (→ SCHLAGER) which relies on excessive sentimentality.

SCHÖNE LITERATUR → BELLETRISTIK

SCHÖPFUNGSMYTHEN (myths of creation) = Ursprungsmythen

These appear in almost all cultures as mythical representations of the creation of the world, men and gods. The usual pattern is akin to the biblical account of creation by a pre-existing creator from pre-existing chaos, but also widespread is the anthropomorphic myth of the separation of the Sky Father and the Earth Mother. → MYTHOS.

E.W.H.

SCHRIFTLEITER → REDAKTEUR

SCHRIFTSPRACHE (written or literary language) = Literatursprache → UM-GANGSSPRACHE

SCHRIFTSTELLER (writer, author, esp. of prose)

SCHRIFTTUM → LITERATUR

SCHULDRAMA = Humanistendrama

Developed in the schools and universities during the 16th century, with the aim of improving students' command of Latin and their skills of rhetoric. The texts used were either dramatizations of biblical stories or Roman comedies, chiefly those of Terence (c.195–159 B.C.), although later Greek dramas were also performed. The *Schuldrama* was unquestionably the most important form of theatre in Renaissance Germany. Performances were not restricted to pupils and teachers but open to all citizens who were thus exposed to a more serious form of drama than that offered by the → FASTNACHTSPIELE. The *Schuldrama* was an important purveyor of humanistic ideas of the → RENAISSANCE and in the sphere of dramaturgy it reintroduced the unities of Classical Greek drama on a neutral stage → SUKZESSIVBÜHNE. *Schuldrama* was an integral part of the Protestant and Catholic (→ JESUITENDICHTUNG) education systems.

Because of its popularity the plays became less esoteric and Latin was increasingly blended with German, to the extent that even the popular → KNITTELVERS was utilized. However, by the end of the 17th century *Schuldrama* could no longer compete with the travelling professional theatre groups and the newly established court theatres and gradually declined in importance.

SCHUNDLITERATUR = Schmutzliteratur

Highly contemptuous term for literature of no artistic value. → TRIVIALLITERATUR.

SCHUTZFRIST (term of copyright)

Period during which a literary work may only be published with the consent of the copyright holder(s).

SCHUTZUMSCHLAG (book jacket)

Detachable paper cover which protects the binding of a book.

SCHWANK

1. Lighthearted dramatic piece of little aesthetic merit which aims at entertaining its audience in a cheerful manner. It avoids all problems and criticism and does not develop characters. It neither mocks nor satirizes its subject-matter but strings events and stereotyped figures loosely together.

2. Short narrative in prose or verse about a peculiar idea or event either for a didactic purpose or for mere entertainment. When performing the latter function *Schwank* frequently employs crude and even obscene language.

A.O.

SCHWARTE

Originally a book bound in pigskin, now a pejorative term for an old and fairly large book.

SCHWEIFREIM = Zwischenreim

Rhyme scheme frequently used in the six-line stanza: aabccd. . . .

SCHWULST

Slightly pejorative term for the elaborate and metaphorical style of the Baroque, which now appears artificial and pretentious. Recent scholarship, however, has attempted to rehabilitate the term by seeing *Schwulst* as the authentic expression of the particular spirit of the time as it was manifest throughout Europe. *Gongorismus* and *Kultismus* are examples of *Schwulst* in Spain, *Marinismus* in Italy, *Euphuismus* in England, and → PREZIOSITÄT in France.

SEKUNDÄRLITERATUR (secondary literature)

Critical works about literature. → PRIMÄRLITERATUR.

SEKUNDENSTIL

Naturalistic technique, in which, in order to give an impression of reality, the writer attempts to reproduce the actual time-span of minute noises, movements, etc., by describing them in explicit detail.

SELBSTBEKENNTNISSE → BEKENNTNIS

SELBSTVERLAG

Publication by an author of his own work, at his own expense.

SEMANTIK (semantics) = Bedeutungslehre

The study of meaning in language, i.e. the relationship between words and the real world and the system underlying the words we use. Semanticists aim ultimately to be able to make statements about language which will be applicable to all natural languages.

One may distinguish between lexical semantics and sentence semantics. Lexical, or word semantics looks at the meaning of individual words and their functions. The most obvious of these is denotation — words refer to features of the world about us (referents) and in the process classify our environment: compare boy, girl, tree *vs.* man, woman, bush. The lexical semanticist is interested in discovering the features languages use to distinguish meaning. One form of such analysis is 'componential analysis', which uses features such as ± animate, ± human, ± adult etc. By this means the words of a semantic field may be systematically compared, and concepts such as synonymy and antonymy explained. But not all meaning is denotative: words such as 'if', 'when', 'the' have quite different functions which become apparent only in the context of a sentence. Sentence semantics investigates the meaning which arises from the grammatical interaction between the words of a sentence. At this level the study of meaning is inseparable from the study of syntax. The verb 'give' presupposes a giver, a recipient and a gift, so that the syntactic structure of the sentence must provide for the inclusion of all these participants. Linguists have as yet not solved the 'chicken or the egg' question of whether abstract syntactic structures are later filled with meaning or whether the inherent meaning of a word such as a verb determines the syntactic structure.

But meaning is conveyed by other means too, e.g. the contextual factors associated with an utterance, such as intonation, gesture and intention, e.g. "You had better finish that work today (!)" While retaining the same words and syntax the sentence could, by change of intonation, be made to express advice, or a threat.

A.F.G.

SENDBRIEF

Publication in the form of a letter; e.g. Luther's *Ein Sendbrieff von dem harten büchlin widder die bauren* (1525).

SENKUNG

Unstressed or short syllable of a metrical foot. →METRIK.

SENTIMENTALISCH →NAIV UND SENTIMENTALISCH

SENTIMENTALISMUS →EMPFINDSAMKEIT

SEPARATUM →SONDERDRUCK

SHAKESPEAREBÜHNE (Elizabethan stage) = Dreifelderbühne

The stage of the Elizabethan playhouse consisted of three acting areas. The largest and most important of these was the forestage which projected into the audience area, so that the audience was able to view the action from three sides. Behind the forestage was the inner stage, which provided the two main entrances and was sometimes fitted with a decorative curtain. Above this inner stage was the upper stage, which resembled a balcony, and seated spectators and musicians. The multiple acting areas of the *Shakespearebühne* facilitated rapid scene changes which did not interrupt the action of the play being performed. This form of stage was introduced to Germany by the English travelling theatre groups. →ENGLISCHE KOMÖDIANTEN.

A.O.

SIEBEN FREIE KÜNSTE →ARTES LIBERALES

SIGNATUR

1. Signature, autograph.
2. Classification of a library book.
3. Map symbol.

SIGNET → DRUCKERZEICHEN

SILBENLÄNGE → QUANTITÄT

SILBENMASS

The 'quantity' (duration of pronunciation) of a syllable, which establishes the metre in → QUANTITIERENDE DICHTUNG; now also incorrectly applied to → AKZENTUIERENDE DICHTUNG.

SILBENSCHRIFT (syllabary)

Script in which each character represents a syllable; e.g.: the Japanese Kana syllabaries. → BILDERSCHRIFT, → LAUTSCHRIFT.

SILBENZÄHLUNG

The principle of Romance language poetry which counts syllables rather than stresses. Although it has been used in German poetry this form of scansion is not suited to the rhythm of German.

SIMPLIZIADE

Type of novel which developed from the *Abenteuerroman* and → SCHEL-MENROMAN. The classic hero is a simple ingenuous fellow who undergoes a series of adventures.

SIMULTANBÜHNE

Med. stage form, so called because the actors, even when not participating in the drama, and the sets necessary for the various scenes, remained on stage throughout the performance. The term is now also applied to a stage where different actions which take place at different locations simultaneously, are clearly visible to the audience; e.g.: upstairs and downstairs rooms.

SIMULTANTECHNIK

Literary device: the simultaneous presentation of events which occur at different locations and are not necessarily related to the main plot, in an attempt to achieve an approximation of reality, which is experienced as a heterogeneous phenomenon.

SINGSCHULE → MEISTERSANG

SINGSPIEL

Type of *opera buffa*, a less rigid and serious form of opera which replaced the opera seria. In the *Singspiel*, the singing is interspersed with dialogue, with the emphasis on the latter.

SINNBILD → EMBLEM

SINNFIGUR → RHETORISCHE FIGUR

SINNGEDICHT → EPIGRAMM

SITTENKOMÖDIE → SITTENSTÜCK

SITTENSTÜCK (comedy of manners) = Sittenkomödie

Comedy which attacks human follies and social idiosyncrasies in a polished, witty and detached manner. The *Sittenstück* is a mild form of social criticism and is appreciated by sophisticated audiences who enjoy the intellectual brilliance of the dialogue. → KONVERSATIONSSTÜCK, → POSSE.

SITUATIONSKOMIK

Comic effect derived from the situations in which the characters find themselves, as opposed to → CHARAKTERKOMIK.

SKALDE (scald)

Ancient Scandinavian poet and singer, who was employed by kings and princes in the Viking period.

SKIZZE (sketch)

In a simple sense, the term *Skizze* is used to refer to a short fragmentary work which has the appearance of being a draft for an undertaking later to be completed with greater detail and polish. The *Skizze* can be a short dramatic work, as is often the case in English literature, but is often found in German literature in the. form of the prose sketch — a compact piece of largely un-structured prose. The impression of fragmentary incompleteness is essential to this form and it is this which sets it apart from the short story (→ KURZGE-SCHICHTE), while a comparative lack of lyrical elements allows its differen-tiation from the prose poem (→ PROSAGEDICHT). Since it is easier to describe the prose sketch in terms of what it is *not*, it is perhaps not surprising that it has tended to become a collective description for sundry short, otherwise unidentified prose forms.

G.B.

SMERALDINA

Alternative name for →COLOMBINA.

SOFFITTE (ceiling-piece)

The part of the scenery which hangs down to seal off the tops of the flats, usually painted to represent the sky or ceiling.

SOLÖZISMUS (solecism)

Conspicuous error in grammar or syntax.

SONDERDRUCK (offprint) = Separatum

A separate copy of an article in a periodical or in a collection of essays for the use of the author.

SONETT (sonnet)

The sonnet is distinguished by the musical effect of the perfectly balanced structure and rhyme patterns. The one integral stanza is made up of fourteen lines, usually iambic pentameters, which are divided into two parts: the eight line octave (→ AUFGESANG) and the six line sestet (→ ABGESANG), each of which is further divided, the octave into two quatrains (→ QUARTETT) with a parallel rhyme scheme abba, abba, and the sestet into two tercets or triplets (→ TERZETT, → TERZINE) with variable rhyme patterns (e.g. cdc cdc or cde cde etc.). The formal disposition of the whole, which is communicated not only by the rhyme scheme but also by the break or caesura between the two main parts and between the division within the parts, predetermines the disposition of content. Within the bipartite structure, which provides an overall framework for the exposition in the octave and the resolution in the sestet, the movement between the defined stages of development can be either of a progressive or of an antithetic nature, i.e.: either the initial expression of feelings or ideas is carried through a process of refinement and clarification to the decisive and frequently epigrammatic conclusion, or the argument is developed on antithetic or dialectic principles. In either case, the economy and precision in the use of language, required by the brevity and structural precision of the form, make the sonnet one of the most concentrated and articulate forms of poetic expression. The sonnet form, thought to have originated in the 13th century in Sicily from the combination of two strambottos (a popular form of folk-poetry), was perfected by the Italian poet Petrarch (1304–1374). It appeared in Germany at the time of Weckherlin (1584–1653), but made its first real impact during the Baroque e.g. Gryphius (1616–1664), Fleming (1609–1640), mainly because of its antithetic possibilities, which the Baroque poets enhanced by introducing the use of the → DISTICHON and the alexandrine (→ ALEXANDRINER). The form suffered from overpopularization and was ignored by the Enlightenment, but flourished once more in the 19th century, e.g. August Wilhelm Schlegel (1767–1845), Eichendorff (1788–1857), Uhland (1787–1862), etc., and again in the 20th century, e.g. George (1868–1933), Rilke (1875–1926), Heym (1887–1912), Johannes R. Becher (1891–1958) among others.

P.L.

SONG

Differing from its usage in English, where it denotes any vocal setting of a poetic text with or without accompaniment, the term *Song* in German is applied only to satirical-critical didactic lyrical poetry set to music. The *Song* introduced into the German-speaking world after World War I, incorporates elements of older forms, → CHANSON and street-ballad (→ BALLADE), and applies them to a modern situation.

In keeping with the didactic intention of the *Song*, its text and music are of an extreme simplicity. The text often makes a particular point, whether moral e.g. Brecht, *Vom armen B.B.* (1922), or political e.g. Biermann, *Großes Gebet der alten Kommunistin Oma Meume* (1970), deliberately accentuating it by formal means such as alliteration or refrain. In accordance with its origin, the musical accompaniment of the *Song* frequently includes elements of jazz. Its vocal presentation is non-melodious and harsh; singsong intonation is common. Theatrical gestures underline the intended message. A special development of the *Song* in the second half of the 20th century is the *Protestsong* which takes up a particular social issue in a consciously provocative way as a means of expressing peaceful resistance (Degenhardt, 1931–; Süverkrüp, 1934–; Biermann 1936–). → BÄNKELSANG.

E.K.

SORTIMENT (retail book trade)

SOUBRETTE

Comic figure, portrayed as a mischievous and scheming maid-servant.

SOUFFLEUR, SOUFFLEUSE (prompter)

SOZIALISTISCHER REALISMUS (Socialist Realism)

Defined officially by Andrej Zhdanov at the 1st Congress of the Soviet Writers' Union in 1934 as "the true-to-life representation of reality in its revolutionary development". This definition arose out of Soviet debates on aesthetic theory, and represents the rejection of → FORMALISMUS and all attempts to establish specifically proletarian art forms in the early post-revolutionary ferment. Whilst purporting to reject Naturalism, Socialist Realism's demand for verisimilitude made a naturalistic style of realism inevitable. This became most obvious in the Bitterfeld movement (→ BITTERFELDER WEG) when workers berated professional writers for lack of accuracy in their portrayal of production processes. Realism of detail stands in contrast on the other hand to the call for an *optimistic perspective* (→ PERSPEKTIVE). This contradiction was cemented by the rejection of experimental forms such as montage (→ MONTAGE) in favour of 19th century bourgeois realist forms − epic totality and a hero worthy of emulation (→ POSITIVER HELD). Nor was the breadth and slow pace of the novel as suited to the avowed didactic purpose of Socialist Realism as → AGIT-PROP, → REPORTAGE and other forms rejected as constituting part of the so-called → PROLETKULT. In more recent years, the recognition that predictable resolution of conflict and a foreseeable rosy future could alienate the reader has led to the demands of Socialist Realism becoming vaguer, less explicit, with emphasis on the multiplicity of forms it can encompass. Within a general commitment to the society of the GDR for example, writers are no longer required to depict a panorama of a society in transition, but can and are portraying individuals involved in the problems and conflicts of everyday life, in other words the operation of social relations at the personal level.

B.E.

SPANNUNG (suspense)

While the state of suspense is an essential element in all fiction, it assumes major significance for the drama. Pütz (*Die Zeit im Drama. Zur Technik dramatischer Spannung*, 1970) follows Staiger's lead in seeing suspense as the essence of the dramatic, but provides a more differentiated analysis, following Eric Bentley's view that it is "not merely ignorance as to what will happen next, but an active desire to know it. . . aroused by a previous stimulus." This is to be distinguished from mere surprise and in fact exerts its strongest influence when the spectator knows, or at least suspects, the outcome. Thus the dramatic action consists of the actualization by gradual stages of foreshadowed future events and of past moments reconstructed in the present. The sequential framework is built round devices such as indications of time, change of locale, exchanges between characters, entrances and exits. Within this, suspense-stimuli, such as prophecies, curses, dramatic irony (→ IRONIE), intrigues and asides, function as foreshadowing elements; while recollection, homecomings, exposition, recurring characters and situations function as flashbacks. Both affect the immediate lives of the characters in the play in ways which sustain the audience's interest in the 'what' of the events, but more importantly in the 'how, when and where' of their dramatic resolution.

M.M.

SPECULUM → SPIEGEL

SPELL

An old Germanic form of oral literature. It was a short narrative, which was recited before an incantation, relating previous exploits of the demons and spirits being appealed to.

N.B.: The English term 'spell' refers only to the incantation.

SPIEGEL = speculum

Didactic literary genre, which lays down rules and principles for behaviour. During the M.A. such pamphlets were known as → FÜRSTENSPIEGEL or *Ritterspiegel*, princely or knightly codes. The most famous example is Machiavelli's *II Principe* (1532).

SPIEL IM SPIEL (play within a play)

A device found in European drama from the 16th century onwards. The type of play in which it occurs is sometimes called *ein Rahmendrama* — a framework play. It appears in all kinds of drama — Shakespeare uses it in both *A Midsummer Night's Dream* and *Hamlet* — but it is found most frequently in comedy. The degree to which the *Spiel im Spiel* is integrated into the action of the whole play varies, as does its function; it can serve to destroy theatrical illusion, or to satirize dramatic conventions and the taste of the public, or to reinforce the dramatist's message. In German literature, the device occurs in its most extreme form in the comedies of Tieck (1773–1853), which are rooted in the Romantic concept of irony; at one point in *Die verkehrte Welt* four plays are in progress simultaneously on the stage. The best-known framework drama of a serious kind in the modern German theatre is Peter Weiss's *Die Verfolgung und Ermordung Jean Paul Marats* (1964), subtitled "performed by inmates of the Asylum of Charenton under the direction of the Marquis de Sade". →WELTTHEATER.

C.P.M.

SPIELLEITER (director) = Regisseur

SPIELLEUTE (minstrels) = Fahrende

Med. itinerant musicians or poets.

SPIELMANN singular form of → SPIELLEUTE

SPIELMANNSDICHTUNG

The major problem in defining this term lies in the uncertain connection between the → SPIELMANN and the literature often attributed to him. A number of anonymous med. epics, known as *Spielmannsepen*, which do not approach the standard of the major med. heroic epic poems, have been attributed to these minstrels. They are characterized by crude versification, frequent use of hyperbole and direct references to the audience. The subject-matter frequently reflected the interest in the crusades and the newly discovered Orient.

SPIELPLAN (repertoire)

Schedule of plays which a theatre intends to perform within a specific period.

SPONDEUS (spondee)

Metrical foot consisting of two stressed or long syllables ($\bar{x}\bar{x}$). → METRIK.

SPRACHE (language)

A system of signs among whose main functions are: a means of communication, a marker of national, ethnic, regional and/or social identification, and an instrument of cognitive development. Items are arranged in sentences through a set of rules called a grammar. There are universals of language, but each language has specific features which testify to the close relationship with culture and make a perfect translation impossible. All levels of language are of significance in literature — phonological (sound), lexical and semantic (words and meaning), grammatical, and pragmatic (communicative function) — for language is the raw material for literature. Of special importance are the rules for the cohesion of *discourse*, i.e. connected speech (including writing) beyond the sentence. *Sprache* is sometimes used to refer to a register, such as 'poetic language'. Deviations from syntactic or phonological rules or unusual collocations are frequently employed in literary texts as a stylistic device. Language is used by a writer to recreate feelings, thoughts or images. Some authors attempt to recreate or imitate language.

M.C.

SPRACHGESELLSCHAFTEN

Societies formed during the 16th and 17th centuries to promote the use of the mother tongue. Their activities included the standardization of the use of language and the establishment of poetical rules. → PURISMUS.

SPRACHKUNSTWERK → DICHTUNG

SPRACHLICHES BILD (image) = Bild

Stylistic device which utilizes intensified and frequently figurative language, thus evoking a multiplicity of connotations, in order to visualize abstract ideas and concepts.

SPRACHMELODIE

Inflexion, or musical quality inherent in spoken language, and esp. in poetry.

SPRACHRHYTHMUS →RHYTHMUS

SPRACHWISSENSCHAFT

The systematic study of all aspects of language incorporating →PHILOLO-GIE, → PHONETIK, → PHONOLOGIE, → MORPHOLOGIE, → SEMANTIK, etymology, grammar, etc., as well as the sociological, anthropological and philosophical investigation of human speech. As such *Sprachwissenschaft* could best be translated as linguistics, however the German term *Linguistik* refers to modern descriptive linguistics which deals with general theories of language.

SPRECHENDE NAMEN

Names, which by their sound or meaning, suggest the occupation or nature of the character they belong to; e.g.: *Mittler* in Goethe's *Die Wahlverwandtschaften* (1809), a character who always tries to act as mediator.

SPRECHSTÜCK

Term used by Peter Handke (1942–) for his stage texts, which are based on linguistic arrangement and contain no action.

SPRICHWORT (proverb)

Pithy saying which expresses a general truth or observation, and is frequently alliterative and rhyming. →APHORISMUS.

STAATSTHEATER

Theatre owned and financed by the state government. → BUNDESTHEA-TER, →HOFTHEATER, →LANDESTHEATER.

STAB

The alliterative syllable in a *Stabreim.* →ALLITERATION.

STABERL

Stock comic character in Viennese popular comedy. → VOLKSKOMÖDIE.

STABREIM →ALLITERATION

STADTTHEATER

Theatre owned and financed by a municipal authority.

STÄNDEKLAUSEL

Notion that only persons of noble birth and elevated rank qualify as tragic heroes while people from the lower and middle classes feature as comic figures. First formulated by Horace (65–8 B.C.), the *Ständeklausel* became a rule during the Renaissance and Baroque and was in force until the middle of the 18th century when it was made obsolete by the → BÜRGERLICHES TRAUER-SPIEL.

STAMMBUCH

Type of album in which friends are invited to write samples of poetry or intimate messages.

STASIMON (stasimon, stationary song)

In pre-Aeschylian tragedy the *Stasimon* was a song recital by the chorus between scenes with actors. Later it developed into a musical interlude which had no direct connection with the action and formed the first division into acts.

STATIONENSTÜCK

A play of the open form (→ OFFENE FORM). Instead of a strict act division leading to a linear build-up of dramatic tension, a *Stationenstück* presents a sequence of 'stations', i.e. scenes which are complete within themselves. This form of drama was a feature of med. theatre (→ MYSTERIENSPIE-LE, → PASSIONSSPIEL) and was reintroduced by the Expressionists, esp. Strindberg (1849–1912).

STATISCHES GEDICHT

1. → DADAISMUS used this term to refer to a poem created without the inner involvement of the author. Such a poem listed events, impressions and happenings simultaneously without evaluating or ranking them, thus expressing the absurdity of reality.

2. Gottfried Benn (1886–1956) used the term to designate his ideal of 'pure' poetry, mainly his own. Benn was campaigning against → TENDENZDICH-TUNG and aimed to revitalize art by postulating that art should take itself as subject-matter and from this experience he hoped that a new style would be developed.

STATIST → KOMPARSE

STEGREIF (extempore, impromptu) = Extempore

STEGREIFKOMÖDIE

Improvised comedy as in the →COMMEDIA DELL'ARTE.

STEIGENDE HANDLUNG (rising action)

The part of a dramatic plot in which the hero's fortunes rise; the part from the beginning of the action to the turning-point (→ WENDEPUNKT). → FALLENDE HANDLUNG.

STEIGERUNG →KLIMAX

STICHOMYTHIE (stichomythia)

Rapid exchange of dialogue between characters in a play, where each character speaks only one line at a time; a device to increase tension in dialogue.

STICHWORT

1. Cue: last word of a speech in a play, which an actor waits for as a signal to enter or begin his speech.

2. Entry in a dictionary, lexicon etc. = *Schlagwort*.

STIL (style)

Term referring either to the manner in which a text is presented or to the quality of this presentation or both.

When 'style' is used to denote the manner of presentation, it is implied that every piece of work has style as an essential component which cannot really be evaluated as being good or bad, but can only be described as being characteristic of a person, of an epoch etc.

When 'style' refers to the quality of presentation, i.e. if it is said that a text is distinguished by its style or is lacking in style, then there is implied a preconceived concept of 'beautiful', 'economic' or 'functional' writing to which any given text has to conform and against which it can be judged. This is the underlying assumption of all textbooks and courses which set out to teach style or to improve the style of the student.

If, however, 'style' refers both to the manner and to the quality of presentation, it becomes a tool for evaluating and describing a literary text. It will judge the quality of presentation according to accepted norms and rules (e.g. grammar etc.), describe deviations from this standard and attempt to evaluate the aesthetic purposes of such deviations.

A.O.

STILARTEN (types of style) = Genos, —us

Latin rhetoric distinguished between three basic types of style (*genera dicendi*):

a) the plain style (*genus tenue, subtile* or *humile*) which does not employ any ornamentation or figure of speech and was regarded as being the appropriate style for the communication of information.

b) the middle style (*genus medium, mediocre* or *floridum*) which employs a certain amount of ornamentation and figures of speech in order to provide enjoyment in addition to information.

c) the grand style (*genus sublime* or *grande*) which employs all aesthetic means of language to express powerful emotions with the aim of moving the listener.

In the M.A. the three styles were appropriated to social classes (shepherds, farmers, warriors). Modern stylistics has dismissed the idea of normative styles. → STILISTIK.

A.O.

STILBLÜTE (stylistic lapse)

Error or clumsiness in choice of language, resulting in stylistic incongruity.

STILISIERUNG (stylization)

The conscious application of style for the deliberate accentuation of aesthetic effect; this is usually achieved by a simplification of the forms and outlines of the represented object, in order to produce what is unmistakably an artefact.

STILISTIK (stylistics)

1. A normative or descriptive set of rules for the composition of good prose. This is also referred to as *Stilkunde* or *Stillehre*.

2. An academic discipline, part of → LITERATURWISSENSCHAFT, which concerns itself with all aesthetic possibilities of language and seeks to establish criteria for the description and evaluation of a literary text in aesthetic terms. → STIL.

A.O.

STILKUNDE → STILISTIK

STILLEHRE → STILISTIK

STIMMUNGSBILD

Description of a particular atmosphere in an attempt to recreate its mood for the reader.

STOFF = Sujet, = Vorwurf

Stoff has given rise to various theories in which the terminologies are by no means uniform. On the basis of more recent theoretic insights, it has been claimed that the term is of no great consequence if understood only as superficial content and as being closely related to the concepts of → QUELLE, → INHALT and → MOTIV. Instead, *Stoff* should be seen as the totality of formal and thematic components which combine to produce the independent aesthetic world of a piece of literature (→ GEHALT); or as the fictional sphere of a poetic product, originating in and shaped by the language. Its characteristics are its being bound by a particular form, its non-interchangeability with reality, its polyvalence and its interpretability.

In most contexts a more traditional conception of *Stoff* is maintained. *Stoff* is not, as might be supposed, any content matter as the opposite pole of formal structure, it is not everything nature supplies as the raw material of a poetic work, but an external, pre-existent story or plot that has come down to the author through myth and religion as tradition, experience, vision, report or historical event, and has provided the initial stimulus for literary composition. It applies to dramatic and narrative, rather than to lyrical forms. It must be distinguished from the smallest thematic unit, the → MOTIV as well as from the more abstract problem or theme. A *Stoff* may consist of a chain or complex of motifs. The flexible motif texture of *Stoffe* constitutes their variability and has secured for some of them a history of 25 centuries. The term *Stoff* is usually rendered in English as 'theme' which, however, is much less precise than *Stoff* and comprises → THEMA, *Stoff* and *Motiv*.

P.M.

STOLLEN

The first two parts of the tripartite *Minnesang*— and → MEISTERSANG-STROPHE. The two *Stollen* (also known as *Stollen* and *Gegenstollen*) constitute the → AUFGESANG and are followed by the → ABGESANG.

STREAM OF CONSCIOUSNESS (stream of consciousness) = Bewußtseinsstrom

A narrative technique in which the thoughts and emotions of the protagonist are related directly to the reader. The result is a sequence of associations and a diminished presence of the narrator (→ ERZÄHLER). In its most radical form, which eliminates the narrator altogether, this technique is called interior monologue (*innerer Monolog*). It was introduced into German literature by Schnitzler's *Leutnant Gustl* (1901), from which the following example is taken:

Wie lange wird denn das noch dauern? Ich muß auf die Uhr schauen. . . schickt sich wahrscheinlich nicht in einem so ernsten Konzert. Aber wer sieht's denn? Wenn's einer sieht, so paßt er gerade so wenig auf, wie ich, und vor dem brauch' ich mich nicht zu genieren. . . Erst viertel auf zehn?. . . Mir kommt vor, ich sitz' schon drei Stunden in dem Konzert. . .

A.O.

STREITSCHRIFT

Polemical or controversial piece of writing.

STROPHE (strophe)

1. In its original Greek sense, and corresponding to the current usage of the term in English, a *Strophe* is a group of lines of various lengths which formed the first part of an ode or chorus lyric in ancient Greek drama. The chorus sang or recited the *Strophe* as they moved from right to left, and the answering *Antistrophe* (which was identical in structure to the *Strophe*) as they moved from left to right, and the *Epode* (which was different in structure) standing still.

2. Stanza, verse. A fixed number of verse lines, which as a group forms the basic structural unit of a poem.

STROPHENSPRUNG

Form of → ENJAMBEMENT which occurs when a verse line runs on from the end of a stanza to the next.

STRUKTUR (structure) = Aufbau

The term refers to any system of relationships between units which form part of a complex entity. Works of literature are said to have an *äußere* as well as an *innere Struktur*. The *äußere Struktur* is made up of elements which are not peculiar to any individual work but are shared by a number of works, thus helping to constitute categories such as the drama (where the most obvious element of *äußere Struktur* is the system of acts and scenes), or poetry (where the most obvious and most general structural element lies in the system which determines the length of verses or lines in any given poem). Sometimes the *äußere Struktur* determines the character of a work to a very large extent. For instance, in a sonnet (→ SONETT) the distribution of stressed and unstressed syllables, the number of lines in each stanza, the number of stanzas, the distribution of rhymes, all follow pre-established systems of relationships which are those of the sonnet in general and are therefore encountered in a great number of poems. *Innere Struktur*, on the other hand, is made up of systems of relationships which are peculiar to an individual work. These relationships can exist, for example, between characters or other elements of the plot, or between symbols, motifs, and phonemes, etc. All such relationships, whether they form part of *äußere* or *innere* *Struktur*, whether they are obvious or subtle, are essential to the nature of each individual work.

H.W.

STUMPFER REIM → MÄNNLICHER REIM

STURM UND DRANG

The name – taken from the title of a play by Friedrich Maximilian Klinger (1776) – given to a short-lived but significant literary movement which flourished mainly in South-West Germany between 1770 and 1780, and which is generally regarded as marking the beginning of modern literary consciousness. The members of this loose-knit fraternity, most of them students of lower middle class origin, shared a set of beliefs which put them at odds with the existing political and social oder, so that they consciously promoted a revolution in thought, feeling and style with impassioned intensity. They championed nature against culture, the individual against society, feeling against thought and spontaneity against the trained response. The high value placed on original, inventive imagination accounts for the label → GENIEZEIT, a term by which the phenomenon is also known; but *Sturm und Drang* with its operatic overtones of tempestuous passion and undirected drive towards satisfaction, is aptly characteristic of the youthful exuberance expressed.

In a sense, the name is only to be understood as the middle term of a literary-historical sequence, seen as a reaction away from → AUFKLÄRUNG and a preparation for → KLASSIK and → ROMANTIK, but compared with the works which preceded and followed, it must be said that there is often a refreshing realism and directness, not commonly found in German literature. Yet Goethe's early works and Herder's complementary theories dominate over anything else produced by their contemporaries and remain the prime object of attention.

J.S.

STYLE INDIRECTE LIBRE → ERLEBTE REDE

SUBSTANTIVISCHER STIL → NOMINALSTIL

SUJET → STOFF

SUKZESSIONSBÜHNE → SUKZESSIVBÜHNE

SUKZESSIVBÜHNE = Sukzessionsbühne

Type of stage where all the action in successive acts and scenes takes place in the same acting area. Changes in time and place are indicated by different scenery, and thus necessitate the exit and entrance of the actors. The *Sukzessivbühne* replaced the med. → SIMULTANBÜHNE in the 17th century, and has remained the predominant stage form since.

SUMMATIONSSCHEMA

In 17th century German poetry the object is often characterized in a lengthy series of mutually unconnected comparisons with natural phenomena. The final stanza then briefly repeats all those images to give a total impression. This recapitulation also serves to give formal coherence to what otherwise may seem a rather loosely structured string of similes. Poems conforming to such a scheme can also be found in antiquity, the German M.A., the Italian → RENAISSANCE and especially the Spanish 'Golden Age'. In German baroque verse the 'summation' form mirrors important aspects of the prevailing philosophical orientation. There is no difference of rank among the various natural phenomena mentioned in the grammatically and logically uncoordinated comparisons. This agrees with the theocentric views of the age, according to which all elements of the material world were of equal value or worthlessness in the light of eternity.

E.Kr.

SURREALISMUS (Surrealism)

Deriving mainly from Dadaism (→ DADAISMUS), Surrealism was a leading international art movement between the two world wars. It was especially productive in French literature (Aragon, Eluard, Soupault), in the visual arts centred on Paris (Ernst, Masson, Magritte, Miró, Tanguy) and in film (Buñuel). The term had been used by Apollinaire in 1917, and the hallucinatory perspectives of the style had been established by this time by the painter de Chirico. As defined from 1924 in manifestos by the movement's long-time leader, André Breton, Surrealism aimed at freeing the personality and infusing everyday experience with psychological depth through the use of dream, reverie and the apparently chance association of ideas and images, all given new significance in this period by Freud. Unexpected associations of images were thought to evoke revelations of hidden realities. Like the Dadaists, the Surrealists acted as a group, they had a similar passing involvement with extreme left-wing politics and they also opposed the traditional separation of art from life. The term 'surrealist' is also used in a non-historical sense for fantastic art of all periods.

M.A.

SYMBOL

Generally speaking any empirically perceivable object which either (1) represents a non-empirical sphere of a higher or general order e.g. *Wasser = Seele* in *Gesang der Geister über den Wassern* (1779), by Goethe, or (2) renders visible and concretizes the invisible: feelings, thoughts, fate, destiny, e.g. the flowers in V, 10 of Kleist's *Prinz Friedrich von Homburg* (completed 1810, published 1821). Such an object can be man-made (e.g. the cross = Christian faith) or natural (e.g. rose = love). The object can be given its symbolic meaning by (a) tradition and common consent (cross, rose) or (b) by the creative act of an individual (*Wasser* as above, the *Schloß* in Kafka's novel). Some critics would deny that (2) (b) can be called a symbol and would prefer the terms *Privatsymbol* or, particularly in the case of the modern lyric, *Zeichen*; in English 'correlative' has been suggested for (2) (b) (C. Hayes) — not to be confused with T.S. Eliot's 'objective correlative' (→CHIFFRE).

In Germany, the issue has been complicated further by the influence of Goethe's (1749–1832) dictum that, in the case of "true symbolism", "the particular represents the general, not as a dream or a shadow, but as the living, instantaneous revelation of the inscrutable". This definition would exclude (a) wherever the intended meaning of the symbol was quite clear (e.g. the breaking of the flower in Goethe's own *Heidenröslein*), it would, however, allow for (b).

As far as the distinction between symbol and allegory (→ ALLEGORIE) is concerned, it is generally agreed that — whereas the symbol contains its symbolic meaning more or less intrinsically and evidently — allegory is an arbitrary creation whose meaning is extrinsic to the object chosen to portray it (e.g. Horace's use of the ship as an allegory of the state). Allegory would therefore imply "a dominance of theme over action and image" (A. Fletcher) and hence tend to be more abstract than the symbol.

A.V.

SYMBOLISMUS (symbolism)

Term denoting primarily a literary direction in Europe from the second half of the 19th century to the early decades of the 20th; it can also be applied to artistic tendencies derived from or related to *Symbolismus* proper. Beginning as an outgrowth of French Romanticism and enriched by English and German influences, e.g. Novalis (1772–1801), Hoffmann (1776–1822), Wagner (1813–1883), Symbolism normally dates from Baudelaire's book of poems *Les Fleurs du Mal* (1857), and the poetry of Verlaine (1844–1896), Rimbaud (1854–1891) and Mallarmé (1842–1898) completes the Symbolist canon in France by the end of the century. There was no school or movement known as *Symbolismus* in German literature. Rather, individual poets such as George (1868–1933), the early Hofmannsthal (1874–1929), Rilke (1875–1926) and Trakl (1887–1914) assimilated Symbolist influences or developed independently in ways that show affinities to the beginnings in France. Those aspects which critics in German use to define *Symbolismus* are variously attributed to other styles or trends as well, e.g. → IMPRESSIONISMUS, → NEUROMANTIK, → JUGENDSTIL, → ÄSTHETIZISMUS, → DEKADENZ etc. This is confusing but unavoidable in the absence of a Symbolist programme in German. Symbolist writing in both France and Germany is marked by an absence of political commitment, a tendency to become esoteric and a disdain for the experience of the average citizen as the raw material of art. Reality is never taken at face value; rather, the artist looks beyond what is given towards a world of transcendent meanings.

These can only be hinted at, never spelled out, and so verbal symbols tend towards the suggestiveness of music. Poetry has an affinity to magic and poetic language exists on a level high above everyday speech. The reality of the work of art is *purer* than the human situation from which it stems. It is projected from the inner world of the isolated individual and avoids the commonality of experience. Symbolist writing values imagery above statement, fascination above depth of feeling and myth above history. →MODERNE.

A.S.

SYNÄSTHESIE (synaesthesia)

Poetic device facilitating the response to stimuli by senses other than the normally appropriate one; e.g.: a visual response to music if one talks about white and blue notes.

SYNAPHIE

The flowing on of a line of verse into the next one without breaking the metre.

SYNEKDOCHE (synecdoche)

Figure of speech (a kind of → METONYMIE) in which a part of something is used to express the whole, or the whole to express a part. e.g.: 20 Köpfe instead of 20 Personen (→ PARS PRO TOTO); Edel sei der Mensch (Goethe) meaning all human beings.

SYNKOPE (syncope)

The elision or slurring-over of letters or syllables (usually unstressed) within a word.

SYNTAX (syntax) = Satzlehre

The part of grammar which deals with the arrangement of words and sentence constructions.

SYSTOLE

The shortening of a vowel which is naturally long for purposes of versification.→DIASTOLE.

SZENARIUM

1. Comprehensive list of properties, technical devices, and decorations necessary for a theatrical performance.

2. Basic outline of a play around which characters improvise dialogue and actions. →COMMEDIA DELL'ARTE, →STEGREIF.

SZENE (scene)

Although it is customary to subdivide acts of a drama into scenes, this division is often arbitrary and unsystematic, partly because of the uncertainty as to what constitutes a scene. Following the French model, some critics feel that entrances and exits of important characters determine the beginning and end of a scene; others adopt a more pragmatic definition, based either on the function of the scene as a unit in the development of the play's action or, simply, on change of locality or setting. Modern playwrights tend to view the scene as the major structural division, discarding the older models of three, four or five act structures (e.g. → STATIONENSTÜCK). Thus it has become common to adopt various and loose criteria for classifying scenes: function (expositive, or transitional scenes); length (relief scenes, climactic scenes); even mood and atmosphere (crowd scenes, confrontation scenes, battle scenes). → AKT, → AUFTRITT.

M.M.

SZENENANWEISUNG → BÜHNENANWEISUNG

TABLEAU

In drama a static representation to complete a play or an act.

TABLEAU VIVANT = lebendes Bild

Picturesque representation by a static group of people which recreates a famous picture or scene.

TABULATUR

Set of rules governing poetic and musical composition used by the *Meistersinger.* →MEISTERSANG.

TAGEBUCH

1. Diary: book in which a daily record is kept of experiences, thoughts, and observations, usually of a subjective and personal nature.

2. A literary work which, although fictional, is written in the form of a diary.

TAGELIED (dawn song) = Aubade

A special form of the →MINNESANG which describes the parting of lovers at dawn, a literary theme which transcends the boundaries of time and cultures. In its MHG form, the noble lovers are usually in a private chamber in the castle. They are woken by a singing bird or, more frequently, by the watchman who announces daybreak and often warns the lovers with a few words or even a song of his own (*Wächterlied*). The major theme of the (sung) lyric is the sorrow of parting. It is frequently treated by means of a dialogue between the lovers. The earliest *Tagelied* is dated c.1160. The genre is particularly popular in the period of the *Minnesang*, with poets like Dietmar von Aist, Heinrich von Morungen, Walther von der Vogelweide and Wolfram von Eschenbach represented with one or several lyrics. Unlike the *Minnesang*, however, the *Tagelied* continues as a lyric tradition into the 18th century, when it is assimilated into the folk-song.

P.Oe.

TAKT (foot)

Metrical unit made up of several syllables, of which one, at least, is stressed or long. →METRIK.

TANTIEME (royalty)

The percentage of profits payable to any author or composer for each copy sold, and/or for each performance of a literary or musical work until the copyright expires.

TASCHENAUSGABE (pocket edition) → AUSGABE

TASCHENBUCH

1. Pocket-book, notebook.
2. Paperback.

TASCHENBUCHAUSGABE (paperback edition) → AUSGABE

TAUWETTER

A period of *Tauwetter* (*thaw*) may arise in a closed political system where public opinion and literary expression are subject to the strictest censorship. In systems of this kind social and political change can often only be brought about by short periods of a relaxation of censorship and a more liberal manipulation of literature. Even a slight relaxation of pressure might in such a situation lead to a euphoric feeling of liberation and greatly boost not only manifestations of social criticism but all forms of literary and artistic expression. This in turn will be felt as a threat by the ruling establishment and lead to the re-introduction of more restrictive policies, a new 'frost'. The term *Tauwetter* has been used in this sense for the liberalization process after Stalin's death in the Soviet Union on the basis of Erenburg's novel *Thaw* (1954–56). It has also been used in connection with some phases of GDR-literature, and was adopted recently to characterize the literature of the Habsburg monarchy following the relaxation of censorship by Joseph II (1781).

L.B.

TEICHOSKOPIE = Mauerschau

Dramatic device: the report by a person placed in a look-out (e.g. a tower, a wall, a hill etc.) of an event which for various reasons cannot be staged (e.g. a sea battle) but is nevertheless important for the development of the plot.

There is no equivalent term in English.

TEKTONIK → GESCHLOSSENE FORM

TELEGRAMMSTIL

Telegraphic style: abbreviated, clipped, and frequently elliptical style practised by some Expressionists and Impressionists.

TENDENZDICHTUNG = Tendenzliteratur,= Zweckdichtung

Pejorative term for literature whose underlying purpose is to promote a certain viewpoint or ideology, frequently at the expense of its aesthetic quality. Some critics, however, maintain that any literature which communicates a message can be classified as *Tendenzdichtung.* → ENGAGIERTE LITERATUR.

TENDENZLITERATUR → TENDENZDICHTUNG

TENOR (tenor)

The main purport or thought of a discourse.

TERENZBÜHNE → BADEZELLENBÜHNE

TERMINUS A QUO = Terminus post quem

The date after which it can be established that an event must have taken place.

TERMINUS AD QUEM = Terminus ante quem

The date after which it can be established that an event cannot have taken place.

TERPSICHORE

Muse of dancing and later the chorus. → MUSEN.

TERTIUM COMPARATIONIS

The point of comparison between two objects under discussion when they share a common quality.

TERZARIMA (terza rima) = Terzine

Italian form of versification comprising iambic decasyllabic or hendecasyllabic tercets which are interlinked by common rhymes, with the following rhyme scheme: aba, bcb, . . .

TERZETT (tercet)

Three-line stanza. → SONETT.

TERZINE → TERZARIMA

TETRALOGIE (tetralogy)

The Greek tetralogy was a set of four dramatic works, normally comprising three tragedies (→TRILOGIE) and a →SATYRSPIEL.

Term also applied by extension to any set of four related literary works by the same author.

TETRAMETER (tetrameter)

Metrical line consisting of four feet. →METRUM.

TEXTBUCH

Book containing the libretto (or sections of it) of an opera or musical comedy.

TEXTKRITIK (textual criticism) = Editionstechnik

The object of textual criticism is to establish and present the text of a work of literature in accordance with the intentions of its author, and if possible, with his authoritative approval. The editor of this text can be the author himself or a scholar who has been commissioned (usually by a publisher) to present the text for publication after having established the authenticity of its every word. The publication itself can take the form of merely reproducing the text, usually for aesthetic edification and enjoyment, or it can add to the text a scholarly justification including its genesis or history, variants of differing versions and factual explanations of unusual features of the text and its contents with the purpose of paving the way for a critical interpretation. Such additions to the text are usually assembled in an *apparatus* (→APPARAT) following the presentation of the text. This form of dealing with a literary text is termed a *critical edition*, whether of the complete or collected works of an author (which may include diaries and letters), or of an individual work or even of a single poem.

The strongest evidence of an author's intentions lies in the existence of a manuscript of a literary text in the author's own hand. There may, of course, be several manuscripts of the same work, a fair copy, for instance, of a draft or new versions written during different phases of the author's life. A further step in the process of textual criticism is the examination of the earliest printed version of a literary text which appeared with the express approval of the author (→ IMPRIMATUR). If the literary work is republished during the author's lifetime every one of these printed versions has to be carefully scrutinized and compared with extant manuscripts. Should proofs of printed versions be preserved with corrections and changes in the author's hand, these constitute valuable additional material for the process of textual criticism (→ÜBERLIEFE-RUNG). The collection, sifting and collation of all this material and the setting out of all differences between the various versions in the form of lists of *variants* (→ LESART) has been termed by philologists: *recensio*. The process of *recensio* has to be implemented by an examination of the material with a view to its authenticity. This involves not only the examination of different versions of a literary work in manuscript or printed form, but also of biographical, and esp. of autobiographical documents, in letters, diaries, transmitted statements in conversations and — least reliable — in autobiographies proper pertaining to the work in question. The editor's decision-making becomes more difficult if no autographs of the work exist and printed versions alone must be relied upon, in particular if they were not supervised by the author or appeared posthumously. Equally uncertain are copies from manuscripts made by persons other than the author; their text can easily be corrupted by slips of the pen, spelling mistakes, misreadings, even by well-meant corrections and wilful interpolations, or by changes in punctuation. In establishing the final text the editor has to consider the author's spelling and punctuation habits. Regarding the latter, deviation from common rules may well be intentional, emphasizing rhythm, pauses and pace, rather than convention. *Modernization* of texts, i.e. subjecting them to current rules of grammar, spelling and punctuation is now frowned upon. Adhering to the author's habits (after eliminating obvious demonstrable writing, spelling and printing mistakes) is to render a work of literature in exactly the way the author intended it to be, including contemporary flavour and local or dialectal idiosyncrasies, and in the way his contemporary readers received and appreciated it.

Textual criticism not only leads us into an author's workshop and makes us witness the gradual growth and final completion of a literary work of art, it also enables us to penetrate the author's mind and to gain an insight into his psychological make-up.

R.S.

THALIA

Muse of comedy and pastoral poetry. →MUSEN.

THEATERLIED

Light lyrical song inserted in farces and plays. →VOLKSKOMÖDIE.

THEATERREDE

Form of address, usually in verse, common in the 18th century, which formally greeted the audience before the performance of a play.

THEATERWISSENSCHAFT

An independent academic discipline which was established in Germany through the efforts of Max Herrmann and Artur Kutscher during the early decades of this century. At first the emphasis was laid on theatre history as a field of research which could not be adequately covered by *Germanistik*. At present the discipline encompasses the study of all those elements which constitute theatre, as opposed to drama, both past and present: theatre history, costumes, acting styles, theatre architecture, theatre criticism, theatre and law, e.g. censorship, and of course, the audience. Modern *Theaterwissenschaft* tends to see theatre as a complex sociological and historical phenomenon which can only be adequately studied through an interdisciplinary approach. For example, psychological and sociological techniques are being applied to analyse the actor-spectator relationship. Film and television studies are also being incorporated.

This discipline does not see itself as being in the first instance a theatre school, but as an academic pursuit which provides an excellent background for the → DRAMATURG and the theatre critic and, to a lesser extent, for the director.

C.B.

THEATERZETTEL (playbill, theatre programme)

Notice provided by a theatre giving details of the cast, and members of the production-team of a play, and information about the play itself and announcing forthcoming productions.

THEMA

The subject of a literary work; the main matter under discussion.

THEMATIK

Collective term to denote the multiplicity of interrelated aspects of a → THEMA.

THEODIZEE (theodicy)

The philosophical and theological vindication of Providence in the face of evil; e.g. the attempt by Leibniz (1646—1716) to establish earth as the best of all possible worlds. Since the 18th century this has become a central theme in literature.

THEOGONIE (theogony)

The genealogy of the gods, or a poem dealing with this subject.

THESPISKARREN

Humorous term for a travelling theatre. The original Latin term was coined by Horace (65—8 B.C.) who erroneously assumed that the legendary founder of Attic drama, Thespis, used a wagon as his stage.

THRILLER (thriller) → KRIMINALROMAN

TITELSCHUTZ (copyright of a title)

The legal protection enjoyed by authors or publishers which ensures that titles of their works cannot be reproduced or copied without permission.

TITURELSTROPHE

Med. stanza form named after Wolfram von Eschenbach's courtly epic *Titurel* (after 1215). It consists of two rhyming couplets, each line ending with a falling cadence. In general the first line has eight stresses, the second and fourth lines ten, and the third line six. Each line except for the third has a caesura after the fourth stressed syllable. In a later form, the stanza of *Der jüngere Titurel* (c.1270), rhyme also occurs at the caesura of the first two lines producing the rhyme-scheme of a seven-line stanza: ab, ab, c, xc.

TON = Weise

The metrical form and melody of med. lyrics and the songs of the *Meistersinger*. In the M.A. it was not permitted to use the *Töne* of other poets which resulted in an immense proliferation of metric and melodic forms. → MEISTERSANG, →MINNESANG.

TONMALEREI →ONOMATOPOESIE

TOPIK (topics)

Since Aristotle's first treatise on topics as part of his *Organon of Logic*, topics is defined as the theory and the body of principles of persuasive argumentation in the area of probable opinion that lies ahead, both systematically and historically, of axiomatic scientific proof. Topics received its systematic treatment under the heading of invention in → RHETORIK, from where it extended its influence into poetics and, during the M.A. into theology. After the denunciation of probability, traditional wisdom and current opinion in favour of scientific certainty during the Age of Reason, topics was reduced from a theory of the sources of arguments to a storehouse of commonplaces and clichés (Greek: topos — Latin: locus communis — English: commonplace). A renewed critical interest in the persuasive forms of argumentation in disciplines like law, sociology, linguistics, epistemology and literary criticism has developed topics into an analytical instrument for the investigation of the past and present use of persuasive arguments and strategies in areas as diverse as advertising, politics, law, philosophy, history of science and literature. The analysis of topics seeks to show which arguments were offered and accepted at various times and circumstances within a given society and within specific literary genres. It not only researches and records the tradition of a topos/argument, as for example in Curtius's seminal book *Europäische Literatur und lateinisches Mittelalter* (1948), it also assesses the consciously or unconsciously accepted and fostered truth value of topoi within historically changing cultural horizons. Since Aristotle (384—322 B.C.), research into topics looks at the legitimation of the persuasive arguments which create and shape the ideas which are found in debates about the questions and problems of life which in turn influence political decisions. This legitimation is itself subject to the process of historical change, as, for example, in the critique of class interests: Aristotle refers to the wisdom of the 'wisest' or of the 'majority', yet even in antiquity 'reason' was directed against 'commonsense' and today the term applies principally to the 'inherent logic of matter', thus overthrowing the legitimation by the philosopher, poet or writer, which used to be a matter of course. →TOPOS.

W.V.

TOPOS, TOPOI (topos, topoi)

The invention of arguments as the art of open discussion of all human matters is the subject of the central part of → RHETORIK; it is investigated in detail in → TOPIK. The topos is, originally, the place or source where arguments can be found which help to convince the audience or reader of the speaker's or writer's case; later on, the term is applied to the individual argument. Thus in law, the topos 'alibi' harbours many arguments in defence of the accused; in literature traditional topoi such as 'life is a vale of sorrows', 'labour sweetens life', 'life was better in the past' (the topos of the Golden Age), 'nature is wiser than man' or 'good people go to heaven, bad people go to hell' etc. give rise to many diverse and even contradictory arguments and are passed on in the many proverbs, examples, poetic images and social conventions which made up the consciously or unconsciously accepted cultural traditions of societies. Aristotle (384–322 B.C.) was mainly concerned with the 'artificial' topoi which categorize arguments according to their logical provenance, but the above substantive or 'non-artificial' topoi, which are legitimized by one authority or another, are of far greater importance for the writer or literary analyst: they are handed on and continually invented afresh. In this way they offer access to traditional and current opinions as well as insight into the productive imagination of writers in their argumentative interpretation of human affairs. Since Curtius's *Europäische Literatur und lateinisches Mittelalter* (1948), which is much concerned with continuity in literature in form of the constant factors such as poetic imagery in its many variants, thoughts, themes and even archetypes, modern literary criticism has begun to use topos research as an analytical tool for the investigation of past and present thought-processes and the hidden or open interests contained within them. It is, however, important that research should not only catalogue the continuity of topoi through the ages; research must also be directed to the discontinuity that manifests itself in the demise of old and the rise of new arguments, and to the reasons for such changes. Equally, it is necessary to look closely at the meaning of the topos by considering its function in the structure of a given work, so that we may reconstruct the full thrust of its argumentation.

W.V.

TRAGIK

A basic concept of perception of the world applicable to life and by extension also to art; the basic mode of tragedy (→TRAGÖDIE). *Tragik* results from a conflict between two sets of values, one set being represented by supreme powers (e.g. the gods, fate, a universal law, eternal justice etc.) or an institution (e.g. the state, the church, a dynasty etc.) which leads inevitably to the physical or mental destruction of a worthy human being who tries with all the means at his disposal to uphold another set of values, if only as an idea. The human being thus trapped is usually aware of the sacrificial nature of his stance but has no real choice if humanity as a whole is not to be betrayed (e.g. *Othello V*, 2 "It is the cause, it is the cause, my soul"). The destruction of such a being may be experienced either as higher necessity because the old universal order is being restored or as total senselessness because it occurs for no humanly comprehensible reason. *Tragik* is thus constituted by the fact that the tragic human being is compelled to act as he does but in doing so brings about his own downfall.

A.O.

TRAGIKOMÖDIE (tragicomedy) = Mischspiel

Dramatic genre subject to much confusion. The best attempt at definition so far has been by Guthke (*Geschichte und Poetik der deutschen Tragikomödie*, 1961). The concept was already known to and accepted by Socrates (470–399 B.C.) and Aristotle (384–322 B.C.), and the term was facetiously coined by Plautus (254–184 B.C.). *Tragikomödie* was rejected as a genre by Cicero (106–43 B.C.) and other classical purists, but revived by →RENAISSANCE Humanist writers and critics to justify an indigenous tradition and its link with the classical tradition of essentially distinct tragic and comic dramatic genres, producing a combination of opposite and extreme emotions rather than the middle way of Guarini's pastorals. In pre-18th century drama (Beaumont and Fletcher, Haugwitz, Hallmann) *Tragikomödie* could be one or more of four things: (1) a mixing of high and low class dramatis personae, (2) a mixture of high and low styles, (3) a blending of comic and tragic subject-matter or plots or (4) a happy end to a tragic story and vice versa. The last is the most frequent criterion. The 18th century purists rejected the genre. It was replaced by →WEINERLICHES LUSTSPIEL or sentimental comedy which avoided extremes of emotion. The 19th century German and French Romantics (Schelling, Hugo) stressed the mingling of extremes, often referring to individual scenes from Shakespeare. Later writers championed it as expresssion of a modern loss of an encompassing metaphysical order. 20th century theory (Dürrenmatt 1921–, Pirandello 1867–1936, Ionesco 1912–, Pinter 1930–) points out that in tragicomedy the comic and tragic heighten rather than diminish each other and that all comedy is in essence tragic. The common denominator of tragic and comic modes is that the individual protagonist is in conflict with some accepted norm. Tragicomedy is to be distinguished from grotesque-absurd drama as more realistic and as disorientated rather than pessimistic; it is less exaggerated and more genuinely tragic and comic than melodrama. A German example is: Dürrenmatt's *Der Besuch der alten Dame* (1956).

S.H.

TRAGISCHE IRONIE (dramatic irony) → IRONIE

TRAGÖDE (tragic actor)

TRAGÖDIE (tragedy) = Trauerspiel

The artistic presentation of → TRAGIK in the form of a stage play. This presentation underwent changes throughout history as the notion of *Tragik* changed (e.g. the M.A. with their strongly dominating Christian philosophy did not really allow a tragic conception of the world as the suffering endured by the moral human being during his lifetime would be rewarded after death).

Tragedy as an art-form was developed by the ancient Greeks and Greek tragedy has served as a model for almost two thousand years. Structural elements such as → ANAGNORISIS, → HAMARTIA, → HYBRIS, → KATA-STROPHE, → PERIPETIE were thought to be constituents of each tragedy, necessary to achieve the desired effect of → KATHARSIS, but the incorporation of structural elements, including the three unities (→ EINHEITEN), and the elevated status of the tragic hero, which was relaxed in the 18th century (→ STÄNDEKLAUSEL), does not guarantee a tragedy. The ultimate test will always be whether or not the play succeeds in portraying the event or situation it is presenting as being tragic (→ TRAGIK).

A.O.

TRAKTAT

Treatise or pamphlet on religious or moral questions.

TRAUERSPIEL → TRAGÖDIE

TRAVESTIE (travesty)

Like the English equivalent, *Travestie* refers to the imitation of the typical subject-matter of a genre or of a particular author and the accompanying substitution of a 'low' or colloquial style for the serious and lofty style of the original.

Though travesties do not play a very significant part in great literature — Johann Nestroy (1801–1862) is an exception — numerous major works incorporate travesty. In *A Midsummer Night's Dream* (1595), the 'rude mechanicals' stage a performance of the tragedy of Pyramus and Thisbe which through their comic ineptitude becomes a travesty. Like parody (→ PARODIE), travesty derives part of its comic effect from the incongruity between form and content which is basic to it, and part from its deflation or ridicule of what is being travestied. Whether mild or savage, travesty is satiric by nature, unmasking what is high-faluting, pompous or hackneyed. →SATIRE.

P.T.

TRILOGIE (trilogy)

A group of three tragedies, each complete in itself, but linked by a common story or theme, which with the →SATYRSPIEL made up the Greek →TETRA-LOGIE. Term also applied by extension to any set of three related literary works by the same author.

TRIMETER (trimeter)

Metrical line consisting of three feet. →METRUM.

TRIVIALLITERATUR = Unterhaltungsliteratur

Trivial literature is always popular light reading (*Unterhaltungsliteratur*), but not all popular literature is trivial literature: trivial literature is literature of inferior artistic quality. In the literary work of art, the criterion which governs the selection and shaping of the material is necessity: every word-image, every device used, derives its function and its significance from the interrelated whole it serves to constitute. The aesthetic whole, formed by this strictly economical use of material and means, provokes reflection, induces insight and reveals meaning. Trivial literature has no such integrated form. The aim is not reflection, but the stimulation of emotion, effect for effect's sake. The criteria of necessity and economy give way to arbitrariness and accumulation. The vague word-images, the extravagantly used metaphors, the contrived symbols, the lyricisms are all chosen arbitrarily for their evocative potential and are replaceable by any equivalent that would achieve the same effect. The order of appearance is also arbitrary, so long as the range of emotional stimulus is extended. The means become an end in themselves, and as there is no meaningful context to sustain the artificially stimulated effect, the stimulus must be continually renewed. The accumulation of evocative motifs covers and merges the entire range of emotions and keeps the reader in a continual state of vibration — as long as the book lasts. Superficial details from the familiar contemporary scene are incorporated to lend to trite story and empty sentiment the semblance of validity. For the same reason the more pretentious author, with the pseudo-cultured philistine in view, incorporates the stilistic traits of recognized poets or cultural eras.

Why the phenomenal demand for trivial literature in the modern world? Too little research has been done in the field for that question to be answered adequately, but the following explanation (Killy, *Deutscher Kitsch*, 1951) is convincing. Trivial literature has taken over the function of the fairy-tale. When stripped of its contemporary trappings and evocative effects, the material of trivial literature shows a marked resemblance to that of the fairy-tale: both present the same basic human types, both order the complexities of the world into a clear-cut, moral pattern, revealing the basic conditions of human existence, both stimulate the reader's imagination and enable him to participate in the illusory resolution of real life's inextricable problems. This fulfils a basic human need, which is not otherwise satisfied in the modern world. Man cannot live without the illusions, the pictures which the imagination creates of the workings of the world, but this need is becoming increasingly more difficult to meet: literature is foreign to the average man in the street, the traditional fairy-tale is outmoded and the Bible has become an unknown book. The masses turn to trivial literature.

But in modernizing the world of the fairy-tale, trivial literature has secularized it: stripped it of its supernatural dimension and replaced its timeless universal values with the semblance of contemporary relevance. The hollowness of the result is veiled by false sentiment. Trivial literature exploits and foils the need to which it owes its existence. → KITSCH.

P.L.

TRIVIUM → ARTES LIBERALES

TROCHÄUS (trochee)

A metrical foot of two syllables in which the stressed or long syllable is followed by an unstressed or short syllable (x́x). → METRIK.

TROPE (trope)

Figure of speech: any rhetorical device which invests a word with more than its literal meaning.

TROPUS (trope)

The addition or amplification in Gregorian chant, and later in med. religious drama.

TYPOGRAPHIE (typography)

The art of type-setting and composing; the arrangement or appearance of printed matter.

ÜBERBRETTL → KABARETT

ÜBERLIEFERUNG

The tradition of a text, e.g. oral or written. In → TEXTKRITIK, *Überlieferung* specifically means the tradition of the text, as it can be verified by the study of manuscripts and other documents.

UMARMENDER REIM

Rhyme scheme, in which one rhyming couplet is enclosed by another: abba, cddc. . .

UMFANG

The physical dimensions or number of pages of a (literary) work.

UMGANGSSPRACHE (colloquial spoken form of language) → SCHRIFT-SPRACHE

UNGEBUNDENE REDE → PROSA

UNIKUM

The only copy (of a book) in existence.

UNIVERSALPOESIE → FRÜHROMANTIK

UNMITTELBARKEIT

An author's or narrator's total and immediate involvement with his creation, and with the emotions and ideas expressed therein. → DISTANZ.

UNREINER REIM (imperfect rhyme)

Occurs when the rhyming sounds are not identical; e.g.:
Ach neige,
Du Schmerzenreiche (Goethe, *Faust I.*)

UNTERHALTUNGSLITERATUR → TRIVIALLITERATUR

UNZIALEN (uncials)

Type of script used since the 5th century. It consisted of capital letters only (→ MAJUSKELN, → KAPITALE) and was more rounded in appearance than the script used previously. Later, the term *Unzialen* was applied to the non-ornate capital letters at the beginning of a book or a chapter. → INITIALE.

URANIA

Muse of astronomy. → MUSEN.

URAUFFÜHRUNG (première)

The very first production of a work. → ERSTAUFFÜHRUNG.

URBILD (archetype, prototype)

Original model or form of something.

URHEBERRECHT (copyright)

The exclusive right of an author and his heirs to control or publish his work. At present it expires fifty years after the author's death. → VERLAGSRECHT.

URSPRUNGSMYTHEN (myths of creation) → SCHÖPFUNGSMYTHEN

UTOPIE (Utopian literature)

Term derived from Thomas More's *Utopia* (1516). Utopia, literally meaning nowhere, was the name he invented for an imaginary island with an ideal political, social, and legal system. The term *Utopie* is thus applied to a literary genre, whose main feature is the presentation of idealized societies.

UT PICTURA POESIS (let the poem be like a picture)

Phrase from Horace's *Ars poetica*; it has been interpreted as meaning that literature should be descriptive and try to 'paint' its subject-matter. Lessing in *Laokoon* (1766) establishes literature as an independent art-form with its own laws.

VADEMEKUM (vade-mecum)

Pocket-sized handbook or manual on a particular subject.

VAGANTENDICHTUNG

Literature of the 12th and 13th century travelling students and scholars of Europe, esp. Germany, France and England. Some wrote ribald and satiric Latin verses which were termed Goliardic as they attributed them to a mythical Bishop Golias.

VARIANTE → LESART

VERBALSTIL

Style characterized by the frequent use of constructions using verb-forms. → NOMINALSTIL.

VERBLÜMTE REDEWEISE

Style in which thoughts are expressed in an oblique and allusive manner.

VERFREMDUNGSEFFEKT (alienation effect)

Also *V-effekt* in Brecht's dramatic theory.

Technique in literature or art which makes that which is depicted strange and unfamiliar, in Russian formalism called *ostranenie*. Central aspect of Brecht's epic theatre (→ EPISCHES THEATER) where *Verfremdungseffekt* is used to evoke critical distance rather than empathy in the spectator, in order to arouse active response or argument on political and social questions. The production aims to discourage vicarious experience or catharsis (hence non-aristotelian theatre), *showing* events instead of creating illusion. Brecht (*Kleines Organon für das Theater*, 1948), devised the *Verfremdungseffekt* to punctuate the action and prevent the audience from identifying with the characters. *Verfremdungseffekt* may be visual, such as placards with slogans or films projected above the stage; aural, as in songs, addressing the audience directly or commenting on the action; physical, where house lights are on, smoking is permitted, actors dress on stage, wear masks or move among the audience. Similar techniques are widely used in experimental, alternative or street-theatre, whether political or not, and in new performances of classical plays. Alienation or shock effects also abound in modern art, poetry, music and dance.

M.St.

VERGLEICH (simile)

Stylistic device: the comparison of one word or concept to another in order to enrich the associative qualities of the expression. The *Vergleich* is much shorter and far more compact than → GLEICHNIS or → PARABEL; e.g.: stumm wie ein Fisch.

VERGLEICHENDE LITERATURWISSENSCHAFT (comparative literary studies) = Komparatistik

Vergleichende Literaturwissenschaft today comprises a spectrum of critical approaches applied to a range of literatures. *Vergleichende Literaturwissenschaft* can be traced back to Goethe's humanistic interest in the literatures of the world (*Weltliteratur*) which he saw as an expression of universal human consciousness. Taken up by French and German scholars in the early 19th century, *vergleichende Literaturwissenschaft* developed in opposition to narrow, nationalist tendencies and the concentration on national literatures in sharply defined departments. *Vergleichende Literaturwissenschaft* was originally concerned mainly with indicating suitable themes and subject-matter for examination, whereas more recently attention has been focused on its methods. *Vergleichende Literaturwissenschaft* disregards national boundaries and includes the comparison of one work with another, one artist with another, literary movements, literary works with other art forms, or such particulars as themes and motifs. To avoid the dangers of merely impressionist judgement, *vergleichende Literaturwissenschaft* has now shifted to methodological questions and makes increasing use of a number of theories, especially translation theory, linguistic structuralism, semiotics, Marxist theories, phenomenology, reception aesthetics and psychoanalytic approaches. Comparisons of works and their contexts can thus be formulated in terms of theoretical premises, declared procedures, and defined goals. Based on such theories *vergleichende Literaturwissenschaft* claims to act as an umbrella discipline subsuming generic, stylistic, historical, genetic, or sociological criticism. As a result of the combination of its multiple theoretical base and its readiness to study all kinds of literary texts, *vergleichende Literaturwissenschaft* encourages a certain hermeneutic self-awareness and highlights both the systemic nature of *literariness* and the manner in which literary discourse is integrated into its enveloping aesthetic and ideological structures.

H.G.R.

VERLAG (publishing company)

VERLAGSALMANACH → ALMANACH

VERLAGSRECHT
Either the full copyright or parts of it which the author (→ URHEBER-RECHT) transfers to the publisher.

VERLAGSSIGNET → DRUCKERZEICHEN

VERLEGER (publisher)

VERLEGERZEICHEN → DRUCKERZEICHEN

VERRAMSCHEN
The practice of selling recently published unsold books at reduced prices.

VERRISS
Totally negative and destructive review of a performance or book.

VERS (verse)
In literary criticism *Vers* always refers to a single metrical line. In general usage, *Vers* is sometimes used as a synonym for stanza (→ STROPHE).

VERSALIEN (majuscules) = Majuskeln
Capital letters at the beginning of each verse.

VERSANDBUCHHANDLUNG (mail-order bookshop)

VERSBRECHUNG → ENJAMBEMENT

VERSCHLEIFUNG
Slurring over a syllable for purposes of versification.

VERSCHRÄNKTER REIM
Rhyme scheme: abc abc or abc bac.

VERSENKUNG
Adjustable part of the stage floor which can be lowered to make characters disappear.

VERSETZSTÜCKE
The mobile parts of the theatrical set; e.g.: furniture, trees etc.

VERSFÜLLUNG → FÜLLUNG

VERSFUSS → FUSS

VERSKUNST → METRIK

VERS LIBRE → FREIE VERSE

VERSMASS → METRUM

VERSUCH → ESSAY

VERWANDLUNGSSTÜCK → AUSTATTUNGSSTÜCK

VERWERTUNGSGESELLSCHAFTEN

Associations of writers which concern themselves with the clarification of authors' rights as far as the use of their work is concerned; e.g.: books in libraries, recording, filming, etc. of books.

VIELGESTALTIGKEIT

The use of more than one type of metrical foot in a single verse line.

VIERZEILER (quatrain) = Quartett

Four-line stanza with the rhyme scheme: aabb, abab, or aaaa. → SONETT.

VOLKSAUSGABE (inexpensive edition) → AUSGABE

VOLKSBALLADE (folk-ballad)

A sub-genre of the → VOLKSLIED.

A ballad is a narrative poem, usually in strophic form, which is either sung or recited (→ BALLADE). The term *Volk* is ambiguous and in this context has lead to controversies in the past. It is now generally understood to mean 'the lower strata of a society'. *Volksballade* thus refers to a narrative poem sung by the common people who, regardless of the original author, treat it as their 'property' transforming it, consciously or subconsciously, in the course of time.

Although basically epic, the folk-ballad has marked lyrical qualities (refrain, repetitions), but is also dramatic (scenic structure, strong conflicts). Its style tends to be ornamental (rhetorical questions, exclamations). Stereotyped phrases and rhymes, repetitions, 'gaps' in logical progression, even unintelligible phrases are characteristics of the oral tradition.

The folk-ballad reached its peak in the 15th and 16th centuries when the first manuscript and printed collections appeared. It was rediscovered by the *Stürmer und Dränger* (→ STURM UND DRANG) who were inspired by it to write ballads themselves e.g. Bürger (1747–1794), Goethe (1749–1832), and modern authors too e.g. Brecht (1898–1956), Biermann (1936–) have modelled some of their songs on the *Volksballade*.

E.K.–R.

VOLKSBUCH (chap-book)

A collection of prose tales of an entertaining, partly didactic nature, popular in the 15th and 16th centuries. Its sources were (a) indigenous and (b) literary themes. The first group was collected from anecdotes current among the common people, (*Dil Ulenspiegel*, 1515; *Historia von D. Johann Fausten*, 1587). The second group comprises mainly translations and adaptations of French courtly epics and romances (*Die schön Magelona*, 1527; *Die Haimonskinder*, 1604), as well as classical and Italian works. The term *Volksbuch* is applied even to these collections of literary origin as they became widely known to the common people with the invention of book-printing; they were simplified to suit popular taste and were changed from edition to edition regardless of who the original author was. After the → STURM UND DRANG movement had awakened a new interest in *Volksbücher* the Romantics revived them by editing them and writing their own versions.

E.K.–R.

VOLKSBÜCHEREI (public lending library)

VOLKSBÜHNE

Organization of theatre lovers which tries to attract people to theatrical performances with reduced ticket prices, and aims to promote theatre generally.

VOLKSDICHTUNG

Notion that a people collectively creates literature: a view which was dominant during the Romantic period, but which is not held by modern scholars. The term is currently used to refer to anonymous literature which, after a long oral tradition, was collected and recorded during the 18th and 19th centuries. →MÄRCHEN, →VOLKSBALLADE, →VOLKSLIED.

VOLKSKOMÖDIE (popular comedy) = Volkstheater

Taking → KOMÖDIE in the widest sense of the word, this somewhat infelicitous term is used to cover all kinds of metropolitan popular theatre, not only – though largely – comical (→POSSE, →SINGSPIEL, →ZAUBERSTÜCK), but also comprising dramatized romances, legends and fairy-tales e.g. *Donauweibchen, Zwölf schlafende Jungfrauen*, as well as melodrama and plays appealing through lavish sets and stunning stage effects (*Spektakelstücke* and *Pferdeko-*

mödie). Parodies of serious drama and opera also featured prominently. All these plays would normally incorporate the comic figure of → HANSWURST and his descendants *Kasperl, Thaddädl, Staberl* etc. This popular theatre, aimed at a broad spectrum of the people, has its roots in the M.A., and in the Baroque, as well as in → COMMEDIA DELL'ARTE. It survived repeated attempts by Gottsched (1700–1766) to regulate the German stage; in the later 19th century incorporating more and more foreign, especially French influences, it gradually gave way to *Operette* and → BOULEVARDKOMÖDIE. Plays from Vienna especially dominated the German stage (including the Weimar theatre), other main centres were Hamburg and Berlin. *Volkstheater*, as opposed to court theatre or high literary drama, refers to the same concept; → VOLKSSTÜCK is generally used in a narrower sense, it lives on in the works of Brecht (1898–1956), Horváth (1901–1938), et al.

F.W.

VOLKSLIED

Since Herder (1744–1803), the concept of *Volkslied* has become twofold in German. In addition to the musical term with the same meaning as 'folksong', i.e. combination of melody and text, it is also specifically applied to a certain poetry, whether this combines with melody, or not. These verses of popular use, whose authorship is mostly unknown, are passed on by word of mouth from generation to generation, thereby undergoing constant change, yet preserving the essence of certain recurring situations in human experience; often related to specific customs, festivals or ways of life or work of a confined ethnic group, but with a universal meaning. The *Volkslied* does not as a rule seek a new approach to a topic, but reshapes traditional elements and topoi. This unrefined, seemingly artless poetry, where mood prevails over logical progression, was praised by the Romantics who upheld it as a model of poetic expression, and who initiated steps for its preservation, e.g. Arnim and Brentano with their collection *Des Knaben Wunderhorn* (1806–8). The structure of the mainly lyrical verse is as simple as its statements; though variations abound, the *Volkslied* is usually composed of rhymed stanzas of four lines with four accents per line, while ballads often directly imitate the English Chevy Chase form.

G.C.

VOLKSMÄRCHEN → MÄRCHEN

VOLKSSÄNGER

19th century Viennese street singers who sang popular songs (→ GASSEN-HAUER) with instrumental accompaniment.

VOLKSSTÜCK

Comic genre which originated in Vienna towards the end of the 18th

237

century. As the name suggests, it is a play about 'das Volk', for 'das Volk', meaning the lower echelons of society in contrast to the traditional aristocratic dramatis personae and audiences. There are two distinct developments in the *Volksstück* tradition. The earlier one is associated with the → VOLKSKOMÖDIE where the term *Volksstück* is used as a loose synonym for a number of comic genres: → ZAUBERSTÜCK, *Lokalposse* (→ POSSE), → BESSERUNGSSTÜCK. The second development occurred during the later part of the 19th century when it came to mean any regional play, written in dialect, with a rural setting which aimed chiefly at cheap entertainment, although frequently with an underlying didactic purpose. Since the 1920s the *Volksstück* has been rehabilitated as a respectable literary form, particularly through the influence of Horváth (1901–1938) who reversed the conventions of the second tradition. Urban replaces rural setting; petite-bourgeoisie and proletariat feature instead of peasants; the fluctuations of a capitalist market economy replace nature to provide the requisite 'blows of fate'. Horváth also isolated the urban dweller's loss of an authentic language as the key to his inability to master private and social problems. These themes have been continued by a new generation of dramatists in the 1960s and 1970s. Today one must differentiate between the *Volksstück* and the critical *Volksstück* which reacts against the expectations associated with the former to become almost an anti-genre.

C.B.

VOLKSTHEATER → VOLKSKOMÖDIE

VORABDRUCK

The full or partial publication of a literary work in newspapers or magazines before it appears in book form.

VORAUSDEUTUNG

Important structural device esp. in prose: the foreshadowing of future events. → PRÄFIGURATION.

VORBILD → QUELLE

VORFABEL → VORGESCHICHTE

VORGANG → HANDLUNG

VORGESCHICHTE = Vorfabel

Those events of the plot which took place before the play started and which must be related to the audience to facilitate a proper understanding of the action. → ANALYTISCHES DRAMA.

VORMÄRZ

The literary period before the outbreak of the revolutions in Germany and Austria in March 1848. This literature is characterized by an overriding interest in social and political issues. It is sometimes dated from the 1830 revolution in France and the emigration of Börne and Heine to Paris; and sometimes from 1835 when the censors of the German Diet (*Bundestag*) clamped down on a number of radical writers including Heine (1797–1856), Gutzkow (1811–1878) and Laube (1806–1884) who were accused of conspiring against the established order and lumped together under the name *Das Junge Deutschland* ('Young Germany'). In their prose these writers developed a trenchant Hegelian criticism of religious, moral, social and political conditions in Germany. The plays of Büchner (1813–1837) and Grabbe (1801–1836) are closely connected with this movement. Some critics (e.g. Jost Hermand) would only use the term *Vormärz* for the decade after 1840 when political interests also became dominant in Austrian, German and Swiss lyrical poetry, e.g. Anastasius Grün (1806–1876), Freiligrath (1810–1876), Herwegh (1817–1875), Keller (1819–1890), and the verse epic, e.g. Heine, Lenau (1802–1850). At that stage, the ideas of early socialism also had an impact on German radical writing. The defeat of the revolutionary movements in 1849 brought the → TENDENZDICHTUNG of the *Vormärz* to its end. Its traditions lived on in the German labour movement; they achieved new significance in East Germany after 1945 and in the FRG in the wake of the radical movements of the 1960s.

L.B.

VORSPANN

1. Credits at the beginning of a film.

2. Shorts: excerpts of a forthcoming film.

VORSPIEL (curtain-raiser)

Short dramatic piece (frequently one-act) performed before the main play.

VORSTADTTHEATER

In the 18th and 19th centuries, a theatre situated in a suburb, which concentrated on the performance of → VOLKSKOMÖDIE, as opposed to the → HOFTHEATER, situated in the inner city.

VORSTELLUNG (performance)

VORTRAG

1. Talk or discourse on radio or television : lecture.

2. Recitation (of poetry).

VORWURF → STOFF

WÄCHTERLIED → TAGELIED

WÄLZER

Colloquial term for a very large and thick book.

WAGENBÜHNE

Type of stage used in the late M.A. for the performance of religious plays. The scenery was mounted on a wagon in front of the audience. By using a succession of wagons for different scenes it was possible to perform the play simultaneously at different places.

WAHLSPRUCH → DEVISE

WAISE

A non-rhyming line surrounded by rhyming ones, esp. by rhyming couplets.

WALTHERSTROPHE

Variation of the → NIBELUNGENSTROPHE. The → ANVERS of the fourth → LANGZEILE has six feet instead of four.

WANDERBÜHNE (strolling players)

Travelling theatre group.

WASCHZETTEL (publisher's blurb)

Article containing information about a text and its author prepared for the reviewer by the publisher. → KLAPPENTEXT.

WECHSELGESANG

Alternating dialogue between two people in the form of a song. They may each sing a line or a stanza in turn.

WEIBLICHER REIM (feminine rhyme)

Rhyme which ends on an unstressed or short syllable. → REIM.

WEIHNACHTSSPIEL (nativity play) = Krippenspiel

Med. religious play; dramatic representation of Christ's birth performed at Christmas. →DREIKÖNIGSSPIEL, →GEISTLICHES DRAMA.

WEIMARER KLASSIK →KLASSIK

WEIMARER REPUBLIK (Weimar Republic)

Proclaimed on the 9th Nov. 1918 by the Social Democrat leader Philipp Scheidemann, Germany's first parliamentary democracy was named after the city of Weimar, where the Constituent Assembly took place on 6th Feb. 1919. The Weimar Republic was politically polarized from the outset and resented both by conservative nationalists and by socialists. The legend (originating in the German Supreme Command) that the civilian government had 'stabbed the army in the back' by agreeing to the armistice, and the signing of the draconian peace terms of the Treaty of Versailles in June 1919 by the new Republic's Social Democrat leaders, gave wide currency to the belief that the Weimar Republic in particular, and the institution of parliamentary democracy in general, represented the betrayal of German national aspirations. The socialist opposition, on the other hand, resented the Republic for its neglect of thorough-going economic and social reforms.

By the mid 1920s the utopian socialist works of activist expressionists such as Toller and Hiller had lost much of their appeal, and in the relatively stable middle years of the Weimar Republic (after the currency reform in the wake of the inflation of autumn 1923 until the onset of the Great Depression in October 1929) more sober expectations and more realistic styles prevailed (→ NEUE SACHLICHKEIT). The middle years of the Weimar Republic saw the concentration of wealth, power and influence in ever fewer hands. Not only Marxist writers such as Brecht (1898–1956), but also liberal supporters of the Weimar Republic such as Heinrich Mann (1871–1950), Thomas Mann (1875–1955) and Döblin (1878–1957) were critical of social inequalities and the persistence of the authoritarian spirit of Wilhelmine Germany in the bureaucracy, the legal system and in schools and universities. Writers in sympathy with National Socialism denounced the whole range of pro-Republican as well as socialist writers as part of an international liberal, Marxist and Jewish conspiracy and as rootless *Asphaltliteraten* concentrated in the big cities, especially in the capital, Berlin. With the onset of the world depression in October 1929, massive unemployment created further political polarization. The Nazi Party's electoral support increased nine-fold in September 1930. While writers who supported the National Socialists diverted attention from the economic origins of the rapidly deepening social inequalities by proclaiming an organic 'unity' of the German people based on 'Race, Blood and Soil' (→BLUBO), Brecht developed a didactic theatre (→ LEHRSTÜCK) following from his studies of Marx. It was designed to make the audience and players consider the origins of economic and social antagonisms in the capitalist system and to encourage revolutionary solidarity amongst the working classes. The failure of the various anti-Nazi forces in the Weimar Republic to form a common front facilitated Hitler's rise to power. Most major writers fled Germany soon after he became Chancellor on 30th Jan. 1933. (→EXILLITERATUR).

R.A.

WEINERLICHES LUSTSPIEL (sentimental comedy) = comédie larmoyante, = empfindsames Lustspiel, = rührendes Lustspiel

The German *Weinerliche Lustspiel* has similarities to Richard Steele's sentimental comedies. It was influenced by the French *comédie larmoyante* originated by La Chaussée (1692–1754). It was to appeal not only to reason and common sense but to the heart. As a reversal of the satirical comedy it set out to praise the positive qualities in man: virtue, unselfishness, compassion, loyalty, generosity.

Its aim was to move the audience to floods of tears (hence the name) instead of arousing unsympathetic laughter. As the precursor of the → BÜRGERLICHE TRAUERSPIEL in Germany it was still a comedy of types. Gottsched (1700–1766) objected to its classification as comedy, suggesting the term → TRAGIKOMÖDIE. The main exponent in Germany was Gellert with three plays *Die Betschwester* (1745), *Das Loos in der Lotterie* (1746) and *Die zärtlichen Schwestern* (1747) and a discourse *Pro comedia commovente* (1751). In the plays of Krüger (1723–1750) and Weisse (1726–1804) satire was often intermingled. The tradition was then trivialized in the popular sentimental → RÜHRSTÜCK (Iffland 1759–1814, Kotzebue 1761–1819) and attacked by Schiller (1759–1805), Goethe (1749–1832) and Tieck (1773–1853). There are elements of the *Weinerliche Lustspiel* in Lessing's *Miß Sara Sampson* (1755) and *Minna von Barnhelm* (1767). →LUSTSPIEL.

S.H.

WEISE →TON

WELTANSCHAUUNG (philosophy of life)

A basic and personal notion of the essence and purpose of the world and of human life which governs a person's decisions and actions, in contrast to a systematic philosophical or scientific concept.

WELTCHRONIK

Popular med. chronicle about the origin and history of the world according to the Bible.

WELTGEIST

The prevailing spirit of the times, of an age or a period.

WELTGERICHTSSPIEL

Form of med. → BIBLISCHES DRAMA; principal themes are man's damnation and the wrath of God.

WELTSCHMERZ

The term first appeared in Jean Paul's *Selina oder Über die Unsterblichkeit der Seele* (1827), but the roots of the malaise and its first symptoms surfaced at the end of the 18th century. The symptoms are moral and emotional torpor, vague discontent, and scepticism, all of which lack any specific objective cause. Its basis is generally atheism and despair at the predominance of evil in the world. The first poet to be associated with *Weltschmerz* was Byron (1788–1824) who made it an almost fashionable pose in Europe. It became a feature of post-Napoleonic European literature.

This 'mal du siècle' affected the Italian, Leopardi (1798–1837), and the Frenchman, Musset (1810–1857), as well as German writers such as Lenau (1802–1850), Grabbe (1801–1836) and Büchner (1813–1837). All fit Kierkegaard's (1813–1855) description of the artist as one who fashions his 'deep torment into beautiful music', a credo which views pain and suffering as the only means to sharpen the artist's apprehension of beauty in the world. In this respect *Weltschmerz* found a positive literary expression and was far more profound than a mere pose or transitory intellectual fashion.

C.B.

WELTTHEATER (theatrum mundi)

The image of a theatre in which humanity acts out its part before God's eyes is a traditional element in Western writing. Based on concepts derived from pagan antiquity and early Christianity, it reached its full moral philosophical development in the 12th century. At that time the idea of the world as a stage became associated with the notion of the 'heroes of virtue' who joined God in contemplating mankind's performance. Expressing an emphatically theocentric outlook, the *Welttheater* was an appropriate allegory for the existential preoccupations of the 17th century. It represented its sense of the transitory and illusory nature of earthly life and so became a popular figure of speech in baroque literature (→ BAROCK). While it was a common motif in other genres as well, the world theatre metaphor in the context of the then prevailing tendency to see microcosmic correspondences of the macrocosm in all phenomena contributed to the prominence of the drama. Especially the frequently used device of a play within a play (→ SPIEL IM SPIEL) is in this connection significant as a reflection on the ontological aspects of theatre. The dramatic treatment of the view of the world as a stage culminated in 17th century Spain, whence in the early modern era several German *Welttheater* plays derived their inspiration.

E.Kr.

WENDEPUNKT (turning-point)

1. In drama the *Wendepunkt* is the moment of peripeteia (→ PERIPETIE) or reversal in the hero's fortunes, when the rising action gives way to falling action. In tragedy the *Wendepunkt* introduces the destruction or fall of the hero; in comedy the hero's good fortune.

2. In the theory of → NOVELLE, the term is usually said to have been first introduced in 1829 by Ludwig Tieck (1773–1853), but the term had earlier been used by August Wilhelm Schlegel (1767–1845) who wrote in 1803/04 that "the Novelle requires definite turning-points, by means of which the major blocks of the story are made evident". Tieck maintained that the *Novelle* will always have that extraordinary and striking turning-point which distinguishes it from every other narrative form and defines it as "this twist in the story, this point from which it takes unexpectedly a completely different direction". Many theorists of the Novelle after Tieck retained the idea that the *Wendepunkt* was an essential characteristic of the *Novelle*, but this is no longer generally accepted. However, because the *Novelle* in its concentration and succinctness has affinities with the drama, the presence of a recognizable *Wendepunkt* is common to many *Novellen*.

E.W.H.

WERKIMMANENT (intrinsic)

The term has become known in the phrase *werkimmanente Interpretation* (→ INTERPRETATION). This was the German variety of → NEW CRITICISM and became the predominant method of post-war literary scholarship in the German-speaking countries. Its main exponents were Wolfgang Kayser and Emil Staiger. The aim of *werkimmanente Interpretation* was to analyse, explain and evaluate a text in aesthetic terms, i.e. to establish whether or not a given text can justifiably be regarded as a work of art and if so, why. It therefore concentrated on questions of the aesthetic relevance and value of a work to the present-day reader and on a very close analysis of the text. This method has encountered two main criticisms: (a) that it is ahistorical and (b) that it regards the work in isolation. The uncritical and unreflected repetition of these criticisms and the claim of some exponents of this method that *werkimmanente Interpretation* was the only legitimate way of studying literature contributed to bringing it into disrepute with present-day literary scholarship. The critics however are guilty of attacking the method for doing exactly what it explicitly sets out to do: namely to establish the aesthetic relevance for the present-day reader of a text written in an earlier period. It is also incorrect to claim that *werkimmanente Interpretation* completely disregards all extrinsic aspects of a work. On the contrary, all extrinsic aspects (such as the genesis of the work, its sources, the author's biography etc.) were studied for the purpose of providing valuable clues and guidelines, but they were not admitted as proof or evidence. Proof or evidence in this method could come only from the work itself and from nowhere else. The concentration on close textual study and on questions of aesthetics, which are central to any study of literature, should ensure that this method still retains a central place within → LITERATURWISSENSCHAFT, although not to the exclusion of other methods.

A.O.

WERTUNG

Evaluation, in art as anywhere else, depends on the criteria applied to whatever is evaluated. In literary criticism, no lasting consensus about these criteria has ever been reached. Hence, the problem of *Wertung* — what constitutes a work of literature, and how we determine the relative quality of a given work — has never been solved. Answers that have been given have only been valid for homogeneous groups of people, the main bases of such homogeneity being the period in which they lived, the social status and the religious or political convictions they shared. Most contemporary scholars agree that the criteria for evaluating a work of literature depend so much on the historical situations of readers that no generally valid criteria will ever exist. But although, in theory, it seems impossible to overcome this relativism, the agreement among 'educated Germans' about the value of individual literary works of the past has not fluctuated as drastically as the absence of a theoretical basis for objective evaluations would suggest. Apparently the system of basic values, of which such value judgements are symptomatic, has gone unquestioned for a long time. During the 1960s and 1970s however, scholars became increasingly aware of the unsolved problem, and much was written about it. This indicates that the basic values of society are no longer taken for granted. The discussion of the problem of *Wertung* is indeed symptomatic of the more general uncertainity about our philosophical, religious, political and social values which all influence our taste. In this situation, scholars avoid explicit value judgements on works of literature. Implicitly however such judgements are constantly made: whoever compiles an anthology, edits a text, offers a course or does research on specific works, has already decided that in one way or another the works selected are worth the effort.

H.W.

WIDMUNGSGEDICHT

Poem which appears at the front of a text, and may introduce or comment upon the work, or may be in the form of a dedication.

WIEGENDRUCKE → INKUNABELN

WIEGENLIED (lullaby)

Cradle-song characterized by simple lyrics, and regular rhythms reminiscent of the rocking motion of a cradle.

WIENER VOLKSKOMÖDIE → VOLKSKOMÖDIE

WIRKLICHKEIT

The term is used in German both for (1) the 'reality' created in a work of literature and for (2) the 'reality' of the external world. Both aspects are the subject of current controversy. The 'reality' of the external world includes not only nature and the physical world of man-made objects, but extends to the psychology of the individual and the interactions of individuals in society. The traditional belief that it was possible to have an objective view of external reality was brought into question as a result of the work of Albert Einstein (1879—1955) on the theory of relativity, which drew attention to the impossibility of excluding the observer from the act of observation. In literary criticism this refutation of objectivity in the observation of 'reality' was developed by Richard Brinkmann. The 'reality' of a work of literature is not a reproduction of external 'reality' but is formed by the language and structures of the given work (→ MIMESIS): it need not even correspond to external reality, and is not to be judged by any such correspondence (→ LITERATUR). In its creation of 'reality' a work of literature remains autonomous, even though it may draw its material from the objects and relationships of external 'reality'. The world of a work of literature is real when it convinces through consistency, and this can be achieved in the → MÄRCHEN, in the utopian novel or in science fiction just as much as in works of literature set in a recognizable milieu or society. → FIKTION.

E.W.H.

WITZ

This word embraces aspects of both English *wit/witticism* and *joke*. From the early 19th century the second meaning became prevalent in German. The structure of a *Witz* (joke) is traditionally based on reason rather than emotions. It is constructed in a linguistically imaginative way, and its form is very important both in written and oral presentation; the joke is seen as one of the basic 'primary forms' of literary communication by Jolles (→ EINFACHE FORMEN). There is a build-up towards a → POINTE, producing an unexpected discrepancy between expectation and outcome which causes comic relief. This may be achieved by the creation or recounting of a humorous situation, it may be based on polysemy in language (→ WORTSPIEL, pun), or the two may be combined, i.e. there are situational and verbal aspects. Freud has shown in his analysis of jokes (1905) how they are used to evade or destroy sexual and other authoritarian taboos. Situations of extreme repression and censorship give rise to socio-political jokes, these being often the only possible form of protest and survival. (In the German context: jokes in Nazi Germany or the GDR; Jewish jokes.) There are many stereotype jokes, such as those about absent-minded professors or regional characters, such as Graf Bobby (Vienna) and Tünnes

(Cologne).

WITZBLATT (comic, satirical magazine)

Magazine of a humorous and satiric nature, usually illustrated.

WOCHENSCHRIFTEN →MORALISCHE WOCHENSCHRIFTEN

WORTHÄUFUNG = Häufung

Stylistic device esp. prevalent during the baroque period: the successive listing of synonymous words which could lead to whole registers of words. → SCHWULST.

WORTSPIEL (pun, play on words)

XENIEN

Highly satirical type of epigram (→ EPIGRAMM) in the form of rhyming couplets, which was used by Goethe (1749–1832) and Schiller (1759–1805) to ridicule their adversaries.

ZÄSUR (caesura) = Caesur = Schnitt

Strong pause or break in a verse line.

ZÄSURREIM

Rhyming of the word at the caesura with the word at the end of the line.

ZAUBERPOSSE →ZAUBERSTÜCK

ZAUBERSPRUCH (incantation, spell)

Highly stylized and metrically arranged formula recited for the control of forces normally beyond the control of human beings; e.g.: afflictions and illnesses, the weather, demons etc.

ZAUBERSTÜCK = Zauberposse

Special genre, mainly of the Viennese popular theatre (→ VOLKSKOMÖ-DIE) in the late 18th and first half of the 19th century. Commonly thought to derive from baroque catholic theatre with its superstructure of personified allegories, and angels and devils; other influences include Gozzi (1720–1806) and Wieland (1733–1813). Man appears controlled by allegorical figures (Envy, Hatred, Melancholy, etc.) or by supernatural figures from folk-legends (Melusine, Rübezahl, Alpenkönig), magicians, witches. A special sub-genre is the → BES-SERUNGSSTÜCK, where human failures are corrected. The treatment was (at times) both serious e.g. Raimund's (1790–1836) late plays and parodic e.g. Meisl (1775–1853), Nestroy (1801–1862), and was as diverse as *Die Zau-berflöte* (1791) and Nestroy's *Konfuser Zauberer* (1832). It owed some of its popularity with the audience to special stage effects representing the inter-vention of supernatural powers. Authors used it because censorship was more lenient towards the unreal world of the *Zauberstück*, though this is often only a thin guise. The influence of the *Zauberstück* can be seen in Grillparzer (1791–1872) and even in Hofmannsthal (1874–1929).

F.W.

ZEICHENSETZUNG →INTERPUNKTION

ZEILENSPRUNG → ENJAMBEMENT

ZEILENSTIL

Style of Germanic poetry in which the end of a sentence and the end of a → LANGZEILE coincide, as opposed to *Hakenstil* (→ ENJAMBEMENT).

ZEITGEDICHT

Poem in which the author, by emphasizing and illustrating an aspect or theme characteristic of a particular period, attempts to convey the spirit of the time.

ZEITROMAN

Novel which aims to give a comprehensive picture of an era. For this reason, it not only portrays society but attempts to incorporate all philosophical, artistic, religious and political issues of that period. Frequently this type of novel degenerates into → TENDENZLITERATUR, but there are notable exceptions; e.g.: Musil's *Der Mann ohne Eigenschaften* (1930 ff).

ZEITSCHRIFT (periodical, journal, magazine)

ZEITUNGSROMAN

Novel printed in instalments in newspapers, frequently of minor aesthetic value. → FORTSETZUNGSROMAN, → ILLUSTRIERTENROMAN.

ZENSUR (censorship)

The scrutiny of publications, films, plays, etc., or parts of them with the aim of possible suppression on the grounds of obscenity, subversiveness etc.

ZERSINGEN

The involuntary changing of the text of a popular song, esp. a → VOLKS-LIED, which occurs through frequent and often inaccurate rendering.

ZIMMERTHEATER

Very small, intimate theatre: miniature form of the → KAMMERSPIELE.

ZITAT (quotation, citation)

ZOTE (obscene joke)

ZUEIGNUNG (dedication) → WIDMUNGSGEDICHT

ZUG (trait)

An aspect or part of a motif or a smaller, structurally less important version of a motif. →MOTIV.

ZWECKDICHTUNG →TENDENZDICHTUNG

ZWILLINGSFORMEL

Twin formula, consisting of two antonyms which are frequently linked by alliteration or rhyme; e.g.: Leben und Tod, Himmel und Hölle.

ZWISCHENAKT (entr'acte)

The interval between the acts of a play, when music, or a short dramatic piece might be played. →INTERLUDES, →ZWISCHENSPIEL.

ZWISCHENREIM →SCHWEIFREIM

ZWISCHENSPIEL

Short comic piece played between the acts of a play.

CONTRIBUTORS

A.C.   =   ANNE CAMPBELL
Canberra College of Advanced Education
Australia

A.F.G.   =   ALYTH F. GRANT
University of Otago
New Zealand

A.O.   =   Dr. AUGUST OBERMAYER
University of Otago
New Zealand

A.S.   =   Prof. Dr. ANTHONY R. STEPHENS
University of Adelaide
Australia

A.V.   =   Dr. AXEL VIEREGG
Massey University
New Zealand

B.C.   =   Prof. Dr. BRIAN L.D. COGHLAN
University of Adelaide
Australia

B.E.   =   Dr. BARBARA EINHORN
Brighton
England

C.B.   =   CHRIS BALME
University of Otago
New Zealand

C.G.   =   Dr. CHRISTIAN GRAWE
University of Melbourne
Australia

C.P.M.   =   Prof. Dr. C. PETER MAGILL
Aberystwyth
Wales

D.R.	=	Dr. DAVID ROBERTS Monash University Australia
E.K.	=	Dr. ERNST KELLER Monash University Australia
E.K.-R.	=	Dr. EVA KORTSCHAK-RUFF University of Melbourne Australia
E.Kr.	=	Prof. Dr. EGBERT KRISPYN University of Georgia U.S.A.
E.P.	=	ELENA POLETTI University of Otago New Zealand
E.S.	=	Prof. Dr. EGON SCHWARZ Washington University U.S.A.
E.W.H.	=	Prof. E.W. HERD University of Otago New Zealand
F.G.S.	=	Dr. FLORENCE G. STONE Dunedin New Zealand
F.K.	=	FIONA KENNEDY Wellington New Zealand
F.V.	=	Dr. FRIEDRICH VOIT University of Auckland New Zealand
F.W.	=	Dr. FRED WALLA University of Newcastle Australia

G.B.	=	Dr. GEOFF. BROAD Auckland New Zealand
G.C.	=	Dr. GERALD CHRISTELLER Victoria University of Wellington New Zealand
. G.S.	=	Prof. Dr. GERHARD SCHULZ University of Melbourne Australia
H.H.	=	HEINRICH HESSE University of Melbourne Australia
H.R.	=	Assoc. Prof. Dr. HORST G. RUTHROF Murdoch University Australia
H.W.	=	Prof. Dr. HEINZ WETZEL University of Toronto Canada
H.W.N.	=	Prof. Dr. HANS-WERNER NIESCHMIDT University of Waikato New Zealand
J.J.W.	=	Dr. JOHN J. WHITE University of London King's College England
J.N.-B.	=	Dr. JAMES NORTHCOTE-BADE University of Auckland New Zealand
J.M.E.	=	Prof. Dr. JOHN M. ELLIS University of California Santa Cruz, U.S.A.
J.M.L.	=	Prof. Dr. J. MARTIN LINDSAY University of Western Australia Australia

J.S.	=	JOHN STOWELL
		University of Newcastle
		Australia

K.F.	=	Dr. KAY FLAVELL
		University of Liverpool
		England

L.B.	=	Prof. Dr. LESLIE BODI
		Monash University
		Australia

L.W.	=	LISA WARRINGTON
		University of Otago
		New Zealand

L.Z.W.	=	Dr. LIVIA Z. WITTMAN
		University of Canterbury
		New Zealand

M.A.	=	Dr. MARION ADAMS
		University of Melbourne
		Australia

M.C.	=	Assoc. Prof. Dr. MICHAEL CLYNE
		Monash University
		Australia

M.H.	=	Dr. MICHAEL HERD
		Wellington
		New Zealand

M.M.	=	Assoc. Prof. Dr. MICHAEL MORLEY
		Flinders University
		Australia

M.N.	=	Assoc. Prof. Dr. MARLENE NORST
		Macquarie University
		Australia

M.S.	=	MARTIN SUTTON
		University of Auckland
		New Zealand

M.St.   =   Dr. MARGARET STOLJAR
Australian National University
Australia

P.L.   =   Dr. PATRICIA LOPDELL
Massey University
New Zealand

P.M.   =   PHILIP MANGER
University of Canterbury
New Zealand

P.Oe.   =   Dr. PETER OETTLI
University of Waikato
New Zealand

P.R.   =   PHILIPPA REED
University of Auckland
New Zealand

P.T.   =   Dr. PHILIP THOMSON
Monash University
Australia

R.A.   =   Dr. REINHARD ALTER
University of Western Australia
Australia

R.C.P.   =   Dr. ROGER C. PAULIN
Trinity College, Cambridge
England

R.F.   =   Dr. RODNEY W. FISHER
University of Canterbury
New Zealand

R.G.   =   Prof. Dr. REINHOLD GRIMM
University of Wisconsin
U.S.A.

R.H.   =   Dr. RAY HARLOW
University of Otago
New Zealand

R.P.　　=　ROLF PANNY
　　　　　Massey University
　　　　　New Zealand

R.S.　　=　Prof. Dr. RICHARD SAMUEL
　　　　　Brighton, Victoria
　　　　　Australia

S.H.　　=　Dr. SILKE HESSE
　　　　　Monash University
　　　　　Australia

U.B.　　=　Dr. ULF BARTHOLOMAE
　　　　　University of Canterbury
　　　　　New Zealand

V.K.　　=　Dr. VOLKER KNÜFERMANN
　　　　　University of Waikato
　　　　　New Zealand

W.H.B.　=　Prof. Dr. WALTER H. BRUFORD
　　　　　Edinburgh
　　　　　Scotland

W.S.S.　=　Dr. WILLIAM S. SEWELL
　　　　　University of Otago
　　　　　New Zealand

W.V.　　=　Prof. Dr. WALTER VEIT
　　　　　Monash University
　　　　　Australia

OTAGO GERMAN STUDIES

Vol. 1 *Festschrift for E.W. Herd.* Edited by August Obermayer.
Dunedin 1980. 311pp. ISSN 0111-3283. NZ$26-00

Contributions by:

T.E. Carter
Tony Barta
Richard Brinkmann
W.H. Bruford
Leonard Forster
Reinhold Grimm
J.A. Harvie
Paul Hoffmann
Gerhard Kaiser
Michael Kessler
Con Kooznetzoff
Günther Mahal
Hans Mayer
John Milfull
Hans-Werner Nieschmidt
August Obermayer
Peter Russell
Gerhard Schulz
W.S. Sewell
Kathryn Smits
Axel Vieregg
K.E. Westerskov
Livia Z. Wittmann

Available from:

Department of German
University of Otago
P.O. Box 56
Dunedin
New Zealand.